# Race, Law, and Higher Education in the Colorblind Era



This book provides detailed analysis of Supreme Court judgments which have impacted the rights of minorities in relation to higher education, and so illustrates ongoing issues of racial discrimination throughout the American education sector.

*Race, Law, and Higher Education in the Colorblind Era* brings together the many racial disputes that have been adjudicated by the Supreme Court to investigate the politics of colorblindness in the post-civil rights era. Through a reading of these various cases as a form of continuing racial discourse, this book focuses on the ways in which racial disputes operate within a clearly entwined colorblind narrative that invalidates racial justice for minorities. By investigating how the Supreme Court has understood racism and the concept of race across its history, this volume demonstrates how colleges and universities must navigate the often contradictory and perilous landscape of 'diversity' in attempts to integrate historically disadvantaged minorities.

This book will be of interest to researchers, academics, and postgraduate students in the fields of sociology of education, multicultural education, and legal education.

**Hoang Vu Tran** is an Assistant Professor of Curriculum, Culture, and Educational Inquiry in the College of Education at Florida Atlantic University, USA.

## Routledge Research in Higher Education

**Data for Continuous Programmatic Improvement**
Steps Colleges of Education Must Take to Become a Data Culture
*Edited by Ellen B. Mandinach and Edith S. Gummer*

**Grounding Education in the Environmental Humanities**
Exploring Place-Based Pedagogies in the South
*Edited by Lucas F. Johnston and Dave Aftandilian*

**Success Factors for Minorities in Engineering**
*Jacqueline Fleming and Irving Pressley McPhail*

**Exploring Institutional Logics in Technology-Mediated Higher Education**
*Neelam Dwivedi*

**The Phenomenological Heart of Teaching and Learning**
Theory, Research, and Practice in Higher Education
*Katherine H. Greenberg, Brian K. Sohn, Neil B. Greenberg, Howard R. Pollio, Sandra P. Thomas, and John T. Smith*

**The Tenure-Track Process for Chicana and Latina Faculty**
Experiences of Resisting and Persisting in the Academy
*Edited by Patricia A. Pérez*

**Higher Education in Nepal**
Policies and Perspectives
*Edited by Krishna Bista, Shyam Sharma, and Rosalind Latiner Raby*

**Race, Law, and Higher Education in the Colorblind Era**
Critical Investigations Into Race-Related Supreme Court Disputes
*Hoang Vu Tran*

For more information about this series, please visit: www.routledge.com/Routledge-Research-in-Higher-Education/book-series/RRHE

# Race, Law, and Higher Education in the Colorblind Era

## Critical Investigations Into Race-Related Supreme Court Disputes

Hoang Vu Tran

Routledge
Taylor & Francis Group
LONDON AND NEW YORK

First published 2020 by Routledge

2 Park Square, Milton Park, Abingdon, Oxon, OX14 4RN
605 Third Avenue, New York, NY 10017

*Routledge is an imprint of the Taylor & Francis Group, an informa business*

First issued in paperback 2020



*Library of Congress Cataloging-in-Publication Data*
A catalog record for this book has been requested

ISBN: 978-0-8153-6123-7 (hbk)
ISBN: 978-0-367-78582-6 (pbk)

Typeset in Sabon
by Apex CoVantage, LLC

To my parents—Vũ Tuyết Giáng and Trần Văn Sâm.

# Contents

*Preface* ix

Introduction 1

SECTION I
**Foundations of Colorblindness, Whiteness, and Racial Subordination** **9**

1 Judicial Colorblindness and the Problem of Racism 11

2 Commitments: Of Methods and Interpretation 21

3 A Historical Synergy: Law, Whiteness, and the Hegemony of Racial Subordination 33

SECTION II
**Revisiting and Revising 'Settled' History** **53**

4 The Politics and Whiteness of *Brown v. Board of Education* 55

5 (Un)Equal Protection and Disproportionate Harm to Minorities 72

6 Affirmative Action = Discrimination (to Whites) in the Colorblind Era 85

SECTION III
**Critical Contemporary Perspectives** **103**

7 After *Fisher v. University of Texas*: Racial Justice or Whiteness Rising? 105

8 Diversity Trending Up, Affirmative Action on Life Support, and the Perilous Status of Asian Americans 123

9 Future Directions 140

*Selected Readings List* 148

*Index* 154

# Preface

It is March and the end of another school day approaches at Northwood High School in Irvine, California. All day, senior Andrew Chau's mind has been elsewhere from classes, lectures, and homework. Andrew just wants to go to the comforts of his home and the privacy of his own room to get on his computer. Far from not caring about his education, Andrew has been distracted from school precisely because he is nervous with anticipation to find out the next destination in his educational journey. He woke up this morning to an email notifying him that he could log onto a college admissions portal to find out Harvard's decision on his college application. He could have done so immediately this morning, but the anticipation, nervousness, and anxiety forced him to delay finding out until after school. In the best-case scenario, he would share the wonderful news of Harvard acceptance with his schoolmates and teachers, and surely be the envy of many at his ultra-competitive school. But what if Harvard rejects him? He knew he would not be able to immediately relay the unfortunate news to his friends and teachers. Does he just go through the day listlessly and pretend everything was fine and internalize the bad news and disappointment to himself? This is why he waits until the school day is over to check at home, alone, and in the privacy of his own room. Andrew knows the uncertainty of going through the day and thinking about logging on would be excruciatingly difficult, but at least no news is still not bad news.

To understand Andrew's Harvard admissions anxiety, one must understand Andrew's educational trajectory—not entirely, but at least briefly. Ever since he was in middle school, his days have resembled a rotating rotisserie of activities directly or tangentially geared toward positioning and preparing him to apply to the most exclusive universities in America. There were pre-SAT preparation programs from Kaplan that started in middle school, two consecutive summer SAT boot camps from Elite Educational Institute every day for a full two months each summer, and the year-round individual tutoring intended to keep his standardized test-taking acuity sharp in between summer programs. This is all in addition to Andrew's difficult class load *in* high school. The only non-AP or IB class he did not take was volleyball, which he only began enjoying this senior year because it is a spring sport—after college application season. The time commitment was tremendous. Not everyone had a jam-packed academic schedule like Andrew. But not everyone had the collective academic goals that Andrew and his parents had planned for him years ago. Harvard, and a few other elite institutions, was the explicit goal. To be a competitive candidate, time, hard work, and most importantly, money was needed. Northwood is a public high school, but the afterschool preparation programs, individualize tutoring, SAT summer boot camps, and private college counselor all added up to tens of thousands of dollars. Not only did Andrew commit time and effort, his parents made incredible sacrifices financially to position their son in the best possible competitive position.

Andrew is finally home, alone in his room and ready to check his admissions decision from Harvard. His palms sweaty, chest pulsating ever faster. He is so nervous and shaking that it takes him three tries to correctly key in his login credentials. The letter opens and Andrew is devastated after reading only the first few sentences; he does not bother to read the rest of the rejection letter. He feels as if all the anxiety and nervousness of the day culminated into a gut wrenching, sinking feeling in his stomach. Just like that, he went from Harvard hopeful to Harvard reject. He was (still *is*) one of the top students at his ultra-competitive school. His weighted GPA would have been a perfect 5.0 but for his volleyball participation. He was in the 99th percentile of SAT test takers both times he took the test and actually improved his score to 1570 the second time, barely missing a perfect 1600 on the combined verbal and math sections. That night after breaking the news to his parents, the family gathered at the dinner table. Mom and Dad offered words of encouragement to their son, insisting that he was still in contention for other elite schools. Furthermore, they reminded him that he was already accepted into UCLA and Berkeley, two of the most famous and competitive public schools in the U.S. However, underneath their veil of encouragement, mom and dad were likewise disappointed and dejected.

The years and months leading up to Andrew's application process, his parents had resisted talking about any negativity regarding Asian American students and elite college admissions. However, the suspicions, rumors, and whispers percolated through email groups and community conversations. When Andrew was in 8th grade, a California state senator attempted to introduce a state constitutional amendment (SCA5) to amend the California constitution to once again allow public colleges and universities to consider race in admissions decisions. Along with many other Asian American families in Irvine, Andrews' parents viewed the proposed amendment as a direct threat to Andrew's admissions chances at the University of California. Mom and Dad were not too active in the campaign that successfully mounted enough opposition for the amendment to be indefinitely shelved, but they did forward opposition emails to their social and professional circles, most of whom were also in opposition. But Harvard is different. Harvard and other private institutions are only bound by federal law regarding the use of racial considerations in admissions. And current federal policy allows universities to consider race in admissions decisions. Andrew's disappointing news was just too overwhelming for them to resist further the gushing negative feelings about college admissions and its apparent Asian American bias. Mom and Dad had intimate knowledge of Andrew's hard work from the past several years. In their minds, he could not have possibly accomplished more than what he profoundly presented in his application. But it just was not enough. To Mom and Dad, the only thing Andrew could have changed was something he had no control over: his race.

---

Jesse Aguilar is a senior at Century High School in Santa Ana, California. Century has a supermajority of Latino/a students (mostly Mexican American) who are predominantly working class. It is springtime and Jesse is excited that he is on track to pass all of his classes and graduate. Many of Jesse's friends and classmates will have to attend summer school to make up missing credits or failed grades in order to graduate. Many more will simply end their high school career without earning a diploma. Jesse plans to attend Santa Ana College in August with the hopes of transferring to a California State University or University of California campus in two years. Jesse and his parents always prided themselves on pursuing a good education and going to college. In his sophomore year, Jesse took the pre-SAT offered for free at his school for the first time. His counselors and teachers advised Jesse the test would be a good diagnostic for him to assess his performance on the test so that he can begin preparing for the actual SAT either at the end of his junior year or beginning of senior year. Jesse did not have a good experience with the pre-SAT. During the three-hour test, he lost interest and concentration after the first two sections of reading and math. He bubbled in the rest of his answer sheet just so that it appeared he completed the test. The reading sections were just too much. He was able to understand the overall themes of the passages, but was unable to quickly answer the succession of questions and thus often ran out of time. On the math section, the questions were vaguely on formulas and computations he remembers from geometry and pre-algebra class, but it had been a while since he worked on them specifically. Jesse's test results and overall test taking experience left him with a daunting realization: he was far from being minimally prepared for the real SAT and preparation classes were not offered at school; he would have to study on his own or pay for a private program.

Offering SAT preparation programs for students is nowhere near the top of the priorities list at Century High. In fact, many wealthier schools also do not offer any SAT/ACT preparation programs knowing middle class and wealthy families would rather turn to the private sector for test prep services. Century High administrators must tackle more pressing issues such as retaining qualified teachers, hiring enough instructors to alleviate overcrowding, and finding enough resources out of the yearly budget to fund essential programs and services for students. It would be nice if Century administrators had the extra resources to offer college access programs to assist college-aspiring students like Jesse, but the realities of an overcrowded urban school serving majority minority working class students dictates that scarce resources go to more urgent needs and expenditures.

The University of California and California State University[1] systems require applicants to submit an SAT/ACT score for admissions consideration. To Jesse, his terrible test taking experience and the lack of preparation opportunities available at school essentially precluded him from applying to the UC or CSU. However, he was not deterred. Going to college in Jesse's mind was always geared toward attending Santa Ana College. The distance to the local community college was essentially the same as the distance to his high school. Although a high school diploma was not necessary to attend community college, Jesse was advised by his high school counselor that graduating from high school would enable him to take degree-earning classes immediately and not have to be enrolled in remedial courses. This was the consistent advising he received from his high school counselor throughout his high school career. As the end of Jesse's senior year was quickly approaching, he could not help but feel a sense of achievement that he would graduate and begin community college in the fall at Santa Ana College. Century High's difficulties are not unlike other American urban schools that serve a majority minority poor student population. Overcrowding, lack of resources, and a perpetual exodus of qualified staff and teachers collectively compound to make the learning environment for students like Jesse difficult. At Century, the rate of dropouts and students who finish high school without earning a diploma is high and graduation rates are not high enough. As such, Jesse is justified to feel a sense of accomplishment for his college trajectory.

---

Northwood and Century High are a world apart. But on an Orange County map, they are physically no more than seven miles from each other. Notwithstanding the notorious Southern California traffic, the drive should be about fifteen minutes. These two Orange County public schools produce drastically different educational experiences. At Northwood, the expectation for students to attend college is a foregone conclusion. It is not simply just a matter of attending college, but which one. These expectations are not unfounded. Northwood exists within a broader educational ecology of high achievement and excellence. A student at Northwood like Andrew is nurtured from home to school to afterschool to home again in a never-ending cycle of educational excellence and opportunity. There is never a moment, an aberration, in the day where the educational message is anything but to expect the best. At Century, a student's everyday educational cycle is defined by decisions not to ensure the best, but a minimum. Hamstrung by scarce resources at school and a lack of cultural capital at home, college expectations morph to just graduate-from-high-school-aspirations in a seven-mile journey of spatial educational metamorphosis. Taken together, Jesse and Andrew's respective excitement and disappointment with their college paths should not be surprising, but expected. The two students' excitement and disappointment are products of their educational ecologies. Jesse is authentically excited to graduate and attend community college because all the messages in his educational everyday have painted a portrait of mediocrity and low expectations. Andrew and his parents are genuinely disappointed, perhaps even angry and resentful, of his Harvard rejection because he has been groomed in his educational world to expect nothing but the best precisely because he has experienced only the best.

Although Jesse and Andrew's educational experience may appear to be worlds apart, they are a product of the same public educational system. From local, to state, to federal, the exact same interaction of laws and policies create poor and rich schools. Arguably, the most consequential reason for inequality in public education is because schools draw a significant portion of its expenditures from local property tax. Poor areas produce poor schools and wealthy areas produce wealthy schools. American public schools have been funded this way at least since the Civil Rights Era. In fact, the disparity that local property taxes create in schools was deemed not a violation of any federal laws or constitutional guarantees in 1973. The inequality between Northwood and Century high schools is directly tied to the amount of property taxes available to each district. In addition, the quality of public schools represents a massive calculus for families when they identify communities and areas to purchase family homes based on their financial capabilities. Just these two variables, the local property tax public school funding structure and the home purchasing decisions of families, have impacted and perpetuated the racial and economic composition of schools unlike any other variables. The predictable educational experiences of students in schools such as Century or Northwood are institutionally determined outcomes of these larger structural dynamics. As such, since the Civil Rights Era, or at the very least since 1973, generations of Americans have been nurtured through a public educational structure where inequality and racial segregation are as American as apple pie.

Jesse and Andrew's college aspirations stories should be familiar to all observers who are even casually familiar with public education in the U.S. Every year in the spring, scores of incredibly high-achieving students are disappointed, angry, or even vengeful when the most elite and exclusive universities send out those dreadful rejection letters. At the same time, many students at poor schools are relieved to receive diplomas from severely underfunded high schools derisively labeled as drop-out factories due to larger factors well beyond their control. As the arc of history has continued to bend toward inequality, a peculiar development has cemented itself in education. Aggrieved students from rich schools have all available legal recourses to voice their sense of college admissions injustices while the doors of justice are effectively shut against students who wish to challenge the structural dynamics of their segregated and poor schools.

Aggrieved students and families rejected by elite schools have targeted the use of racial considerations in college admissions and educational policy making as the culprit of their disappointment. In response, folks like Andrew and his family have been willing partners with conservative and right-wing legal groups who, together, have consistently challenged the constitutionality of racial considerations in education. With the exception of the school assignment case in Seattle (to be discussed further in Chapter 2), all of the momentum in challenging affirmative action since the early 2000s has been focused on eliminating the use of racial considerations in college admissions. However, students like Jesse and their families have effectively been prohibited from utilizing the legal process to challenge the constitutionality of hyper-segregated and drastically underfunded schools. Effectively since the early 1970s, the United States Supreme Court has constitutionalized into federal policy that any amount of hyper segregation and unequal funding of public education is permissible so long as it occurs across arbitrary district lines.[2] Thus ushering in a *laissez-faire* colorblind formation of educational segregation and unequal school funding created by the free-flow of capital via home purchasing decisions and directed-flow of property taxes to local schools.

Although broadly related to education, readers may react that elite college admissions disappointment and the state of segregated and poor public schools have little to do with each other. I respectfully disagree. The legal terrain on race and education since at least the Civil Rights Era has directly orchestrated the formation of segregated and poor schools while inviting a steady stream of anti-affirmative action challenges. That is, the constitutional terrain on race and education that opens wide the doors of justice to aggrieved students like Andrew likewise shuts the same doors to students like Jesse. To defenders of public education and those who champion the democratizing promise of schools, this should be deeply troubling. Critically investigating the formation of this legal terrain on race and education is the project of this book.

## Notes

1. The CSU requires an SAT/ACT score unless an applicant has a 3.0 GPA or better on an index of required courses determined by the CSU system.
2. *San Antonio v. Rodriguez* (1973) and *Milliken v. Bradley* (1974).

# Introduction

In 2008, Abigail Fisher, a white student, sued the University of Texas at Austin after she was denied admissions as an undergraduate student. Fisher blamed her rejection on the University's race positive holistic admissions program. UT Austin's holistic review takes into account racial considerations as one factor in a multitude of factors in its admissions process. In addition to standardized test scores and high school GPA, the University of Texas evaluated applicants on considerations such as extracurricular activities, parents' educational background, location of high school, and race. Fisher claimed she had suffered racial discrimination due to the school's use of racial considerations and therefore argued holistic admissions violated her constitutional equal protection rights guaranteed under the Fourteenth Amendment. With much anticipation during the spring of 2013 for the Supreme Court's decision, the opinion was rather tame and anti-climactic. Rather than issue a verdict on whether or not the University of Texas' holistic admissions policy was constitutional, the Court instead punted and remanded the case back to the lower appeals court on procedural grounds. Perhaps the University of Texas and their proponents welcomed the decision because the Court did not affirmatively strike down its race positive admissions policy.

The Fifth Circuit Court of appeals reheard the case via a three-judge panel and sided with the University of Texas' usage of race positive admissions. Predictably, the case returned to the Supreme Court as Fisher's legal team, funded and supported by a plethora of conservative foundations and think tanks, repeatedly stated that they will only accept the Supreme Court's opinion as the final say. At most, the Supreme Court would maintain the status quo of using racial considerations as one factor in a number of factors in higher education admissions. At worst, and this was a scenario that legal scholars increasingly predicted, the Court's five conservative justices would form a majority bloc and ultimately do away with the University of Texas' race positive admissions program. In a somewhat surprising outcome, conservative justice Anthony Kennedy joined with the liberal wing to preserve the permissibility of racial considerations in college admissions. The final 2016 *Fisher* (2016) decision maintained the status quo of using race in college admissions. What the decision did not do was signal an end to future legal challenges on the permissibility of racial considerations in higher education.

For race positive advocates who campaign for racially conscious policies in education, government, employment, and other civil institutions, the Court's assault on race positive considerations in public policy has been relentless. As this book will show, the Court's sixty-year history since *Brown v. Board of Education* (1954) has produced a judicial history that has been at best hostile toward race positive policies and at worst prolongs the racial disparity that many social and civil policies have attempted to address. As a result, a decision from the Court in favor of maintaining racial considerations for the University of Texas and its proponents is a small consolation when viewed against a larger history of affirmative action and race conscious policies. Although sixty years since *Brown* is a significant period, six decades is merely a fraction of the Court's long history adjudicating racial issues. Thus, equating the positive decision in *Fisher* in favor of race positive holistic admissions as a victory to affirmative action policy represents a short view that is limited to the sixty years since *Brown*. Important legal developments notwithstanding, this short view neglects the longer legacy of the Court's decisions concerning race. The Court's racial decisions for the past sixty years are built on the foundations of its racial decisions of at least the last two hundred years. Taking a longer view preceding the *Brown* case reveals a history that suggests the race positive decision in *Fisher* is not a complete victory for the project of affirmative action, but represents the latest maneuver in an ongoing retrenchment of whiteness and white privilege.

## Goals

This book reviews the Supreme Court's colorblind jurisprudence since *Brown v. Board of Education* and argues that its uptake of racial issues is a refraction of American society's problematic 'colorblind' imagination of race and its general unwillingness to confront the material realities of racial stratification and subordination. More critically, colorblindness in the law represents a reactionary racial project intended to reinvent and reposition white racial privilege. The jurisprudential turn (more on this in Section II) toward colorblindness following *Brown* and the Civil Rights Era occurred not simply because of individual conservative Supreme Court justices exercising an independent constitutional interpretation, but represents a broader social-civil uptake of the significance of race in the construction of public policy. Furthermore, viewed as a vehicle for upward mobility, education is as an institution that may either eliminate or reproduce social inequality. As a result, the Court's decisions on issues of race and education have a direct relationship in determining the democratic potential of public education.

Particularly as the law relates to educational policy, I will show that the Court's racial ideology cannot be severed from its material manifestations and consequences, specifically in education. That is, the Court acts as more than just an umpire enforcing the rules of fair play in education when it comes to the usage of race in policy practices. Rather, with a careful analysis of its contemporary educational cases, I explore whether or not the Court's rulings help establish the normative, or commonsense, uptake of race in civil society. Finally, if education is inhibited from fulfilling its potential to democratize a racially stratified society, what then does education represent as a cornerstone of U.S. democratic promise? In addressing this last issue, I engage the academic literature on race and whiteness studies in education to open a process of inquiry that questions, if education is unable to deal with the material manifestations of race is it itself an affirmative agent in the stratifying process; one that is given the sanction of law?

In Ian Haney López's (2006) seminal work *White by Law: The Legal Construction of Race*, one of López's main questions pertaining to the relationship between the law and race is whether or not law operates as an ideological system and therefore constructs social belief systems. Additionally, if the law in fact operates as an ideological system, Haney López asks how the system then creates and upholds ideas about race. *White by Law* is a critical examination into the processes, methods, and justifications utilized by federal and supreme courts in the construction of racial meanings in the early 20th Century. To Haney López, the courts were more than just legal arbiters reflecting existing socio-racial practices. Rather, courts, justices, and lawyers actively *constructed* racial meanings by using a combination of scientific evidence and commonsense knowledge, thereby actively shaping the nation's racial understanding. The bulk of López's analysis focuses on cases from the first half of the 20th century.

Beginning with the latter half of the 20th century, a radical shift occurred in the way the Supreme Court adjudicated issues of race. In the first half of the century before *Brown*, the Court vacillated between using scientific evidence or common sense in order to establish acceptable racial categories. For instance, in *Ozawa v. United States* (1922) the Court utilized a scientific anthropological understand of race to deny Takeo Ozawa the right of land ownership. At the time, land ownership was only legally permitted for Whites and Blacks. The Court was not persuaded by Ozawa's claim of white personhood because of his Japanese ancestry. Rather, the Court located whiteness to those belonging to the Caucasian race, geographically from the Caucasoid region. Thereby in *Ozawa*, the Court utilized a scientific geographical approach to determine whiteness. In response, Bhagat Thinh sought to take advantage of the Court's ruling because of his ancestral ties to the Caucasoid region as an Indian Sikh. In a case decided by the same Court with the same justices a few months after *Ozawa*, the *United States v. Thind* (1923) Court abandoned its scientific definition of race by elevating a common social understanding of race. The court rejected Thind's claim of white personhood ruling that although he was from the region of the Caucasus mountains, he was not socially understood as white. The Court concluded that although Thind is Caucasian by virtue of geography, it did not necessarily make him white as a matter of common everyday understanding. Whereas the Court in *Ozawa* and *Thind* were unapologetic about taking up the issue of race, even contradictorily, the Court since *Brown* now shows either a disdain toward race or simply refuses to recognize the importance of race altogether.

## Purpose

Post *Brown v. Board of Education* and the Civil Rights Act of 1964, U.S. society entered the 'colorblind' era of race relations. Much has been written about this colorblind era, a discussion this book will neither comprehensively address nor critique, but will engage as a constraint in legal jurisprudence regarding colorblindness' effects on race and education policy. Related to this era is the development of a colorblind jurisprudence by conservative (mostly) and centrist (a few) Supreme Court Justices since the landmark *Brown* decision. Therefore, I wish to appropriate Haney López's study by interrogating a particular ideological type of jurisprudence forwarded by his framework: the colorblind constitutional jurisprudence. In this analysis, I will map out the historical development of how the *idea* of a colorblind constitution became the *practice* of colorblind jurisprudence. Through this historical process, I aim to show that the development of a colorblind jurisprudence is fundamentally anchored and dependent on a purposeful misrecognition of race and racial history that culminated in the treatment of *Brown* and the Civil Rights Era as a *tabula rasa* absolving American society from its past racial sins. That is, colorblind jurisprudence effectively viewed *Brown* and the Civil Rights Act as ushering in a blank slate of meritocracy, where race is believed no longer to play a significant role in the organization of society.

By reviewing the emerging literature of whiteness studies, I argue that a constitutional colorblind jurisprudence amounts to an 'act of whiteness', perhaps one that is more difficult to identify and address because of its elusive racial sensibilities. As a consequence, racial stratification and the manifestation of white privilege continue as social problems because judicial colorblindness refuses to recognize the salience of race or understands race as simple difference by reducing and stripping its institutional and material manifestations. From this perspective, the Supreme Court then becomes a theatre where the state insulates, protects, and legitimizes structures of white racial domination, particularly in education. A goal of this study is to advance the understanding of the synergy between whiteness and the law by looking at judicial colorblindness not primarily as a legal theory, but what Zeus Leonardo (2007) calls an instantiation of whiteness.

Finally, the assault on racial considerations in public policy does not appear to be slowing down. Beyond educational policy, judicial colorblindness is also peeling back Civil Rights Era protections designed to prevent racial discrimination in voting, housing, and employment. The common ingredient in all of these assaults is the Court's colorblind definition of 'discrimination'. This study will attempt to show that since *Brown*, a majority of major race cases has showed the conservative learning Court has more often than not failed to grasp the nature of racial stratification and subordination. Its failures have proven tragic not only to the specific racial issues presented at the time, but also casts a long antagonistic shadow of difficulty for future race related disputes. The Court continues to hear cases attacking racial considerations in and beyond education. Therefore, it is paramount to know the Court's historical trajectory where it carefully crafted a constricting and limiting definition of discrimination.

## Clarifying Legal Terms and Concepts

Two short explanations are in order. First, by jurisprudence I mean how the court views the constitution and adjudicates legal disputes based on this view. By implicating colorblind jurisprudence, I am critiquing one particular view, which critics and self-professing Justices (conservatives mostly) characterize as a fundamental belief in the declining significance of race. Although related, colorblind jurisprudence is not necessarily synonymous with what Eduardo Bonilla-Silva has called the colorblind era in American civil society. But as this book will show, colorblind jurisprudence is a critical component in the *ascendancy* of colorblindness as the dominant U.S. racial discourse. Supreme Court decisions have material significance in civil society, but in speaking of judicial jurisprudence, the investigation begins first and foremost with the Court's ideological methodology in hearing, determining, and settling constitutional disputes pertaining to issues of race, thereby constructing a clear albeit contradictory relationship between the law and race. That is, although the Court has routinely espoused so-called colorblind virtues and principles, its decisions striking down race positive policies are ultimately racial in that they prolong or intensify racial stratification, thereby presenting the paradox of 'color-conscious colorblindness'. Additionally, the colorblind judicial approach is by no means representative of the entire court. Arising out of *Brown* and the Civil Rights Era, judicial colorblindness has been the philosophical approach adopted by all conservative justices and a few centrist justices. However, progressive justices commonly favor the interpretation of the constitution as a 'living document', thus allowing, and at times favoring, race to enter into constitutional interpretation.

Second, my collective references to terms related to the Court and judicial colorblindness recognize that nearly every major case on race conscious policies since *Brown* has resulted in a right leaning majority that consistently views racial classifications as insidious at best and unconstitutional at worst. As a result, references to 'the Court' and 'judicial colorblindness' are only directed toward the majority and its concurring opinions, not dissenting opinions often authored by progressive Justices who reject judicial colorblindness. Although they are important in airing their objections, dissenting opinions have absolutely no binding legal ramifications and at most represent a text of conciliatory comfort to those on the losing side of the Court's majority decision. Therefore, unless otherwise noted, utterances, references, and articulations of 'the Court' and 'judicial colorblindness' refer only to majority and concurring opinions, representing the dominant framework that is indicative of the Court's judicial trajectory since *Brown*.

The following is an overview of the book's sections and chapters.

## *Section I*

Section I establishes the conceptual and ideological commitments necessary to critically investigate the symbiotic relationship between law and racial subordination. Chapter 1 introduces the concept of colorblindness both as a legal doctrine and popular social discourse on race and racism. Colorblindness, at best, views racial problems with ambivalence, and at worst, dismisses the existence of racism altogether. This chapter briefly touches on the early history of *Brown v. Board of Education* and the Civil Rights Era and documents a time when critical race consciousness was in fact central to governance and policy making—albeit short-lived. However, a sharp epistemological break occurred, with colorblind jurisprudence playing a central role, that has ensured the hegemony of colorblindness since *Brown*. Chapter 2 explores the methodological and interpretive commitments necessary to investigate the problem of colorblindness. Paul Ricoeur's concept of hermeneutics and Critical Race Theory are explored in order to locate judicial colorblindness and colorblind discourse as a site of contestation. Here, colorblindness is treated not simplistically as a legal doctrine, but a majoritarian narrative that produces racialized consequences. Chapter 3 explores the historical synergy of the law, racial subordination, and whiteness, understood as a racial discourse. The history of race and law in the U.S. can be categorized in three eras with slavery, Jim Crow 'separate but equal', and the modern colorblind era. Rather than signaling an end to racism, these eras are representations of particular practices of racism and racial understanding. Moving from period to period, this chapter charts the ongoing conversation on racial subordination and attempts to locate the source of subordination and inferiority: from biology, to culture, to personal choice. Most importantly, the chapter identifies the ongoing conversation on racial subordination not only to investigate the problem of racial subordination, but to indict whiteness.

### *Section II*

Section II examines canonical race disputes before the Supreme Court in the modern era from a critical race vantage point. Chapter 4 revisits the significant *Brown v. Board of Education* decision and views the opinion as a political maneuver of racial appeasement. With the hindsight of history, *Brown's* failure to usher in substantive educational equity for black children leaves its legacy as nothing more than a hollow symbolic victory for racial justice. Perhaps more critically, *Brown* is an act of whiteness that ushers in a new racial discourse ensuring the permanence of racism. Chapter 5 explores a specific new manifestation of racism in the post-*Brown* era: disproportionate racial harm to marginalized communities via 'colorblind' (read: race neutral) practices. *Brown* and the Civil Rights legislation shifted the public and civil conversation on race and racism. As a result, the Court was forced to adjudicate persistent racial inequalities under a new regime of racialized practices. With few exceptions initially, the Court repeatedly failed to fully grasp the evolving nature of racially subordinating practices, thereby not only missing repeated opportunities to address institutional manifestations of racism, but more critically sanctioned a stamp of approval to its colorblind forms. Chapter 6 investigates the history of affirmative action policies—modest democratic attempts to ameliorate specific institutional manifestations of racial inequality. As a product of the Court's colorblind jurisprudence, coupled with its inability and unwillingness to fully grasp the evolving nature of racial subordination, the constitutional world on race is completely upside down. Affirmative action policies, because they purposely (as it should) center race and racism, are adjudicated with viciousness and dismissive suspicion. As a result, the doors of 'equal protection' have been effectively shut against claims of institutional racism, while open and inviting to Whites who make dubious claims of victimhood from affirmative action policies.

### *Section III*

Section III concludes the book by presenting two peculiar phenomena in the colorblind era, and offers modest future directions for those committed to Civil Rights and confronting racial inequality. Chapter 7 situates the fortuitous *Fisher v. University of Texas* affirmative action decision that did *not* eliminate the use of racial considerations in college admissions. The chapter argues that, if placed within its broader anti-Civil

Rights context, *Fisher* is little more than a footnote to the consistent and orchestrated campaign to eliminate all vestiges of Civil Rights protections for subordinated and insular communities. Chapter 8 argues that despite the ubiquity of diversity as a celebrated ideal, affirmative action as a mechanism to achieve diversity has been all but defeated. As a sad consequence, democratic institutions such as colleges and universities are left cherishing a celebrated concept without any effective tools. These racial dynamics constitute a peculiar public discourse where minorities are now pitted against one another in the affirmative action debate. This discursive maneuver is necessary because the vitality of the white victim has all but enjoyed its last minutes of fame, thereby necessitating a new preferred victim: enter Asian Americans. Chapter 9 closes by offering an accessible and necessary proposal on future directions clustered around legal and educational issues.

---

Today, inequality, disparity, and racism are ever present in education in areas such as segregation, funding, and discipline. Rather than focus its energies and exacting scrutiny on addressing and potentially fixing these widespread educational problems, the law generally, and the Supreme Court specifically, choose to side with elites who claim to be 'victims' of discrimination because they were not admitted to exclusive institutions such as Harvard. Yes, racism and discrimination remain in education. I hope this book shifts our legal and social discourse to focus on actual victims of racial subordination.

## Section I

# Foundations of Colorblindness, Whiteness, and Racial Subordination

# 1 Judicial Colorblindness and the Problem of Racism

In tracing the decline of Jim Crow racism to the rise of *laissez-faire* racism, Bobo and Smith (1998) argue that the economic basis for Jim Crow had eroded, therefore racial attitudes changed with the structural conditions of group life. First, Bobo and Smith show that the civil rights movement systematically attacked the political underpinnings that were the cornerstones of Jim Crow racism. The *Brown* decision, the Civil Rights Act of 1964, the Voting Rights Act of 1965, and other political successes permanently altered the structural and economic basis for overt practices of racial subjugation such as segregation in education. Furthermore, Bobo and Smith suggest that if racial attitudes describe the material conditions of everyday life, it stands to reason that Jim Crow attitudes would eventually ebb away in popular acceptance. However, despite these monumental changes, Blacks and other people of color remained systematically segregated and economically disadvantaged well beyond *Brown* and the Civil Rights Era. These continuing social conditions must be differentiated from the economic and attitudinal underpinnings of the Jim Crow era. The decline in Jim Crow economics and attitudes signified the end of a *particular practice* of racial subjugation, *not* the end of racial subjugation itself. As numerous authors have pointed out, segregation and economic inequality continue today under the banner of *laissez-faire* racism flanked by the discourse of colorblindness. Continuing Bobo and Smith's analysis, the ebb of Jim Crow racial attitudes in the public was replaced by the flow of colorblindness as the new mainstream racial discourse.

The continuing social conditions of racial inequality lead Whites to believe that they stand to lose something tangible if political and legislative efforts are made to improve the lives of people of color, such as affirmative action and other race-based preferences in education. This belief is further solidified due to a colorblind sensibility in the post-Civil Rights Era. In a colorblind perspective, individuals are their own worst enemy if they experience any form of inequality because we live in a largely egalitarian and meritocratic society. As a result, people of color and their 'culture of poverty' are to blame for ongoing conditions of segregation and economic disparity. *Laissez-faire* racism in the era of colorblindness produces two related consequences. First is the individualized and free-market ideal that one receives what one works for. Second, because of the dogmatic belief that a colorblind society is largely fair, social policy and governance should not favor minorities over Whites; in fact, there are no racial groups, just a 'nation of minorities', as Justice Powell famously wrote in the first affirmative action case from 1978. Taken together, it is not a paradox for Whites to hold increasingly egalitarian racial principles while opposing strong forms of affirmative action intended to produce more racial equality. As Ian Haney López (2006) argues, contemporary colorblindness is a set of understandings that dictates how people apprehend, make sense of, and act on race.

However, the process of racialization is constantly contested and is neither smooth nor guaranteed. One important site for the ongoing contestation of racial meaning lies in the law and its interpretation in the courts. As colorblindness has become the dominant racial ethos, colorblind jurisprudence in the courts has played a commanding role in promoting a particular colorblind vision through public policy while simultaneously invalidating various race positive policies. Together, colorblindness as a mainstream racial discourse in society and judicial colorblindness in the Courts has worked symbiotically to reinforce a particularly vicious civil and social order, one that makes it all but impossible for social and civic policy to effectively tackle racial stratification and subordination. In the Court's function as arbiter of social and civil disputes, adjudicating issues of race have the potential to drastically reshape society. In this way, the willingness of the Court as a whole to reject or accept the persistence of racial inequality becomes paramount.

In general, there are two types of constitutional approaches. Progressive justices favor a 'living document' approach in interpreting the constitution. Justices favoring the 'living document' perspective argue for a 'spirit of the law' reading of the constitution. This approach allows freedoms, rights, and ideals, believed foundational to framers of the constitution, to be rearticulated and interpreted according to the social norms of contemporary society. One justification for the 'living document' interpretation argues that an evolving society and its norms require a constitution to reflect its values. For instance, Thurgood Marshall (1987) argued the original framers of the constitution would in no way ever imagine for someone like himself, a black jurist and descendant of slaves, to be Supreme Court justice despite the fact that he was hailed as the nation's first black Supreme Court justice upon his nomination to the Court. Marshall's observation is rather astute, clearly showing the ideals of justice, freedom, and liberty evolved over time to allow what was once an inconceivable proposition to move into the realm of possibility and eventual reality. However, conservative justices tend to take a 'strict constructionist' (also known as 'originalism') and textual jurisprudential approach favoring above all else a 'letter of the law' interpretation at the time the policy, law, or amendment was adopted. This perspective believes in first analyzing the literal text of the constitution. If the direct texts are not sufficient in answering a constitutional question, Justices then seek to interpret the intent of the framers of the constitution along with the common practices at the time of the law's adoption. 'Strict constructionists', or originalists, view the constitution as a document containing rights, freedoms, and values that are set in stone, not malleable to an evolving society. For instance, the late conservative justice Antonin Scalia has argued against a 'living document' interpretation of the constitution by saying that the constitution is in fact, dead—not living, because its values, ideals, and intents are written and must be respected according to its authors, not modern-day jurists. Originalists argue that there is a specific legislative process that must be followed in amending or adding constitution rights, freedoms, and values. Additionally, originalists argue that adding constitutional amendments specifically requires two-thirds ratification by the states and thus belongs to the political process and legislative branch, not a process located in the judicial branch or a responsibility of the Supreme Court.

However, the apparent uniformity of strict constructionists runs into difficulties when the Court deals with issues related to race. For instance, the Court has routinely held it unconstitutional for public universities to use racial classifications in admissions policies. But when universities attempt to curb racial hate speech, these efforts have not survived constitutional review. Therefore, the Court has made curious distinction between public and private forms of racial discrimination. Whereas a university is not allowed to use racial considerations, private individuals and groups within a university are constitutionally protected to discriminate along racial lines. Thus, a strict constructionist interpretation of the constitution deals with race on a superficial level without a proper understanding of the nature of racial domination and subordination.

Judicial colorblindness is a relatively recent jurisprudential spawn of the 'strict constructivist' perspective. The literal 'letter of the law' reading of the 'equal protection clause' of the Fourteenth Amendment and Title VI of the Civil Rights Act of 1964 are foundational to judicial colorblindness. Section 1 of the Fourteenth Amendment, better known as the 'equal protection clause', states, 'no state shall deny to any person within its jurisdiction the equal protection of the laws'. Additionally, Title VI of the Civil Rights Act prohibits any institutions receiving federal financial assistance from implementing any programs or activities 'that discriminate on the ground of race, color, or national origin'. Therefore, a 'letter of the law' reading of these two pieces of law provides the theoretical foundation of judicial colorblindness. Here, colorblindness in the law does not literally mean the inability to see color (read: race). Courts see race, but refuse to acknowledge the structural and institutional harm of race, therefore absolving itself of any culpability in its inaction toward structural racism. In the eyes of colorblind legal perspective, race is any and all forms of differentiation with little regard to whether structural or material harms are attached to those differentiations. Or as Justice John Roberts wrote in *Parents Involved* (2007), 'The way to stop discrimination based on race is to stop discriminating based on race'. As a result, justices who adopt a colorblind jurisprudence see no substantive or procedural difference between laws that enforce segregation, e.g. Jim Crow, and those that attempt to remedy segregation, e.g. race conscious school assignment programs and affirmative action policies.

This particular colorblind interpretation of Title VI and the equal protection clause is emblematic of the anti-classification principle of the modern equal protection tradition. Although *Brown* prohibited racial segregation in public education, Riva Siegel (2004) argues that the decision inaugurated a great debate about equality and the possibilities, or limits, of equal protection. From this great equal protection debate, two principles emerged: anti-classification and anti-subordination. For many, the principle of anti-classification embraced a particular conception of equality committed to individuals over groups. That is, anti-classification rejects laws and policies that classify individuals based on race, sex, religion, ethnicity, or national origin. This account of the anti-classification principle repudiates an alternative conception of equal protection, the anti-subordination principle. Advocates of the anti-subordination principle share the commitment that laws and governmental practices should not enforce or further perpetuate the subordinated status of historically oppressed communities. Anti-subordination, a legal scholarship tradition established by Yale scholar Owen Fiss (1976) during the critical Civil Rights Era two decades after *Brown*, fundamentally recognizes the subordinate status of minority groups as a consequence of white domination and racial stratification. Here, it is important to differentiate between recognizing the inferior social and cultural statuses of racial minorities as a result of institutional racism, rather than enforcing some notion of inherent inferiority based on biology. As a result, Fiss argued that laws should not aggravate or perpetuate group subordination. Furthermore, the anti-subordination principle argues that courts must review with great care the laws that *burden* minorities and adopt a model of equality that focuses on structural processes of domination instead of simplistic uptakes of difference.

## The Burden of Strict Scrutiny

Decided in 1978, *Regents of the University of California v. Bakke* was the first affirmative action case in education adjudicated by the Supreme Court. The *Bakke* decision is a landmark case for several reasons (discussed further in Chapter 6). For instance, *Bakke* declared affirmative action quotas unconstitutional but accepted 'diversity in the classroom' as a permissible constitutional justification for racial considerations in higher education admissions. However, lesser discussed but perhaps the most significant consequence of *Bakke* is that justice Powell's opinion established a majority bloc that mandated that all future legal disputes concerning race conscious policies would be adjudicated under strict scrutiny, the Court's most stringent and exacting examination. In other words, the *Bakke* Court established the parameters where future democratic attempts to address educational and social inequalities via race consciousness, such as *de facto* segregation and university admissions, would be subjected to 'strict scrutiny' which views all racial considerations automatically suspect. In reviewing statutes and government action against the potential violation of constitutional rights such as 'equal protection' or statutory rights under Title VII, the Court utilizes a hierarchy of standards. Strict scrutiny is the most stringent standard of review followed by intermediate scrutiny and rational basis review.

| | *Rational Basis Review* | *Intermediate Scrutiny* | *Strict Scrutiny* |
|---|---|---|---|
| State Interest | Legitimate, can be merely conceivable—need not be actual | Must be genuine and important | State interest must be compelling |
| Law's Relation to State Interest | Must be *rationally* related, or non-arbitrary | Must be Substantially related | Must be *necessary to achieve the purpose*, and discriminating policy is 'narrowly tailored' |

Rational basis review simply requires that the government show the law in question is 'rationally' related to state interests. The Court utilizes this lowest standard of review on benign classifications like prohibiting the sale of alcohol to minors. To illustrate further the lax requirement of rational basis review, a law's relation to state interests only needs to be conceivable; whether or not the law is smart or sound policy is of little concern. To illustrate this point, Justice Thurgood Marshall has said, 'the constitution does not prohibit legislatures from enacting stupid laws'.

However, strict scrutiny is a much more difficult standard. The Court has consistently ruled that all government classification of race requires strict scrutiny as the standard of review. Therefore, strict scrutiny immediately renders all racial classifications constitutionally suspect. As a result of this high threshold, proponents of race conscious educational policies fight a difficult legal battle just to get the Court to recognize that race matters. Major race cases in educational policy since *Brown* such as *Bakke*, *Grutter*, *Parents Involved*, and *Fisher* have shown the difficulty posed by a colorblind jurisprudence in fulfilling *Brown's* promise of equal educational opportunity. Due to the requirement of strict scrutiny coupled with a colorblind jurisprudence from conservative Justices, proponents of race conscious polices are severely handicapped in the legal fight.

## Antisubordination and Anticlassification: A False Dichotomy?

Legal scholars Jack Balkin and Reva Siegel (2004) suggest the standard story of the Court's jurisprudence in the latter half of the 20th century is that the views of Owen Fiss and other anti-subordination proponents were soundly rejected by the Court in favor of an anti-classification principle. However, Balkin and Siegel argue that the Court initially embraced both anti-subordination and anti-classification equal protection principles depending on specific practices, shifts in trends over time, and social contestation and struggle. Today, anti-subordination principles are not embraced by contemporary conservative Supreme Court Justices. Conservative justices not only adopt the anti-classification principle, but a particular version grounded in colorblindness. Justice Thomas explained:

> *Brown I* itself did not need to rely upon any psychological or social-science research in order to announce the simple, yet fundamental, truth that the government cannot discriminate among its citizens on the basis of race. . . . At the heart of this interpretation of the Equal Protection Clause lies the principle that the government must treat citizens as individuals, and not as members of racial, ethnic, or religious groups.[1]

On the surface, colorblind jurisprudence is seductive. The allure of colorblindness is spurned by the popular conception of blind justice, popularly depicted by the blindfolded statue of lady justice holding a scale balancing truth and fairness. The appeal of blind justice is that any member of society, whether rich or poor, black or white, young or old will get a fair shake before the blind eyes of justice and will be treated according to a uniform application and enforcement of the law. Beyond this, the impression of blind justice gives the justice system a sense of authority and righteousness *because* it is perceived as fair and just.

But Justice Thomas' belief that *Brown* did not need to rely on psychological or social-science arguments exposes the essence, and therefore fallacies, of judicial colorblindness. By sidestepping the psychological and social effects of institutionalized racism, judicial colorblindness foreclosed possibilities that the Court could fulfill an anti-subordination equal protection promise. That is, how can a colorblind Court address the effects of racism when it does not recognize the institutional and structural apparatuses of race? Although conservative Justices routinely cite *Brown* in striking down racial classification policies, Balkin and Siegel remind us that *Brown* animated both anti-subordination and anti-classification norms. Reflecting the anti-classification principle, the *Brown* Court ruled that 'separate but equal' was inherently unequal because members of society were separated based on racial classification. Additionally, the *Brown* Court recognized anti-subordination principles by holding that segregation has a detrimental effect upon minority children and would generate a feeling of inferiority unlikely ever to be undone. In other words, *Brown* recognized that educational segregation contained elements of both classification and subordination. Educational segregation harmed black children not simplistically because they were prevented from going to all-white schools, but that their all-black schools were systematically and structurally inferior, thus reinforcing the inferiority and superiority between black and white schools.

The landmark *Brown* case represented a chance to end *de jure* racial classification *and* afford substantive equal protection to subordinated groups, thus incorporating both anti-classification and anti-subordination elements. However, a careful examination of the social and political battles over *Brown's* enforcement mandate exposes *Brown* as a case that is today revered as a hallowed moment although it achieved little substantive change in regard to alleviating the subordinated status of black students. More critically, *Brown* should also be remembered as a significant moment that led to the birth of judicial colorblindness for conservative justices for the next sixty years and beyond—a conservative jurisprudence that has consistently been utilized to rule against the integrationist interests of *Brown* via a strict anti-classification constitutional approach.

## Why Does a Critical Analysis of Race and Law Matter?

Within the context of constitutional review and jurisprudence, it appears that Justice Harlan's famous dissenting proclamation in *Plessy v. Ferguson* (1896) that 'our constitution is colorblind' has been the ideological vision championed by conservative justices in order to methodologically prohibit race-based quota set-asides, and more generally speaking, affirmative action policies in and beyond the institution of education. In fact, including *Fisher*, only one other race conscious policy practice in education has survived constitutional review by the Supreme Court. Having survived strict scrutiny, the permissible law school admissions practice preserved in *Grutter v. Bollinger* (2003) was filled with restrictive limitations on exactly how the University of Michigan could move forward considering race. The Court in *Grutter* provided stringent criterion of procedural substance for all race positive state action, requiring it to be 'narrowly tailored' and 'of last resort'. However, even though it approved a permissible government practice of racial consideration, the opinion contained a clear disdain and suspicion for the salience of race, with swing vote Justice Sandra Day O'Connor noting perhaps race positive policies will no longer be needed twenty-five years into the future. If we take seriously Justice O'Connor's predictions, we are not far away from her predicted post-racial utopia. Although a colorblind reading of the constitution has been utilized to strike down almost every affirmative action-related policy, it would be a mistake to read the two as simply in opposition to each other. As Eduardo Bonilla-Silva (2001) and others have asserted, we are currently in a colorblind era of racial understanding. Comparably, it would be difficult to suggest that anyone is reasonably proclaiming that we are also in the affirmative action era. Colorblindness has achieved a common sense and ideological hegemony that shows no signs of slowing down; in fact, it seems to be speeding up. This social uptake has reached far beyond the confines of law. Rather, colorblindness is more than just how Supreme Court Justices read the constitution. Colorblindness reflects a methodical politics of governance and represents an antagonistic ideology in direct opposition to the long struggle for justice in a society where racial stratification remains the dominant organizing principle.

*Brown v. Board of Education* is rightly regarded today as a significant case, but Derrick Bell (1995) argued that *Brown* represents little more than a hollow symbolic victory rather than the substantive holy grail of racial justice that its stature conjures contemporaneously. Specifically, within the context of education, *Brown* was the first official governmental recognition of the debilitating and oppressive inner workings of racialization and segregation. In *Dred Scott v. Sanford* (1857), the unequal treatment of Blacks and Whites in the law was justified as a simple reflection of the supposed inherent superiority and inferiority of Whites and non-Whites. Having to take account of the newly passed Fourteenth Amendment guaranteeing equal protection, the *Plessy* Court continued white supremacy and institutional manifestations of white privilege by deploying the infamous 'fallacy argument'. The *Plessy* court argued that if enforced separation of the two races creates a badge of inferiority for Blacks, it is a construction solely created by Blacks and not the government. Perhaps above all else, *Brown* is a landmark case to the extent that it was the first Supreme Court case to confront directly the constitutionality of 'separate but equal'. In previous cases,[2] the court accepted 'separate but equal' as constitutional and its method of review focused on enforcing *Plessy's* mandate, as opposed to adjudicating whether or not the doctrine of 'separate but equal' was in fact constitutional. Of course, *Brown* famously ruled that segregation is in fact inherently unequal and therefore cannot be made equal. Unequivocal as these words are, the language of enforcement requiring desegregation spelled out in the second *Brown* decision (popularly known as *Brown II*) was everything but exact, clear, and decisive. Thus, although the initial *Brown* decision represented the first state recognition of the stratifying role of race in civil society, the resulting political pushback against desegregation by segregationists, coupled with the Court's increasing colorblind tendencies, has turned *Brown* into the final state recognition of the stratifying role of race in civil society. Effectively, *Brown* is now the standard cite of the birth of colorblindness by ushering in a new era of strictly anti-classification adjudication by originalist and conservatives on the Court.

This brief history is necessary to understand the contemporary rejection of affirmative action policies in favor of a colorblind reading of the constitution, specifically, and a colorblind vision of society, more generally. Keeping in mind the presence of racial stigma codified in *Dred Scott*, which continued in *Plessy* and *Brown* (I will have more to say about this in Chapter 2), adherents of colorblindness today argue that affirmative action policies create racial stigmas for racial minorities via race conscious policies that consider race. An extension of this conversation could suggest colorblindness is a post-race ideology, only to be pulled back into the ugly and distasteful racialized social organizations via affirmative action policies. However, equating colorblindness with a post-racial society is only possible if one sees *Brown* and the civil rights era as representing the end of the continuing significance of race in society. One needs only to look at the current Court's oral arguments in *Fisher* to confirm Cornel West's (1993) sentiment that race still matters.

Conservative Justices on the Court during oral arguments for *Fisher* showed skepticism toward the University of Texas' (UT) holistic admissions that used race as one of its 'Achievement Index' criteria. However, UT only used the achievement index for 8% of its admitted students during the in-question 2008 admission. The other 92% of admissions came from the state of Texas' 'Top Ten' program that guarantees admissions to any UT campus for students who finished in the top ten percent of their high school graduating class. Thus the Top Ten program is allegedly strictly empirical and race-neutral. Amicus briefs, Abigail Fisher's legal team, and the conservative court questioned why the university would need to use a constitutionally suspect racial classification when it can just default to its Top Ten percent, which would survive constitutional review and apparently produce the desired critical mass of diversity. This racial sleight-of-hand typifies the tendency of colorblindness. Texas' Top Ten percent admission program only produces the desired diversity because Texas high schools are severely racially segregated. Therefore, the top ten percent from a majority-minority school would produce a strong representation of minority students eligible for automatic admission to the UT. Nevertheless, the Court's disfavoring of Texas' holistic admissions for the Top Ten percent does not prove the declining significance of race, but further underscores the stratifying importance of race. This colorblind manipulation shows that colorblindness is in fact not emblematic of a post-racial society, but rather the latest manifestation of an ideological and political practice of racial governance that prolongs, reinforces, constructs, and perpetuates white superiority.

It is short sighted and betrays racial history to read colorblindness in the law as simply and only a constitutional jurisprudence, or one that is used to strike down affirmative action and race conscious policies. More broadly, colorblindness is cut from the same cloth of overt racism and assumed white superiority since *Dred Scott*, 'separate but equal' in *Plessy*, and *Brown's* unenforceable 'in all deliberate speed' desegregation mandate. Colorblindness operates with the effectiveness of political maneuvers of the past in guaranteeing and sustaining the privileges of Whites over people of color. As civil society stands on the cusp of more legal edicts on race and law, it would be a mistake to read any decision against race positive holistic admissions as a move signifying the end to the significance of race in U.S. society. It would more accurately represent the latest moment in the conservative Court's trajectory in solidifying racial stratification and subordination in society by turning a blind eye to the significance of race. Irrespective of its animosity toward usages of race in public policy, the conservative Court clearly recognizes race still matters, apparent from its championing of Texas' Top Ten program as the favored mechanism to produce diversity. Echoing Justice Blackmun in the *Bakke* case, the only way to get beyond race is to first take account of it; there is no other way. Because race still matters, colorblindness as a political ideology of governance becomes the latest act of whiteness *par excellence*. As an ideology of difference, colorblindness cannot be severed from its roots in slavery, Jim Crow, 'separate but equal', and racial segregation.

## Notes

1. *Missouri v. Jenkins*, 515 U.S. 70 (1995). Thomas Concurring Opinion, pp. 120–121.
2. For instance, in a case decided four years before *Brown*, the Court in *Sweatt v. Painter* ordered the University of Texas Law School to admit Heman Sweatt as its first black student because the alternative law school for blacks was deemed not tangibly and intangibly equal to the white-only flagship school in Austin, Texas. In *Sweatt*, the Court did not reject *Plessy's* 'separate but equal' doctrine, but enforced it.

# 2 Commitments

## Of Methods and Interpretation

These two statements should be uncontroversial: we are currently in the colorblind era and the Supreme Court has played a significant role toward its development and continuing preservation. Colorblind ideology dismisses the centrality of race as a source of social conflict and as a worthwhile concept for public institutions, such as the Supreme Court, to consider in legislating or adjudicating social problems. In an updated version to their seminal racial formations project, Michael Omi and Howard Winant (2014) argue that contemporary manifestations of colorblind ideology in politics, policy, and education have hijacked the dream of colorblindness from Martin Luther King Jr. and other Civil Rights activists. We can include the founding fathers of Critical Race Theory (CRT) in the category of Civil Rights activists. Colorblind ideology today represents the exact opposite of the race-centric methodological commitment of CRT. It is not by happenstance or accident of history that colorblindness has become our hegemonic racial discourse despite the continuing persistence of racial stratification and subordination in society. In areas such as housing, the criminal justice system, and education, the persistence of racial stratification and subordination are well documented. Despite the overwhelming evidence of racial problems, the Court continues, at best, to approach racial issues with ambivalence, and at worst, completely reject racial issues as worthwhile problems in which to intervene. Understanding the genesis and epistemology of this apparent paradox is the methodology of this study.

This chapter examines the methodological and interpretative commitments necessary to approach the paradox of colorblindness. First, the leading section provides a contemporary judicial example where colorblind jurisprudence by the Supreme Court has all but eliminated the importance of racial considerations in legal disputes. The example is meant to represent the paradoxical nature of the Court's colorblind jurisprudence in relation to the racially significant nature of social problems that come before the Court. The second section discusses hermeneutics, or the science of interpretation, as a methodological tool in order to take up the Court's colorblind arc. That is, in proceeding to take up the Court's colorblind ideology, its ideology must be understood as what Zeus Leonardo (2003) would call interpreting the problem of domination. Therefore, Paul Ricoeur's (1976) work on hermeneutics and Leonardo's discussion of critical hermeneutics guide our understanding of the Court's ideology by locating it as a problematic site of legal interpretation. Finally, the third section discusses how we can go about utilizing critical legal hermeneutics under the methodological commitments of Critical Race Theory. The working definition of hermeneutics as a 'conflict of interpretation' will be utilized as an instructive force in CRT's methodology of counter storytelling, scenarios, narratives, testimonies, and chronicles. The method of counter storytelling is particularly important as it provides an alternative narrative to explain the Court's ongoing unwillingness to confront and address racial problems.

## The Consequence of Judicial Colorblindness

In *Parents Involved in Community Schools v. Seattle School District No. 1* (2007), the Supreme Court ruled against the Seattle School District's usage of a racial tie-breaker in its school assignment policy. The Seattle School district allowed students and families to apply to any school within the district. Inevitably, some schools were oversubscribed and required the district to use a number of tiebreakers for student assignment. One of the tiebreakers utilized race with the explicit goal to maintain student body diversity within racial percentages reflective of Seattle's overall student population. At the time, the racial breakdown for Seattle's public school students was approximately 41% white and 59% non-White. For example, if a school was oversubscribed, the district would affirmatively make assignment decisions taking into account the race of students in order to maintain a diverse student body reflective of the district's racial breakdown. Before the Court's final ruling, the National Academy of Education (see Linn & Welner, 2007) commissioned a committee to review all *Amicus Curiae* filings with the Supreme Court, which supported either petitioners or respondents. *Amicus Curiae*, also known as 'friend of the court' briefs, are briefs or reports that interested third party groups, individuals, and organizations can submit to the Court in support of either side of the legal dispute. Out of sixty-four reports, the committee found at least twenty-seven to include substantial discussions of social science research. The committee identified five key questions addressed by the research, three of which were:

1. Is racial diversity in a school environment associated with improved academic achievement?
2. Is racial diversity in a school environment associated with intergroup relations?
3. Is racial diversity in a school environment associated with improved long-term effects?

The committee found the totality of reviewed research data answered all three questions in the affirmative. However, conclusions in social science research are always measured and cautioned against sweeping generalizations. For example, in reviewing the question of racial diversity and its association with academic achievement, the committee cautioned that because different analytic approaches were utilized, the impact of school diversity on student achievement was likely to vary across different studies.

When opposing *Amicus* briefs do not disagree over methodology, they disagree over conclusions. In support of race conscious student policies, the American Education Research Association, American Psychological Association, and American Council on Education supported research that concluded African American students who attended desegregated elementary and secondary schools were more likely to attend predominantly white colleges. In response, opponents of race conscious policies acknowledge the same likelihood, but argued the available research could not justify whether the results were a product of desegregation, or other facially non-racial variables such as standardized test scores. Given the diverging opinions apparent in *Amicus* briefs on research methodology and conclusions, conservative Justice Clarence Thomas concluded that the inconclusive social science research cannot plausibly support integration interests, let alone enough to satisfy the Court's standard of strict scrutiny to allow the usage of race as a 'discriminatory factor' in public policy. As a result, whereas proponents of race conscious policies must apparently present incontrovertible research evidence to prove 'compelling interests', opponents need only question research methodology or undermine conclusions. Here, the Court's standard of strict scrutiny is an ally and a weapon for those who reject the necessity of race conscious public policies.

This striking circumstance of opposing *Amicus* briefs from *Parents Involved* perhaps reveals the ultimate goals of each respective side. Whereas groups and foundations in favor of racial considerations provided substantial academic research speaking to the positive educational outcomes of a diverse educational environment, opponents simply poked holes in the social science research. As a result, a methodological approach studying educational diversity was defeated and undermined by a method of obstruction. As the ruling from *Parents Involved* shows, obstruction won thanks to the rigid and almost impossible framework of strict scrutiny that leaves little room at the table for social science research within the context of education, law, and conservative colorblind jurisprudence.

## Hermeneutics and Interpretation

In order to comprehend the Court's colorblind position on issues of race, the role of hermeneutics must be a central concern. Hermeneutics, or the science of interpretation, can be understood as the site to locate the conflict of interpretations. In the context of the colorblind court and current educational issues, the hermeneutical process is needed to fill the incredible gap that exists between the Courts' colorblind language and the racially significant material life it allegedly describes. In studying the Court's historical decisions on race related issues in the colorblind era, its colorblind language *must* be judged against the force and influence of material history. In other words, when conservative justices continually dismiss the salience of racial subordination in favor of colorblind and race-neutral solutions, their language should be made to answer for the ongoing persistence of racial stratification in society. Therefore, a hermeneutics of the Court's colorblind jurisprudence requires that we both understand the Court's decisions, but also go beyond the Court's colorblind language to understand its larger impact in society. In other words, it's an understanding of legal significance and social consequence.

Ricoeur's (1976) hermeneutics framework stresses the important distinction between language and discourse. To Ricoeur, discourse surpasses language because it is within a discourse that language finds its meaning. Without a discursive context, such as a historical conjuncture in the colorblind era, language can be lost in meaning and become an abstraction without specificity, referent, and substance. We often witness this phenomenon within constitutional originalism and colorblind jurisprudence. For instance, conservative Justice Clarence Thomas has routinely stated that he sees no difference between *de jure* practices of racial discrimination (e.g. Jim Crow Laws) and affirmative action policies. Referring to an affirmative action practice ensuring minority participation in construction contracts during the 1990s, Justice Thomas stated:

> There is a moral and constitutional equivalence between laws designed to subjugate a race and those that distribute benefits on the basis of race in order to foster some current notion of equality. . . . In my mind, government-sponsored racial discrimination based on benign prejudice is just as noxious as discrimination inspired by malicious prejudice.[1]

Justice Thomas' moral and constitutional equivalence is only made possible because the language of discrimination has been institutionalized via colorblind jurisprudence and has simply become a linguistic exercise removed from its historical context. If the language of discrimination were in fact tied to material history, there is absolutely no equivalence in comparing a Jim Crow system of methodical racial exclusion with an affirmative action system that promotes inclusion. Ricoeur emphasizes the importance of history in providing the discursive context that gives language meaning by arguing the knowledge of history is not removed from the historical condition. In other words, research of history, or in this case, retelling history, cannot be severed from the consciousness of those who live and make history. Underlining Ricoeur's point, Leonardo stresses that because the force and influence of history is common to all subjects, it is interpretive understanding that becomes malleable as a result of the conflict of interpretation. Therefore, we can conclude that in the context of Justice Thomas' alleged moral and constitutional equivalence, the force and influence of Jim Crow racial subordination is ever present as is any perceived historical significance of affirmative action. However, it is Justice Thomas' selective interpretation of these historical conditions that allows him to equivocate the two as one and the same.

Leonardo (2003) argues that as a methodological tool, a critical hermeneutics is needed in order to allow social actors to critique meaning systems that construct illusions out of history. That is, as a form of ideology critique, critical hermeneutics complicates the everyday, the taken-for-granted, and the 'common sense' assumptions that explain social problems as 'natural'. Oftentimes the constructed illusions of colorblindness do little to portray accurately the material basis of history, but they nevertheless are instrumental in shaping future history. This is a common occurrence in the political Right's anti-affirmative action language. Despite the lack of empirical evidence, anti-affirmative action positions routinely cite the tried-and-true mantra that Whites are rejected from positions in schools and industries *because* of affirmative action, or even more falsely, because of their whiteness. In Gramscian theory (see Anderson, 1976), the ideological hegemony of the anti-affirmative action mantra has in fact been utilized to shape legal history concerning race positive considerations in employment and public education.

As a response to the hegemony of colorblindness, a critical hermeneutics is necessary not only to describe the formation of judicial colorblindness, but also to change it. Leonardo (2003) argues that an important function of critical hermeneutics is to reveal fallacies or taken-for-granted master narratives that have gone unquestioned such as individualism, historical facts, and objectivity. Leonardo's point echoes the important tenet central to hermeneutics: interpretations are never neutral. Therefore, along with the myths of rugged individualism, history's facticity, and science's objectivity, the Court's colorblind trajectory should similarly be exposed. In this way, the Court's colorblindness is not just simplistically a constitutional jurisprudence, but an interpretive discourse that buttresses racial domination in society.

## Critical Hermeneutics, CRT, and Storytelling

If colorblindness is poison to race positive policy making, then Critical Race Theory (CRT) is the antidote. Perhaps the most foundational commitment that informs the pedagogical, methodological, and basic insight of CRT is the centricity of race and racism in society. In order to expose and lay bare the centricity of racism, CRT scholars have adopted the methodological practice of presenting stories, parables, histories, and scenarios in order to underline the legitimacy of experiential knowledge from the perspectives of people of color. Additionally, the importance of CRT's method of storytelling is to present a counter-narrative, or what Daniel Solorzano and Tara Yosso (2002) call an anti-majoritarian story. Here is where critical hermeneutics and a critical race method of storytelling come together. An anti-majoritarian story not only centralizes the experiential knowledge of the marginalized, it also exposes the taken for granted and alleged 'naturalness' of dominant, or master narratives. In other words, critical hermeneutics locates the production of master narratives as a site to deconstruct the conflict of interpretation. Specifically, critical hermeneutics reveals the politics behind the Court's systematic suppression of race positive narratives in favor of colorblind sensibilities. By coupling material history with the Court's canonical race cases, we can construct anti-majoritarian stories on law and racial subordination that the conservative Court refuses to acknowledge.

### *CRT and Anti-Majoritarian Storytelling*

Behind a steady and consistent stream of anti-affirmative action decisions, the conservative Court since *Brown* has constructed a master narrative treating the importance of racial subordination in society as a marginal and declining phenomenon. In fact, racial issues have only been adjudicated to further minimize or all together eliminate racial considerations. This of course has two immediate consequences. First and most obvious is the denial of judicial remedy for communities of color. Second, Beverly Tatum (1997) argues despite the heated rhetoric about affirmative action and reverse-racism in these cases, the denial of judicial remedy for communities of color also affirms the persistent advantages for Whites. Tatum uses the concrete example of housing discrimination to emphasize her point. Meaning, when a person of color is denied housing due to discrimination, the apartment that would have otherwise been occupied by that person of color is nevertheless always available to a white person.

Not only does the existence of master narratives prevent minority-centric perspectives to exist, it also normalizes the persistence of racism and white privilege. In other words, majoritarian stories act like a double-edged sword. First, majoritarian stories silence minority accounts that are incongruent with its colorblind sensibilities. Second, it denies the existence of racial subordination and as a result, upholds the 'excellence' of Whites while painting minority struggles as a fundamental consequence of a culture of poverty, lack of personal responsibility, or individual failures.

Whites are not the only ones who tell majoritarian stories; people of color also tell them. In his *Fisher* dissent, black Justice Clarence Thomas cited Richard Sander and Stuart Taylor's 'mismatch theory', arguing that minority students are harmed when 'under-qualified' students are accepted to competitive elite schools because of admissions that consider students beyond 'strict academic standards'. Similarly, black economist Thomas Sowell (1981) claimed the goals and value systems of Mexican Americans have never centered education. Missing from Thomas and Sowell's prescriptions are any historical and material consideration that prevents minorities from enjoying the same educational experiences as Whites.

Here is where counter-stories, or anti-majoritarian narratives are needed. Solorzano and Yosso (2002) suggest the power of the counter-story exists in its ability to convey the experiences of peoples often forgotten or pushed to the margins of society. Additionally, the counter stories also are weapons to expose and challenge the taken-for-granted master narratives of racial superiority and privilege. Importantly, Solorzano and Yosso argue that anti-majoritarian stories need not only be created and told as a direct response to majoritarian ones. That is, if the existence of counter narratives is only in response to master narratives, we let master narratives dominate the discourse under the guise of universality. The authors identify three types of counter-narratives and/or stories: personal stories or narratives, other people's stories or narratives, and composite stories or narratives. Particularly, composite stories or narratives are formed from multiple forms of data and knowledge to reconstruct the experiences of those on the margins. In reconstructing composite stories, authors are able to place racialized peoples in appropriate historical and political situations to indict racism. In order to craft a counter-narrative, it is important for the researcher to unearth sources of data. In the same way that colorblind justices ignore the significance of data on racial subordination, counter narratives must show a 'theoretical sensitivity' and 'cultural intuition' within the process of collecting data to tell a story. Solorzano and Yosso emphasize that a theoretical sensitivity is the ability to have insight which gives not only meaning to data, but a capability to separate the pertinent from impertinent. Furthermore, cultural intuition allows our own personal experiences to extend outward in the collection and analysis of data. Together, the construction of counter narratives require data from multiple sources without consideration as to whether primary sources are more valued than secondary or individual and personal stories. Critically, critical race methodology such as storytelling connects the institutional manifestation of racist policy with its material consequences. Anti-majoritarian stories support the important contention that discussions of race require a substantive discussion of racism.

CRT's methodology of using narratives and storytelling does not come without its detractors. Although scholars have criticized CRT on a number of grounds, the most common critique alleges that CRT abandons western traditions of rational and empirical inquiry by forswearing analysis for personal narratives or subjective storytelling. The prolific legal scholar and Seventh Circuit Court of Appeals judge Richard Posner (1997) argues that when critical race theorists tell stories—e.g. fictional, quasi-fictional, or autobiographical—logical arguments and empirical data are abandoned. Furthermore, Posner dismissively suggests that because reasoned argumentation is repudiated, storytellers reinforce stereotypes concerning the anti-intellectual capacities of people of color.

Additionally, former Ninth Circuit of Appeals judge Alex Kozinski (1997) suggests that with CRT's storytelling methodology, insuperable barriers are raised that has the effect of preventing mutual understanding. For instance, Kozinski cites Derrick Bell's 'The Space Traders' allegorical tale from *Faces at the Bottom of the Well* (1992) where Bell argues white America would overwhelmingly vote to trade all black Americans in exchange for untold treasure. Kozinski suggests that Bell's thesis is untestable and therefore one reaches the dead end of either having to completely agree or disagree with the merits of Bell's allegorical tale. Even some self-professed traditional liberals call CRT folks 'radical multiculturalists' who are waging open warfare on all that is valuable in western society (see Farber and Sherry, 1997). These critics allege that enlightenment concepts such as merit, truth, equality, freedom, and responsibility have all been given the axe and civil academic dialogue has been the unfortunate victim of CRT's emergence. A common theme arises from these critiques in that they all accuse CRT methodology, and storytelling specifically, of forsaking western traditions of rationalism and destroying traditional liberal values.

This debate is not one that will be settled here. However, the back and forth of CRT's methodology and its criticisms is reminiscent of Zeus Leonardo and Ronald Porter's (2010) criticism for the need of 'safety' in race dialogue. That is, similar to the need of Whites' for safety before engaging in critical race dialogues, it appears traditional scholars are likewise advocating for a safe methodological frame of criticism and reason in order to do what they regard as 'proper' intellectual work in eradicating social problems. At the very least, it appears Kozinski, Posner, et al. are mistaking the *modus operandi* of CRT for its end game. CRT's goals are not to supplant western traditions and methodology with storytelling and counter narratives. CRT utilizes these 'untraditional' methodologies as a means to eradicate social debasement and subordination based on race. Rather than accuse CRT of forswearing rational analysis, perhaps critics should question whether rational analysis is doing enough to eradicate racism. The answer seems self-evident, which promulgates the search for a different methodology.

### *The Formation of Counter Narratives*

The influence of law is felt beyond the personal experience of any one individual. For instance, not only do educational laws influence the experience of individuals and families, they shape the formation of entire communities and their relationship with other social institutions. In this way, composite stories are needed to construct a counter narrative to majoritarian stories of colorblind meritocracy and race neutrality. Necessary in this construction is a hermeneutical process of identifying power, influence, and modes of oppression. Most important, critical hermeneutics demands that we not only tell counter narratives as a response to dominant stories, but counter narratives are an attempt to uncover the racialized foundations of dominant stories. In perhaps the most powerful example of counter story telling in regard to the legacy of *Brown v. Board of Education*, Derrick Bell (2004) provides a reconceived version of *Brown*. Bell's powerful counter narrative offers an insightful reframing of the substantive issues that faced black students in light of the shortcomings from the real *Brown* decision.

Bell offers his reconceived version of *Brown* in the manner of a pseudo United States Supreme Court opinion. In explaining the necessity for *Brown* to be reconceived, Bell argues the actual *Brown* decision has become canonical and an American icon embraced as a symbol of the country's ability to forget and forgive our racial sins. It is precisely the illusion that racial problems are somehow behind us that makes *Brown* so troubling. In offering a reconceived version of *Brown*, Bell identifies the discursive histories that mainstream-celebratory memories of the real *Brown* systematically ignore. Provocatively, Bell's reconceived *Brown* would **uphold** *Plessy v. Ferguson's* 'separate but equal' constitutional mandate. That is, Bell would reverse the principal feature that makes the *Brown* case so famous: the end of 'separate but equal'. In doing so, Bell does not abandon his commitment to racial equality, but locates the measure of racial equality as one that must have substantive results, not idealism *sans* material history. Bell's reconceived version of *Brown* argued that striking down separate but equal does not immediately reveal its hypocritical internal logic. Furthermore, actual relief for segregated schools required specific actions, legally monitored action plans, and concrete steps fundamentally designed to provide the educational equity long denied under the fallacy of 'separate but equal'.

It must be pointed out that scores of books and articles have been written about *Brown* since its passage, and Bell's reconceived alternative version is by no means the only attempt to revisit the original decision. However, many works criticize the opinion for its weakness, ineffectiveness, and ambivalent desegregation language. Although I think these approaches are spot on with their critique, they are categorically different from Bell's reconceived version of *Brown*. The approaches of these scholars differ from Bell in the sense that they continue to celebrate the *Brown* Court's overturning of *Plessy's* 'separate but equal' doctrine. It follows then that their critique of *Brown* stems from a fundamental belief in the feasibility of society rejecting 'separate but equal' *and* instituting social and political policies that would produce substantive results indicative of an anti-'separate but equal' position. These scholars critique the Court's prescribed methods (or lack thereof) toward educational equality but accept in the abstract the promise of *Brown*.

Bell's approach to the situation is completely different. The principle aim of his alternative decision is not to tackle *Plessy's* 'separate but equal' doctrine, but to find ways that would better provide black children with quality educational opportunities similar to those long enjoyed by Whites. Bell understood critically that the institutional structures of segregation rested not on a troubling legal doctrine, but on what he calls a 'covenant' that guarantees the superiority of whiteness. In reinforcing 'separate but equal' in his reconceived opinion of *Brown*, Bell does not abandon his desegregationist commitment, but merely recognizes that his desegregationist commitment is not for its own sake, but a means to ensure substantive racial equality. Thus, as much as the reconceived opinion reads as a forward-looking opinion affirming *Plessy*, it is written as a backwards-looking reflection that fully considers the judicial retrenchment and political pushback against desegregation that followed the real *Brown* decision. Bell critically understands America's racial problem as a broadly shared cultural condition that cannot simplistically be fixed by rearranging the rhetoric of equality. That is, complexities and multidimensional practices of racism cannot be engaged just because the Court has eliminated one mantra for another where 'separate' used to be equal, 'separate' is now always unequal. Here lies the crux of why Bell would uphold *Plessy*. Bell would force the Court to implement its 'separate but equal' doctrine so that black children would enjoy the same educational opportunities as their white peers, even if they attended separate schools.

## *The Role of Critical Hermeneutics*

If hermeneutics is the site to study the conflict of interpretations, and critical hermeneutics is a methodological tool to counter and change majoritarian stories, then Bell's reconceived version is a quintessential example of countering and changing the hegemonic narrative of *Brown*. Bell's reconceived version of *Brown* is remarkable not only in its audacity to reject fundamentally a hallowed Supreme Court decision, but because it recognizes that racial stratification and subordination are material conditions. Bell captures a more accurate discursive history of the original *Brown* by electing to focus on its failures without being blindly enamored by its promise. This reconceived version of *Brown* is a direct counter narrative to the broadly shared opinion that the *Brown* case was the finest hour of American Law. In juxtaposing the celebratory and hallowed nature of *Brown* with the fact that the case accomplished so little, Bell engages in a hermeneutical practice of drawing from a material racial history that is available to both narratives. In other words, Bell centralizes the material consequences of retrenchment and political pushback that were direct responses to the original decision. These material realities are surely forgotten or brushed aside in sanguinary representations of *Brown*.

Critical hermeneutics is useful in questioning the hegemonic and institutionalized memory of *Brown*, which Bell argues as akin to a 'holy grail' of American legal decisions. Critical hermeneutics problematizes the interpretative process of how we came to know *Brown* according to its celebrated stature. More broadly, critical hermeneutics, CRT's methodology of composite counter narrative storytelling, and Bell's powerful reconceived example, provide the methodological assemblage necessary to tackle our current majoritarian narrative of judicial and cultural colorblindness. In every contemporary affirmative action case since *Brown*, conservatives on the Court routinely cite the anti-classification nature of the decision forbidding racial distinctions. Equally striking is the absence of attention paid to processes of racial subordination that similarly accompanied *Brown's* anti-classification language. Guided by critical hermeneutics and utilizing CRT's methodology of composite storytelling, critiques of contemporary colorblindness can be made to answer for the substantive racial history of subordination that it refuses to remember. In this way, the combination of critical hermeneutics and CRT's methodology of counter narrative story telling can strike a blow to colorblindness in the same manner that Bell accomplishes in tackling the mythology of *Brown* as the hallowed finest hour of American law.

Methodology transforms into a matter of how we proceed with social science research and about the questions that can be asked or not asked. Zeus Leonardo and Allen (2008) argue that methodology is more than just 'getting meaning right', but about uncovering the ideological tension over meaning and research. Furthermore, Leonardo and Allen suggest that our meanings are neither obvious nor static but rather in a state of flux subject to struggles of representation of history and everyday life. When applied to race related cases that are foundational to the arc of colorblindness, I proceed with careful attention to both the legal language that describes racial problems as well as the racial problems that legal language obscures. My aim is not only to provide an anti-majoritarian story utilizing case law, but to construct a narrative responsive to racial stratification and subordination. In this way, a counter narrative against the hegemony of colorblindness expands the hermeneutical horizon where interpretations of the Court and equal protection do not collide with justice and equality, but instead compliment it.

## Discussion

Colorblindness is a majoritarian narrative that projects a 'raceless', or post-race, meritocratic doctrine. Understood broadly, colorblindness is not only a judicial approach by the Supreme Court but an ideology that has material consequences in and beyond the institution of education. Specifically, the Supreme Court's arc of judicial colorblindness increasingly makes it more difficult for subordinated social groups to achieve the promises of the Civil Rights movement. The rhetorical 'truths' of colorblindness have been adopted by Whites to beat back any and all attempts to enact racially responsive public policies. Furthermore, there is a lurking danger when minority voices adopt majoritarian narratives. This danger is ever present in the Asian American anti-affirmative action complaint filed against Harvard. Brought by the Project for Fair Representation who previously bankrolled the anti-affirmative action challenge against the University of Texas, the new anti-affirmative action complaint alleges race positive holistic admissions discriminate against Asian Americans. To establish a class of alleged 'victims', the foundation set up an advocacy group encouraging Asian American students to voice their displeasure against race positive holistic admissions if they felt slighted by any colleges and universities that practice race positive admissions. Not surprisingly, the foundation found its fair share of Asian American students who were sympathetic to the colorblind arguments of reverse discrimination believing that they too were rejected because of their race (more in Chapter 8). A counter anti-majoritarian narrative is needed to deconstruct the hegemony of colorblindness. Colorblind narratives of alleged reverse-racism are built upon a smoke-and-mirrors regime of mystification and obfuscation. Therefore, a CRT-inspired methodology of counter narrative story telling will go about recording the discursive racial histories purposely forgotten by colorblind narratives.

## Note

1. *Adarand Constructors, Inc. v. Pena*, 515 U.S. 200 (1995). Thomas, J., concurring, p. 1.

# 3 A Historical Synergy

## Law, Whiteness, and the Hegemony of Racial Subordination

Before *Brown* and the Civil Rights legislation, the law and Supreme Court played a clear and unabashed role in subordinating people of color while affirming the socially constructed superiority of Whites. The Court's history of legal racial subordination can be organized into three epochs: slavery, Jim Crow 'separate but equal', and the 'colorblind' era marked by a stream of anti-affirmative action decisions. To grasp the colorblind era, understanding the Court's discursive approach on racial issues during slavery and Jim Crow reveals the ongoing conversation of racial stigma conducted by the Court. The conversation of racial stigma in the law reflected the larger social understanding of race during each historical period. During slavery, alleged racial inferiority and superiority between Blacks and Whites were understood as biologically determined. The fixed understanding of racial difference was reflected in the Court's decisions. Due to the reconstruction amendments following the Civil War that banned slavery, granted citizenship status to former slaves, and guaranteed equal protection under the law, the Court shifted its racial biologism toward a community and social practice understanding.

### Slavery

*Dred Scott v. Sandford* (1857) is perhaps one of the most famous (and infamous) Supreme Court cases in American judicial history, perhaps surpassed only by *Brown v. Board of Education*. The takeaway historical significance of the case is that the decision denied slaves the possibility of citizenship under the constitution. However, the case also represents an intriguing backwards-looking window toward a fascinating era of race relations in American history. That is, the Court's approach to race is one of minimalism and judicial restraint because racial understanding was understood as fixed and biologically determined. Hence, the Court did not need to do much to establish and reproduce alleged racial inferiority and superiority; it merely needed to give its stamp of approval on racial differences. In this regard, *Dred Scott* is important as an iconic representation of the pervasiveness of racial stratification and subordination during this period of race relations. Furthermore, the case shows how easily racial ideologies could be institutionalized via the judicial system. *Dred Scott* represents the institutionalized nature of racial practice during the slave era and how the Court positioned itself as a minimalist perpetrator in relation to racial subordination.

The legal and political question in *Dred Scott* was whether or not southern slave-owning white citizens would be allowed to continue to practice slavery in the new western territories of the Louisiana Purchase. First, the implication of the dispute calls into question the constitutionality of the Missouri Compromise. The Union was concerned with the spread of slavery into the new territories because permitting its spread would effectively allow the Confederacy to expand its economic power against the northern states. In a rather straightforward decision, the Court relied on the Constitution's Fifth Amendment, ruling that Congress' Missouri Compromise effectively deprived slave owners of their property without due process. In other words, if a southern slave owner moved into any area of the newly acquired western territories that banned slavery, the slave owner would no longer be able to exercise the use of his 'property' because slavery was deemed unlawful. As a result, the Court argued the matter was rather simple. The entire Missouri Compromise was invalidated under the straightforward constitutional principle of property rights enumerated in the Bill of Rights.

Rightly so, *Dred Scott* continues to be remembered as an infamous Supreme Court decision because the Court affirmed the status of slaves as property. Beyond the Court's verdict invalidating the Missouri Compromise, the case did not depend on any statutory language or constitutional amendments to find that slaves were property. It simply went without saying. The Court did not go about inventing any new traits or constructions of blackness, it merely *affirmed* what it viewed as the fixed and inherent racial inferiority of slaves. As a consequence, the Court viewed slavery not as an aberration of race relations, but a natural function and reflection of black inferiority. It then follows that the inherent inferiority of black persons, whether old, young, or future offspring, is fixed whether a slave or free. In the Court's decisions, the question of whether black persons are free in the new territories or continued to be slaves from slave owning states is simply a moot question. The fundamental issue was whether or not black persons were property. This question was neither answered with an inventive maneuvering of judicial review nor was it an exercise of judicial activism requiring the Court to find some new constitutional doctrine. Because black persons were believed to be inherently inferior, the Court's approach to the nature of black persons resembled a methodological 'consistency'. That is, the alleged inferiority of black persons was not necessarily found in the constitution because the Court was only drawing on dominant social belief and established practices of their racial inferiority. Therefore, the Court's opinion constitutionalizes the dominant cultural belief that race was biologically determined and fixed. The takeaway of racial stigma in *Dred Scott* is that racial inferiority was neither enhanced nor impeded by the Court, but only affirmed as a function of the 'natural' inferiority and superiority between the black and white races.

## Jim Crow and Plessy's 'Separate but Equal'

If there is a sense of ideological consistency apparent in *Dred Scott*, there is an inconsistency in *Plessy v. Ferguson* (1896). This is not to say that the *Dred Scott* Court should in some way be applauded for its consistency and the *Plessy* Court scorned. But the *Plessy* court maneuvered in an especially disingenuous way to reach the same result as *Dred Scott*: upholding racial inferiority and subordination of Blacks. When Homer Plessy challenged Louisiana's Separate Car Act (segregated railway cars), the Supreme Court was faced with a new challenge: the reconstruction amendments. Passed during a five-year span (1865–1870) immediately after the Civil War, the reconstruction amendments are:

- 13th: Banned slavery, though allowed convict leasing, essentially ushering in a neo-slave practice.
- 14th: Guaranteed due process and equal protection clause, with the latter containing the famous words: 'NO state shall make or enforce any law which shall . . . deny to any person within its jurisdiction the equal protection of the laws'.
- 15th: Grants voting rights to citizens regardless of 'race, color, or previous condition of servitude (*Read: Slavery*)', however, excluded women until the 19th amendment in 1920.

Together, the reconstruction amendments presented the court with a prima facie simple case. One could argue that equal protection in the 14th amendment would simply be read as equal treatment in the eyes of the law. Although a possible straightforward reading of the reconstruction amendments and 'equal protection' would have invalidated Louisiana's separate car act as unconstitutional, the Court's ruling rejecting Plessy's argument signified an equal protection jurisprudence that was only concerned with equality in the letter of the law without concern for substantive equality. The difference in these two distinctions is important because *Plessy* gave birth to the legal doctrine of 'separate but equal'. Rather than reading the totality of the reconstruction amendments as addressing the violence and debasement of slavery as a product of racism, the Court used a technical definition of slavery, which relies literally on the act of physical extraction and forced servitude. In doing so, the majority court strips the full power of the 13th amendment banning slavery. The crucial element to the institution of slavery was the construction of inferiority serving as the ideological justification for decades of violence and oppression. This sense of 'natural' white supremacy and black inferiority was evident in *Dred Scott*. By reducing the discourse of racism to include only slavery, the Court's 13th amendment interpretation and technical definition relegate the violence of slavery to past acts of physical extraction, the slave trade, and an illegal commerce. In doing so, the Court is able to sever the fundamental characteristics of racial subordination from group and economic exploitation resulting from slavery, thereby allowing it to read the dispute in *Plessy* not as an evolved practice of racial stratification, but simply as a reflection of society's new 'separate but equal' racial understanding.

Importantly, *Plessy* continues the conversation of racial stigma in the law that began with *Dred Scott*. The *Dred Scott* Court clearly recognized the alleged 'inherent' differences of the races, which the Court had no problem in legitimizing in law, thereby constitutionalizing a determinant undertaking of assumed biological differences. However, having to deal with the newly passed reconstruction amendments, the *Plessy* Court found itself in a tricky situation of having to rectify the persistence of racial subordination in the face of an 'equal protection' constitutional mandate. The *Plessy* court addresses this problem directly:

> We consider the underlying fallacy of the plaintiff's argument to consist in the assumption that the enforced separation of the two races stamps a badge of interiority. If this be so, it is not by reason of anything found in the act, but solely because the colored race chooses to put that construction upon it.[1]

With one fell swoop, the *Plessy* Court absolves the legal institution from any responsibility in perpetuating racial stratification and subordination, neatly blaming Blacks as the culprit for their own racial subordination, a self-imposed racial stigma. In doing so, 'separate but equal' is constitutional as long as it is equal in the letter of the law, meaning: separate but equal is equal because the law says it is. Charles Mills (1997) observed that it is oxymoronic to think of Blacks as equal to Whites. That is, the internal logic and self-consistency of white supremacy is maintained by the inherent contradiction of equality between Whites and Blacks.

## Critical Race Theory, Whiteness, and Education

*Brown v. Board of Education* famously declared racial segregation in public education unconstitutional. Notwithstanding the significant unanimous decision of *Brown*, the Warren Court did not immediately order schools to desegregate. The legislative battle across many districts, states, and municipalities seeking to ensure equitable educational opportunities for students of color lasted well into the 1970s. Coupled with the existence of anti-miscegenation laws still operating in Virginia for an additional thirteen years after *Brown* (see *Loving v. Virginia*, 1967), one conclusion was obviously clear: racial subordination and stratification continued despite significant legislative and political developments since the end of legally sanctioned slavery. Thurgood Marshall, lead attorney in *Brown* and future Supreme Court Justice, foreshadowed the durability of racial subordination immediately after the *Brown* decision. Amidst understandable euphoria, Marshall warned celebrating colleagues at the NAACP that *Brown* was only the beginning, not the end, in the battle for racial equality. Marshall's prophetic words fundamentally capture the complexities and difficulties related to issues of racial stratification, practice, and privilege. That is, despite *Brown* and *Loving* ending particular practices of racial subordination, white racial privilege continued under new and evolved practices. In short, these cases ended *particular* expressions of racism and their institutional forms, not the end of racism itself. Scholars and activists who shared Marshall's conviction of meaningful racial progress identified the need for a responsive narrative that would capture the continuing existence of racial inequality. Critical Race Theory (CRT) was born within this historical conjuncture of racial progress *and* retrenchment. Inspired by Du Bois' proclamation that the problem of the 20th Century was the 'problem of the color line', CRT and its influential methodology revealed the core problem of whiteness. Through the methodological lens of CRT and whiteness studies, the institution of education has been revealed as a leading contemporary site where racial subordination and white privilege persist.

### *Race*

Representing the height (or lowest point?) of racial biologism, social Darwinism and the eugenics movement of the late 19th century used scientific measurements of crania, nose, jawbones, ears, and head size to calculate racial differences. Moving beyond the alleged 'natural' superiority and inferiority of racial subjects produced by the bio-racial frame, works of W.E.B. Du Bois and the Chicago School of sociology focused on the myriad social problems experienced by people of color. Most significantly, the sociological approach was a significant departure from biological uptakes on race and began building with much clarity the argument that race was socially constructed, not fixed or a natural phenomenon.

The development that race is socially constructed rather than biologically fixed produced Omi and Winant's influential racial formation theory. Howard Winant (2000) summarizes the racial formation approach as one that: views racial identities as unstable and politically contested, understands the intersections of racial 'projects' that combine discursive elements with structural ones, and views these interactions as interpretations of meanings from the individual to the group and local to global. Drawing heavily on Antonio Gramsci's theory of hegemony and Immanuel Wallerstein's (1975) class formation theory as applied to advanced capitalist societies, racial formation analysis argued against any essentialist or transcendental uptakes of race. Rather, racial meanings and discursive practices were inherently unstable and needing constant (re)articulations in order to maintain a racially stratified society.

Although racial formation theory illuminated the nebulous nature of racial meanings, it also provided a sobering realization that the old racial order was not entirely gone. Quite the opposite. Instead, the old racial covenant supporting white supremacy exemplified by slavery and Jim Crow reinvented itself in a contemporary colorblind form that continued white racial privilege, albeit in a more cloaked existence. Understood via its traditional manifestations, white supremacy was best personified by racist institutions like segregated schools, Jim Crow laws, the eugenics movement, or the assumption of white racial superiority. In the evolving history of race relations, it became no longer fashionable and acceptable in the mainstream to spout the wisdoms of David Duke or the KKK, but as a sign of a continued white domination, it became acceptable to reframe racial difference in terms of standards, nationalism, measurable intelligence through standardized tests like the SAT, arguments of cultural deficit, or to altogether dismiss the significance of race. The upshot is that white supremacy continues largely uninterrupted in its 500-year course through non-White ideological conditioning and white signatories of the racial contract.

## *Critical Race Theory*

In law, early Critical Race Theorists such as Derrick Bell, Patricia Williams, Mari Matsuda Kimberle Crenshaw, and Richard Delgado were frustrated at the incredibly slow pace of racial progress following the Civil Rights Era. They believed that the traditional approaches to legal change and social activism no longer produced the amount of progress that was initially thought possible with the emergence of the Civil Rights Era. CRT began directly to challenge the traditional methodology of legal scholarship that focused on doctrinal and policy analysis, which many CRT scholars thought were limited and ultimately insufficient in addressing ongoing racial stratification and subordination. As an analytic lens, Matsuda (1991) views CRT as the work of liberal legal scholars of color to construct a jurisprudence that centered racism in law and also worked toward abolishing racism within a larger project of eliminating all forms of social subordination.

The law and legal processes were the initial targets of CRT criticism, but its methodology has been adopted as an analytical framework in other disciplines. Early CRT legal scholarship exemplified four central methodological characteristics[2]:

1. Racism is normal, not marginal, in America.
2. Story telling is experiential knowledge.
3. Racism requires paradigmatic change, not pragmatic change. Therefore, the incremental change championed by traditional approaches of liberalism is rejected.
4. Civil Rights laws have benefited Whites more than people of color, thereby confirming Derrick Bell's (1980a) 'interest convergence' thesis—a historical conjuncture when the interests of people of color are advanced only when Whites share and will also benefit from the same interests.

By positioning racism as a normal, as opposed to an aberrant, feature of American society, CRT recognizes the endemic presence and permanence of racism. Therefore, by rejecting the position that racism is a marginal phenomenon in American society, CRT also fundamentally rejects dominant ideologies (i.e. meritocracy, colorblindness, race neutrality) that work to mask the continuing persistence of racial power, privilege, and self-interests of Whites in the U.S.

Even in its early days as a developing critical legal approach, CRT was an interdisciplinary methodology because it centers experiential knowledge via methods of storytelling, personal and communal histories, and creative, imagined scenarios. The use of storytelling is a direct counter to dominant ideologies, or majoritarian narratives that claim to portray the existence of a meritocratic society absent of race or describe the supposed declining significance of race in objective, neutral language. Because CRT believes in the persistence of racism, dominant and majoritarian narratives that do not recognize the centrality of racial subordination tend to 'naturalize' privilege and disadvantage. Therefore, anti-majoritarian storytelling serves as a powerful methodological tool in exposing the fallacy of so-called race-neutral or meritocratic narratives about society and social groups.

Perhaps the most striking element of CRT is the assertion that despite *Brown* and the contentious passage of Civil Rights legislation, their implementation nevertheless benefited Whites. In *Brown*, a memorable line from the unanimous Warren Court regarding black students stated:

> to separate them from others of similar age and qualifications solely because of their race generates a feeling of inferiority as to their status in the community that may affect their hearts and minds in a way unlikely to ever be undone.[3]

Surely attending under-resourced and dilapidated schools had a detrimental effect on children of color, but nowhere in the *Brown* decision is there mention of what attending well-resourced schools did for white students. Segregation not only subordinated black children, it also provided the structural foundation for white superiority. By placing the Civil Rights legislation within the context of Cold War geopolitics, Bell argued that the racial advances of Blacks were only made possible within the context of white self-interest. Furthermore, by evaluating the political and social difficulties facing racial remedies, Bell concluded that Whites would never support civil rights policies that threaten their social status unless their group interests converge with racial redress. CRT in legal studies and its methodological framework laid bare a rather paradoxical reality: the persistence of racial hierarchies and protection of white privilege in the era of colorblindness.

## Whiteness Studies

The study of whiteness and white privilege marked a paradigmatic shift in rejecting the assumption that a study of race meant analyzing the racial experiences of people of color. To name a few early scholars, Peggy McIntosh, Noel Ignatiev, David Roediger, Ruth Frankenberg, and George Lipsitz centered the construction of whiteness in a position that is radically different from its usual comfortable status as an unnamed, comfortable, and universal moral center. This radical difference is significant not because racial difference is talked about in a different manner, but the study of whiteness calls into question the entire racial edifice. Whiteness studies reframes all the foundational questions associated with race by henceforth naming whiteness as the problem of race relations.

When Ignatiev (1997) provocatively challenged scholars to name any redeeming characteristic of whiteness, the question fully grasps the constructed nature of race as an ideology that oppresses people of color and produces white privilege. Only several decades old (est. 1988), the study of white privilege and whiteness as a racial discourse has altered the general understanding of race. Whereas Whites were once the anonymous center of the moral, social, political, and cultural universe, whiteness studies favor a critical analysis of the white racial formation. In Peggy McIntosh's (1990) seminal essay *Invisible Knapsack*, privileges experienced by Whites are uncovered as unacknowledged and protected. By identifying everyday white privileges, such as having pleasant neighbors, or being able to go shopping without being harassed, McIntosh spotlights the unremarkable nature of white advantage that is both normative and neutral. Ruth Frankenberg's (1993) interview of white women also speaks to the taken-for-granted characteristics of white privilege. By showing how race and whiteness shape white women's lives, despite their *prima facie* denial of racism or having anything to do with the racial order, Frankenberg documents white women's assertion of expertise in the very issues of which they had claimed previously to have little knowledge. Furthermore, Frankenberg argues that Whites have never been conceived as the problem, a point reflected by McIntosh's when she observes that Whites are educated to think of their lives as neutral and ideal. Therefore when Whites work to benefit others, it is done in the name of charity and benevolence for others to be more like Whites. Thus, we are again guided by a transformation of W.E.B. Du Bois' (1903) ironic question for Blacks (How does it feel to be a problem?) to a literal one for Whites (How does it feel to be *the* problem?). Recognizing that Whites have never been conceived as the problem, David Roediger and Noel Ignatiev have called for the abolition of whiteness (understood as a racial ideology) and its concomitant identity of white people. To many ears, this sounds like a strange proposition. Allow me to explain further.

Appropriating James Baldwin's comment, 'as long as you think you're white, there's no hope for you', Roediger (1994) suggests that because both whiteness and blackness are socially constructed, whiteness is infinitely more false and precisely because of that falsity, more dangerous. Roediger argues that there is no white culture. Although there are Irish songs, Italian neighborhoods, Slavic traditions, or German villages, whiteness is empty and as a result a terrifying social project to build a racial identity based on superiority and inferiority. To Roediger, any movement of anti-racism, class-consciousness, or solidarity with African Americans must arise not only because of a rejection of racial oppression but of whiteness itself. Therefore, in elaborating on the myth of whiteness, Roediger (1994) decides whiteness is not just false and oppressive, it is *nothing but* false and oppressive.

Ignatiev advances Roediger's take on whiteness by denouncing the reinterpretation of whiteness without working toward its abolition. Admittedly, Ignatiev concedes that white abolitionists do not know exactly how to abolish the white race although he offers certain strategies for 'race traitors', an ironic appropriation that describes anti-white Whites. Despite that, he argues that the history of America's original abolitionists can be instructive. By invoking the history of Massachusetts as a sanctuary state for escaped slaves, Ignatiev points out that Wendell Phillips sought to break up the consensus that supported slavery. In an attempt to provide a free zone adjacent to slave states, the original abolitionists argued that it was necessary to break up the union. To Ignatiev, although northern states did not practice slavery, they were nevertheless co-conspirators in the institution of slavery by honoring fugitive slave laws. Phillips rightly believed that in order to end slavery, northern states needed to become sanctuary destinations alongside slave territories. That is, northern territories cannot just be non-slave states: they had to be anti-slave. Drawing from the same essential framework, Ignatiev calls on Whites to reject their whiteness in a move to break up the union of whiteness. Similar to northern territories acting as sanctuary states in rejecting the institution of slavery, Ignatiev argued for Whites to commit race treason by rejecting whiteness, a form of racial sedition. In doing so, Ignatiev believes the abolitionist task is not to win over more people to become anti-racist, but rather to commit suicide as a 'white person' and be born again in building a human community *sans* race.

Not all undertakings of whiteness call for its abolition. Henry Giroux (1997) has argued for media representations of race, such as movies, to serve as discursive spaces where Whites and students of color can critically examine oppressive representations and how they continue to shape contemporary racial conditions. Here, Giroux calls for a critical engagement of whiteness rather than its dismissal. That is, opposite to white abolitionism, Giroux calls for a reconstruction of whiteness. In doing so, Giroux favors a pedagogical approach that provides students a site to reconstruct whiteness, rather than the binary of rejection or absolute acceptance of its normative assumptions. He suggests that whiteness is not intrinsically the problem, but rather how whiteness positions itself within the discourse and practice of race. As a result, whiteness can be rearticulated without the taken-for-granted assumptions and racial privilege of 'whiteness', working toward an anti-racist whiteness. Whether or not a call for the rearticulation of whiteness may seem sexy for white anti-racists, or its total abolition too unrealistic, an overlooked aspect of whiteness is that as much as whiteness is ultimately false and oppressive, whiteness also maintains historical structures of domination. In other words, whiteness may be false, but its means of existence are real. The material manifestations of white domination leads Zeus Leonardo (2004) to argue for an analysis of the conditions of white supremacy, which he explains are the necessary conditions that make 'white privilege' possible. As a result, before whiteness is rearticulated or abolished, its modes of existence in producing material manifestations of white domination must be fleshed out.

## CRT and Whiteness Studies in Education

Gloria Ladson-Billings and William Tate's (1995) essay 'Toward a critical race theory of education' marked an important moment where the framework of Critical Race Theory in law was introduced to educational scholarship. By introducing CRT's methodological framework to educational inquiry, Ladson-Billings and Tate base their discussion of educational inequity on three central understandings:

1. Race is still an important factor determinative of inequity in the United States.
2. More so than justice or human rights, U.S. society is organized by property rights.
3. Therefore, the intersection of race and property rights produces an important tool for us to understanding social, and specifically educational, inequality.

The authors first propose that race continues to be a significant factor in determining inequality in the U.S., which is easily apparent in statistical and demographic data. The most jarring documentation is Johnathan Kozol's (1991) graphic description of the divergent educational experiences between white students in comparison to their black and Latino peers. Second, in locating property rights as the foundation of U.S. society, the authors critically identify *the* central problematic preventing the Civil Rights movement from fulfilling the promise of justice and human rights. Too often, they argue, issues of justice and human rights are conflated with democracy and discussed as coterminous with each other. Doing so ignores the history of the democratic process producing results and realities that are antithetical to justice and human rights. Bell points to the inherent tension that created the Constitution, a document that is roundly considered a great democratic achievement. However, Bell argued that the possibility of individual rights unconnected to property rights was a completely foreign concept to the founding fathers. Thus, Ladson-Billings and Tate conclude that in regard to the issue of democracy in U.S. society, the interests of property rights trumped issues of individual rights and justice.

Taken together, the first two propositions inform the third proposition that the intersection between race and property becomes a powerful analytic tool in understanding educational inequality. A Jim Crow era interpretation of educational opportunities as a literal form of property is not difficult to see. White-only schools represented for Whites not only the privilege of better educational opportunities, but also the 'right' to exclude Blacks. In the post-*Brown* period, a property analysis of educational inequality locates white flight, vouchers, tracking, and 'gifted programs' as the contemporary manifestation of property rights to Whites. Finally, the authors argue that in order to address educational inequality, a critical race perspective must be *the* educational paradigm because CRT offers a new methodological approach that centralizes justice and offers the possibility of radical change from the current order. The application of a critical race methodology and a whiteness studies analytic in education exposes a litany of racially stratifying and subordinating features of education. From teacher work force to policy and delivery of instruction, CRT and whiteness locates the entire edifice of education as the site of necessary radical change.

The problem of whiteness as the normalized moral center is evident in education. In *We Can't Teach What We Don't Know*, Gary Howard (1999) stresses the importance of a multicultural education for an ever-increasing diverse student body. Howard shares his own journey of white identity formation. Reflecting on the legacy of white dominance and locating his own racial identity development as a white person, Howard uses anecdotal stories and accompanying analysis in a project aimed at personal and professional transformation. In response to the reality of a predominantly white teacher workforce serving multiracial schools, Howard calls for the need to have more people of color in the teaching ranks along with policies that encourage dialogue about whiteness and dominance. Howard hopes that a collective transformation can occur that will lead us to *la terra transformative* (land of hope) where race inequality can be healed collectively between Whites and non-Whites. Interestingly, Howard does not assign blame, only locating the enemy in dominance, ignorance, and racism. Howard's analysis does not particularly focus on white people per se, but more importantly on the transformative aspects of knowing and speaking of racism and dominance within a multicultural approach to education.

Christine Sleeter (1993) and Alice McIntyre (1997) go where Howard does not, focusing their analysis on a predominantly white teacher workforce. In doing so, Sleeter critically argues that we cannot just address racism and inequality by educating white teachers because teachers bring to the profession their own perspective of what race means. Therefore, these white teacher perspectives are not simply informed by their education, but more crucially by their own racial experiences and vested interests. In Sleeter's analysis, the focus on white teacher identity development is needed because the goal of education is more than just addressing racism, but to avoid reproducing it.

Perhaps the importance of focusing on white identity is exemplified clearly by McIntyre's participatory action research with thirteen white undergraduate female students. McIntyre maps racial attitudes, beliefs, and how teachers make meaning of whiteness within their relationship to multicultural education. The focus is not on models of development with the goal of a healthy racial identity, or even mapping the various types of white people exemplified in McIntyre's study. Rather, McIntyre conceptualizes whiteness as a social activity that is constantly constructed and reconstructed in different situations. Her research revealed that female white participants found themselves occupying the spatial moral center characterized as Eurocentric. Furthermore, the students believed that they could fix and ameliorate issues of racial domination by accessing their own problematic racial inventories. In various ways, McIntyre's, Sleeter's, and Howard's work shifted studies of race toward an analysis of white racial practice, participation, and consumption.

Similarly in the educational policy, Zeus Leonardo (2007) suggests the federal No Child Left Behind Act (NCLB) is an instantiation of whiteness. Here, Leonardo argues that NCLB reproduces the 'white polity' within the larger context of education as a project of nation creation. In locating U.S. society as one firmly steeped in a racial discourse of colorblindness, Leonardo argues that a fundamental characteristic of the colorblind discourse is its ability to downplay institutional relations and the racialized social system. Therefore, Leonardo observes NCLB's failure to understand educational disparities within a larger context of structural power not only betrays colorblindness, but reinforces whiteness. In other words, Leonardo suggests an educational policy that is purposeful in neglecting racial issues makes the reproduction of inequality and racism neither aberrant nor accidental, but rather becomes a fundamental characteristic of the system. Sadly, it may come as little surprise to Leonardo that NCLB diagnoses structural problems often faced by families of color such as health care, housing, and job discrimination by prescribing fundamentalist approaches such as market solutions, sanctions, and standards that do little to address racial problems, or worse, exacerbate them.

## The State, Education, and Civil Institutions

Omi and Winant's racial formations theory further illuminates the lasting importance of Antonio Gramsci's (1971) theory of hegemony. Taken from the fragmented and unfinished writings of Gramsci while imprisoned by Italian fascists, Gramsci's prison notebooks reflected on the existence of long-lasting, deeply rooted bourgeois democracies that were vibrant in many western European countries. Perry Anderson's (1976) seminal essay 'The antinomies of Antonio Gramsci' went about synthesizing and framing the many disjointed pages of Gramsci's *Prison Notebooks*. Via Anderson's interpretation, Gramsci updates the Marxist tradition to speak for West European countries. It is important to keep in mind Gramsci's contribution while undertaking a CRT approach to the law and education because racial subordination in education does not happen independently from other social institutions. As such, a careful analysis of Gramsci's theory of hegemony informs our critical race analytical approach so we can fully grasp the nature of racial stratification and subordination beyond the institution of education and into civil society more broadly.

### *Gramsci and Theory of Hegemony*

Analyzing the nature of influence, the state, and state exercise of power in capitalist societies, Gramsci contrasts between the West and East. Gramsci identified the East as the Soviet and other Eastern European states. The state in the East, as a body of government, was brittle because it was less integrated with civil networks in society, thus leaving its methods of influence and control limited to forms of physical force and repression. In short, in a czarist nation like Russia, the state was everything. In the West, or more advanced capitalist societies, Gramsci observed that civil society was much more developed, complex, and wide-ranging in its relationship with the state. As a result of this contrast in structures of power, Gramsci observed that advanced states in the West practice power and influence differently than those of the East.

In the West, Gramsci observed that the ability of the state to manufacture consent via its integration with civil society was paramount, as opposed to coercion with the threat of physical force and repression that he viewed standard in the East. Using the concept of hegemony, Gramsci viewed the political apparatus of western democracies to resemble a strategy of a 'war of positions', of 'cultural hegemony', as opposed to a 'war of maneuver' with sweeping acts of violence and brute force more common in the East during revolutionary times. Gramsci noted that power and influence in the East were practiced swiftly and at times with great violence due to the constant threat and use of state sponsored military force as a form of civil and social control. Not so in the West. Developing the Marxist analysis of the bourgeoisie and proletariat, Gramsci saw that bourgeois power in advanced western nations rests upon its ability to win consent from the multiple classes via civil institutions, what Gramsci sees as the many different positions that contribute to a collective political manipulation of the masses. It follows then that within the hegemonic process of the west, coercion and consent are not exclusive but rather governed through consent during times of peace, buttressed by a civic sense of political self-determination due to the masses' participation in the state's many civil institutions. But Gramsci importantly argues that despite this sense of autonomy, the varied civil institutions are still operated by and under the controlling influence of the state.

Additionally, Anderson is careful to note that although the state manifests itself differently between East and West, it is important to remember the state, as a formal governmental body in the West, still maintains its characteristics just like the state in the East. That is, although the use of violence and coercion are less likely in the West because of democratic institutions, Anderson argues that the presence of civil societies as the main method of the state winning consent from the masses neither eliminates nor diminishes the state's ability to use violence through its parliamentary forces in order to quell counter-revolutions and rebellions. Anderson argues that a common mistake of understanding the state in the West is to suggest that the emergence of civil society replaces or diminishes the power of the state. That is, the state can no longer be understood according to its manifestations in the East but must be replaced by a modern understanding of civil society in the West. To Anderson, this would be a grave mistake. Anderson admits that in Gramsci's writings, there are some grey areas because Gramsci makes no formal comparison or differentiation between hegemony through the state or hegemony through civil society. As a result, Anderson acknowledges a common drift is to think of the two as exclusive of each other, with the state resting in the East and well-developed civil society characteristic of the West.

Despite the easy temptation to read into the grey areas as a differentiation between the state and civil society, Anderson reminds his readers that the coercive power of the state is ever present. He speaks of the critical role of the state's core function, of 'armed bodies of men' maintaining a stranglehold monopoly over legitimate violence. Anderson points out that it is within the state's ability to exercise legitimate violence whenever it wants that serves as the lynchpin for its ability to produce consent. Therefore, in the West, civil society does not replace the state, but perhaps more accurately compliments it with a less aggressive function. As a result of this new understanding of advanced capitalist societies, the state and civil society may be read together or separately, depending on how one wants to identify power, influence, coercion, and consent. Nevertheless, the state is ever-present as a fundamental threat of coercive force and its ability to utilize violence is never diminished. More importantly, Anderson suggests that the modes of bourgeois power in the West do not entirely lie in civil society. Additionally, the modes of bourgeois domination can oftentimes neither be classified as coercive nor entirely by consent. Rather, as a consequence of the formal state's shifting position due to its integration within civil society, the conjuncture between coercion and consent represents two modalities on a continuum of influence exerted by the state through force or democratic engagement within historically specific conditions.

Finally, although Gramsci was not the first to use the concept of hegemony (Lenin used it to describe the leadership necessary from the proletariat in order to establish a socialist state), his pioneering contribution to the theory of hegemony identified influence and power in the West as a form of leadership, not domination. That is, hegemony is in fact *not* a study or statement of domination, but the common sense of leadership through its multi-faceted influence over civic life. Gramsci observes that discourses of domination, which emphasize coercion, are limited in their reach. In terms of leadership, influence and power, hegemony is long lasting due to its ability to manufacture consent, and the inherent ability of taking into account or incorporating subordinate interest through direct political participation. In this regard, power and influence in the West could no longer be accurately described as coercive and emanating from a bourgeois class precisely because the multifaceted institutions that participate in the hegemonic process are no longer centralized within the control of the ruling elite, redescribed by Gramsci more accurately as the 'ruling bloc', or the bourgeois class' ability to win the consent of non-bourgeois elements of society, including aspects of the working class. Gramsci therefore abandons naming the hegemonic process as orchestrated by a specific ruling class, but a product of an alliance of a 'bloc' comprised of, using Marxist terms, a diverse social composition from the ruling class to the peasantry.

### *Race, Education, and the Hegemonic Process*

Gramsci's theory of hegemony and Anderson's interpretive review of the *Prison Notebooks* is needed to analyze law, whiteness, and education. In many ways, education writ broadly represents one of the most significant civil institutions where the state can manufacture and sustain consent. However, the institution of education does not act independently of other civil and political institutions. In Louis Althusser's (1971) analysis, education is one in an array of institutions that form a wide range of controlling ideologies. Along with education, Althusser argues there are religious, cultural, and family institutions that are united under a broader controlling ideology propagated by various Ideological State Apparatuses (ISAs). Similar to Gramsci's differentiation of the state and civil society, Althusser distinguishes the ISAs from the Repressive State Apparatus (RSA) in that the RSA is primarily a controlling and suppressing apparatus propagated by police, army, and governments. That is, the RSA represses through fear of prosecution or violence, whereas the ISAs suppresses people out of fear from social ridicule. Specific to education, Althusser believes that the school has replaced religion as the most crucial ISA in sustaining a ruling class ideology against the interests of the working class. Whereas Althusserian and Gramscian analyses are class based following a Marxist tradition, we can also extend the analysis of a ruling class ideology to a ruling racial ideology. By locating the interaction between education and the legal institution, this relationship reveals itself to reinforce the dominant racial ideology of colorblindness that benefits Whites.

The institution of education offers varied possibilities of civic participation for the public. From Parent Teacher Association meetings to one's ability to vote for members constituting a local school board, educational writ broadly represents an arena where heavy civic participation is a built-in feature central to its existence and legitimacy. Due to its promotion of heavy participation across the multimodal institutional processes of education, the state's ability to win consent is relatively easy. In other words, the state's exercise of power in administering the public service of education is publicly accepted so long as a majority of the masses are ideologically conditioned to believe they are satisfied with its delivery. Thereby the educational ISA invokes a common sense among the masses that is inherently contradictory. That is, because there is wide-spread discontent with public U.S. education, satisfaction with schooling is in fact dissatisfying. Regarding the law, there is a different level of civic participation and engagement.

One can argue the public's participation in elections contributes to the appointment of Supreme Court justices. Through the political process, public participation in elections plays an affirmative role in electing political representatives (e.g. Congress) and sitting Presidents who appoint and review justices to the bench of the Supreme Court. Because of this, a case can be made that the Court's power of constitutional and statutory review is also a product of heavy civic participation. Nevertheless, this position stretches too far the definition of civic participation. The form of civic participation offered in education is much more interactive and results driven. To many proponents of neoliberalism, schools are not unlike commodities to be bought and consumed. For the privileged, schools that do not satisfy the 'customer' (read: students and their families) are discarded for 'better' schools (i.e. a better product). This consumerist model of education is perhaps the ultimate model of civic participation in contemporary America, which encourages not only interaction but also results.

The law and the Supreme Court do not function in this way. Significant change on the Court occurs at an agonizingly slow pace, taking at times entire generations to see any substantive difference because seats on the Supreme Court are lifetime appointments abdicated only through retirement or death. For example, during the eight years that George W. Bush was president, he made two appointments to the Court, replacing Sandra Day O'Connor and William Rhenquist. Similarly, President Barack Obama made two appointments, replacing David Souter and John Paul Stevens. Within President Trump's first three years, he also made two appointments replacing the late Antonin Scalia with Neil Gorsuch, and retired Anthony Kennedy with Brett Kavanaugh. Therefore, between three Presidents, we will collectively see six appointments in an eighteen-year span between presidents Bush, Obama, and Trump.

It may appear that a changeover of six justices out of a total of nine in an eighteen-year period is not too slow and can represent some affirmation that voters are responsible for electing presidents and their respective choices for Supreme Court nominations. On the surface level, this is absolutely true. But significant turnover on the Court is not necessarily measured by how many sitting justices leave the bench, but whether incoming justices change the overall ideological balance of the Court. If we measure Supreme Court turnover in this way, then our measurement of six justices in eighteen years becomes, arguably, two justices in nearly two decades. With the exception of Alito and Kavanaugh, the other four appointments were examples of conservatives replacing conservatives and liberals replacing liberals. As a substantive net effect, the Court's ideological balance would have remained the same for nearly the last two decades but for conservatives Alito and Kavanaugh replacing swing voters O'Connor and Kennedy. Indeed, the ideological balance of the Supreme Court has shifted, not because of all the replacements made since the Bush years, but because of two specific appointments replacing swing votes with more conservative justices. The move is slight and subtle, but nevertheless has tremendous consequences for law and civil society. This subtlety in ideological change is representative of the nature of the Court and indicative of what Stuart Hall (2006) calls a 'tendential balance' as opposed to outright domination.

Baring the unforeseen circumstance of a sudden death, justices will strategically schedule their retirements at a time when an ideologically similar President is in office. This is to ensure that the sitting president has the opportunity to fulfill the vacant seat with an ideologically similar jurist in order to avoid drastically changing the ideological balance of the Court in favor of the political opposition. Looking at the six justices who were nominated and confirmed by the senate to the Supreme Court since 2000, the Senate confirmation vote in favor and against were as follows:

- 50–48 Brett Kavanaugh: Replaced Anthony Kennedy
- 54–45 Neil Gorsuch: Replaced Antonin Scalia after a sudden death
- 58–42 Samuel Alito: Replaced Sandra Day O'Connor
- 63–37 Elena Kagan: Replaced John Paul Stevens
- 68–31 Sonia Sotomayor: Replaced David Souter
- 78–22 John Roberts: Replaced William Rhenquist

Of the six incoming Justices, the contentious nature from the confirmation processes of Alito and Kavanaugh is not at all surprising. Believed to be strict constructionists and stalwart conservatives, Alito and Kavanaugh replaced justices whose voting records were swing votes on many crucial political and social issues, especially affirmative action. The confirmation process of Neil Gorsuch was contentious not necessarily because of who he was replacing, but because republican senate majority leader Mitch McConnell had blocked President Obama's nomination of Merrick Garland to replace Antonin Scalia after Scalia's sudden death. McConnell essentially prohibited President Obama the constitutional authority to replace a vacant seat on the Supreme Court. McConnell played politics by arguing that because the vacancy occurred in the same year as the presidential election between Hillary Clinton and Donald Trump, the seat should be filled by the newly elected incoming president. Many observed that McConnell's gambit paid off since he was able to keep Scalia's seat solidly conservative. However, it was a gamble with no risk and big potential reward. If McConnell simply followed constitutional procedure, Scalia's seat would have been filled by President Obama's nominee, thus shifting the Court to the left. Nevertheless, the nature and structure of the Court leads to two prevailing observations: first, the manner in which the Court is constituted is completely political; second, the time it takes for meaningful shifts in the Court's ideological balance lends itself to the impression that it is in fact *apolitical* because it takes so long for substantive change to happen.

The nature of the Court and its interaction with the institution of education lends itself to a bit of a paradox. That is, education at the community, school, family, and individual level is very interactive and encourages multiple forms of participation. However, education is also regulated by laws, the clear examples of which are the canonical Supreme Court cases that have shaped education as an institution. As a result, the relationship between law and education and its subsequent interaction fall within Gramsci's theory of hegemony. Stuart Hall (2006) further illustrates the importance of focusing on the specific complexities of *inter*-relationships within specific manifestations between state and civil society, notably in areas such as the law and education. On the power and influence of the modern state and its hegemonic process, Hall argues that the modern state exercises moral and educational authority through a multi-dimensional process that both punishes and urges, and every other method of persuasion in between. In doing so, the modern state is not a singular 'thing' to be seized or overthrown with a swift move, but a complex bloc of formations which must be the focus of multiple struggles in an entire arena of social and political struggle. Hall's emphasis on the complex formation in modern society as the source of power and influence suggests the formative relationship between the law and education cannot be ignored. Furthermore, Hall has argued that Gramsci is needed to study the prevalence of race and racism in our contemporary era. Hall writes that although there are general features of racism that can be identified across specific historical epochs, their differences may in fact outnumber their similarities. Importantly, the study of race and racism must pay attention to the ways in which the common general features of racial practices are changed and modified by specific historical moments and environments in which they manifest. In this way, we must not simply identify a connection between educational practice and the law in order to identify racial practices, but more critically how the relationship is practiced during varying historical moments. It leads Hall to focus not on racism in general, but *racisms* on a historically specific, concrete level. Finally, Hall believes the importance of Gramsci to racial studies lies in its ability to interrupt the common sense understanding of racism. That is, because racism is understood as destructive, anti-social, and anti-humanitarian, there is a false belief that racism is the same everywhere it is practiced, either everywhere in place or everywhere in time. To Hall, this is a misunderstanding of racism as a historically specific practice that may manifest in different forms and manners from one historical period to the next. Therefore, Gramsci is important in our ability to identify specific historical practices of racism, as opposed to abstractions of race.

## Discussion

These important theoretical and analytical points of departure frame the fundamental optics necessary to understand the Supreme Court's role in education and civil society. It establishes a cornerstone position rejecting the notion that the law is in any way above social and cultural reproach. That is, the law in general, and the Supreme Court specifically, are products of cultural and racial politics. Additionally, guided by the important contributions of Gramscian hegemony theory and Omi and Winant's racial formations analysis, legal and educational institutions are inextricably linked. Although different in form, nature, and structure, both institutions operate constitutively within a specific historical conjuncture apprehended by Gramsci's analysis of the state and civil society. Racial formations theory and whiteness studies further lend themselves to the analysis that power and influence via the inter-action of social institutions is not just a process that ensures class privilege, but also white racial privilege.

As Gramsci, Anderson, and Hall were all careful to note, the state and civil society are neither distinct entities nor are they one and the same. Their peculiarities and similarities rest within specific historical junctures that are shaped by contemporary political movements. Similarly, racial privilege cannot be confused simplistically as a footnote, or reflux, form of class privilege within the orthodox Marxist understanding of the bourgeoisie and proletariat. Racial privilege within the context of the institutional interactions of law and education must likewise be studied under the careful methodologies and optics of Gramscian hegemony theory, Hall's prescription that hegemony theory elucidates studies of racism, and Omi and Winant's racial formations framework emphasizing the iterative nature of racial meanings and practices.

There is an ongoing crisis in education, marked by continuing and increasing segregation at a historical conjuncture more than six decades removed from *Brown v. Board of Education*. However, the crisis is not created by and limited to education. The law is but one institution in a multitude of political and civic apparatuses that contribute to increasing segregation in education. In the colorblind era, the law no longer acts as an enforcer of segregation as it did during the Jim Crow era, but as a barrier against efforts to diversify and desegregate schools. In this way, the law must be made accountable for its roll in furthering segregation and racial privilege in education. Ultimately, this analysis is not about proving the fact of racial segregation in education as there are other more capable studies to this effect (e.g. Kozol, 1991; Solorzano & Yosso, 2001; Orfield & Frankenberg, 2013). But central to the discourse is an attempt to map out the historical trajectory of the Court and its racial rulings. In doing so, the Court's racial practice is revealed as one that has adapted and changed over time, but nevertheless continues to reinforce white privilege and whiteness. Because of this, racial segregation and white privilege in education exists virtually in perpetuity. As education has been the focus of many important race related Supreme Court cases, a new analytical framework that centralizes the role of the Court in perpetuating and producing new forms of racial privilege in education is required.

## Notes

1. *Plessy v. Ferguson*, 163 U.S. 537 (1896), p. 551.
2. See Ladson-Billings, G., & Tate, W. (1995). Toward a critical race theory of education. *Teachers College Record*, 97(1), 47–68.
3. *Brown v. Board of Education of Topeka*, 347 U.S. 483 (1954), p. 494.

## Section II

# Revisiting and Revising 'Settled' History

# 4 The Politics and Whiteness of *Brown v. Board of Education*

## Introduction

*Brown v. Board of Education* (1954) is a significant historical moment in the formation of our current colorblind era. Along with the passage of the Civil Rights legislation, *Brown* sparked the modern Civil Rights movement. Although the case continues to be revered as one of the most important Supreme Court decisions in American legal history, there is an incongruent relationship between our reverence and actual merits of the decision. That is, the less that is actually known about *Brown*, the more famous and hallowed it is received. 2014 marked the 60th anniversary of *Brown*. To mark the anniversary, groups and institutions such as the White House, national newspapers, and universities commemorated *Brown* by celebrating the decision while throwing caution to the wind regarding the continuing difficulties that public education faced on the issue of segregation. The fact that *Brown* is so celebrated juxtaposed with the somber tone of its 60th anniversary celebration is a quintessential feature of Civil Rights 'accomplishments' in the colorblind era. In other words, *Brown* showed promise but its delivery was sorely lacking. Sixty years after *Brown*, the quest for equality and desegregation in education remain elusive. We often come to this conclusion by looking at the current state of segregation in education. In reality, the writing was already on the wall more than sixty years ago. We need only to remember the opinion and the aftermath of *Brown I* and *Brown II* to see that what has transpired over the last sixty years was compatible with the resulting outcome.

In this chapter, the politics of the *Brown* decision is revisited. In the first section, Chief Justice Warren's opinion is dissected to lay bare the necessary maneuvers and compromises required to secure a unanimous decision. Warren understood the severity of the constitutional issue of enforced segregation and believed a united Court was necessary to end segregation in education. As a result of Warren's astute recognition of the seriousness of racial segregation, the Chief Justice's politicking to secure a unanimous decision also watered down the severity of racial segregation as a form of structural racism. In the second section, the opinion's pivot from emphasizing structural harm in favor of individual harm as a consequence of segregation is analyzed. In the spirit of not inflaming the South and to avoid further social cleavages, the decision's focus on individual harm lets Whites off the hook as the perpetrators or agents of enforced segregation. The third section surveys the varied responses to *Brown I* and *Brown II*. The difficulty Blacks experienced trying to attend white schools during this period was a direct result of the politics, appeasement, and compromising nature of Warren's opinions. Finally, I argue that despite the shortcomings of *Brown* over the last 60 years, its legacy is ever more important for combating contemporary colorblindness. *Brown's* continuing importance is marked by a need to remember accurately its language, appeasement, compromise, and at times, violent struggle.

## The Politics of *Brown*

*Brown* has been discussed extensively as a canonical case (see Ogletree, 2004; Patterson, 2001; Bell, 2004). Its most significant legal achievement is ending *Plessy's* 'separate but equal' constitutional doctrine in the field of public education. Additionally, the case has achieved a sort of Holy Grail status in the popular imagination as a shining example of the goodness of American democracy and equality. In this way, its commemoration as a significant historical event has been embroiled in political controversy precisely because its stature in historical memory represents a significant achievement in American society. I do not quarrel with the fact that it was a landmark decision; this fact seems plain enough. However, in all of this celebration, specifics have been lost concerning the political climate and maneuvers that Chief Justice Earl Warren had to enact for the decision to come to fruition. This establishes the peculiar status of *Brown* being celebrated and remembered today for something that it did not really do (meaningfully desegregate school) and revered as a seminal racial moment even though it racially accomplished so little. Because of this, the specific politics of *Brown* is important and should not be forgotten. Here, an important distinction should be made. Much has been discussed and written about the politics of *Brown* after the decision. However, in referring to the politics of *Brown*, I am invoking processes of contestation and appeasement that Warren navigated in order to reach *Brown's* unanimous decision. Less attention has been paid to this aspect in the literature.

In this analysis, 'the politics of *Brown*' is centrally about the political climate that NAACP lawyer Thurgood Marshall, Chief Justice Earl Warren, and the other eight Justices on the Court considered, participated in, and were part of hearing and deciding the case. Furthermore, the text of *Brown* and what it signifies represents an incredibly rich source of historical significance emblematic of the difficult racial climate the Court and the country faced. Collectively, 'the politics of *Brown*' is an engagement in identifying the contemporary political climate of *Brown* as a racial moment in history that is focused principally before 1954 and immediately following the decision. In this analysis, the Court, its Justices, the lawyers, and activists involved are part of a political polity constructing a conversation on race as it relates to segregation in public education. In this way, *Brown* can be brought down from its perch as a hallowed civil rights case so that it can be studied and analyzed not as a significant historical moment, but whether or not *Brown* deserves its historical significance.

### *What's in a Name: Brown or Briggs?*

*Brown* was a consolidation of four related desegregation cases from around the country and one from the District of Columbia, *Bolling v. Sharpe* (1954). Because *Bolling* originated from D.C., it was subject to a Fifth Amendment due process claim as opposed to an equal protection claim, which applies to the states. Nevertheless, the Court consolidated *Bolling* with the other four cases because it similarly hinged on the constitutionality of segregation in public education. As should be obvious, *Brown's* namesake, *Brown v. Board of Education of Topeka Kansas*, hailed from Kansas. The other state cases, including *Brown*, were:

1. *Briggs v. Elliot* (1952): Summerton, South Carolina
2. *Brown v. Board of Education* (1954): Topeka, Kansas
3. *Davis v. County School Board of Prince Edward County* (1952): Prince Edward County, Virginia
4. *Gebhart v. Belton* (1952): Claymont, Delaware

The Supreme Court is an institution steeped in history and tradition. If a case like *Plessy v. Ferguson* (1896) represents the conflict of one person against one government official or representative of a government body, then the case is simply called *Plessy v. Ferguson*. However, when consolidated cases present a multitude of appellants, petitioners, and government actors, the court has an established procedure that it follows in terms of naming and publishing for public records. For consolidated cases, the Court refers to the entire consolidated action via the case that comes first alphabetically.[1] The preceding four-state consolidated cases are listed alphabetically. Therefore, the canonical case that we have come to know as *Brown v. Board of Education* should instead have been called *Briggs v. Elliot* from Summerton, South Carolina. But according to my conversations with Ian Haney López, the fact that we now refer to these consolidated cases as *Brown* rather than *Briggs* is not due simply to an innocent procedural mistake, but a purposeful maneuver by Chief Justice Earl Warren to appease southern justices on the bench to avoid making the case about southern racism. That is, if case-naming tradition was followed, the verdict would have been called *Briggs v. Elliot* and would locate the Court's unanimous ruling right in the heart of the south: Summerton, South Carolina. Haney López argues it was at Earl Warren's doing that the consolidated cases were referred to as *Brown* instead of *Briggs* because Warren did not want the case to be an indictment of southern racism that would only further inflame the South's racial hostility. Only Earl Warren knows his true intentions for this slight change, but this procedural maneuver was one of a number of important concessions.

Compelling as the suggestion from Haney López is, it is still an unverified claim that speaks to the motivation of Warren to appease southern Justices and not turn the *Brown* case into an indictment of southern racism. However, the case's name change was not the only peculiar detail of *Brown* that suggests the Chief Justice, and by extension the entire court, was well aware of the controversial nature of the case. Delivering the opinion of the Court in *Brown*, Chief Justice Warren was also the opinion's author. Although Warren was able to persuade the other eight justices on the unconstitutionality of segregation in education, they had to also agree with his legal reasoning in order to sign on to a unanimous decision. This is an aspect of the Court's procedure that often gets overlooked. For instance, if a case is decided with justices voting 9–0, the decision may be unanimous in the outcome, but not unanimous in reasoning. In these circumstances, it is not uncommon for nine justices to agree on the final outcome, but nevertheless write their own opinions expressing their individual (or plural) justifications. In the unanimous *Brown* verdict, there were no concurring opinions. All nine justices on the Court signed onto Warren's opinion. Therefore, all the justices agreed to both the outcome and the reasoning of the Warren delivered opinion.

### *Outcome Over Reason?*

*Brown's* specific reasons and justifications to end segregation in public education deserve as much focus as its overall outcome. The constitutional question that Thurgood Marshall carefully crafted for the court was:

> [D]oes segregation in public education, even with tangible equality in resources and other aspects, violate the equal protection clause of the fourteenth amendment?[2]

Procedurally, the Court follows specific steps of established practices in settling constitutional disputes, especially when it deals with aspects related to constitutional amendments. Some of these initial steps are (see Stern, Gressman, Shapiro, & Geller, 2002):

1. Text
2. Original Intent
3. Established local practices

Of the five sections in the Fourteenth Amendment, section 1 has become the most scrutinized and has served as the basis for some of the most famous landmark decisions in the Country's history (e.g. *Plessy*, *Brown*, *Roe v. Wade*, *Bush v. Gore*). In its entirety, section 1 of the Fourteenth Amendment reads:

> Section 1. All persons born or naturalized in the United States, and subject to the jurisdiction thereof, are citizens of the United States and of the State wherein they reside. No State shall make or enforce any law which shall abridge the privileges or immunities of citizens of the United States; nor shall any State deprive any person of life, liberty, or property, without due process of law; nor deny to any person within its jurisdiction the equal protection of the laws.

First, to answer the constitutionality of educational segregation, the Court looks at the text of the amendment to see if it provides any guidance. It does not. The text of section 1 says nothing remotely related to education or segregation. Second, if the text provides no illuminating answers, the Justices will investigate the original intent of the framers of the Fourteenth Amendment. The Justices would ask: did the authors of the Fourteenth Amendment intend for the 'equal protection clause' to outlaw segregation in public education? By any stretch of imagination, at the time of the amendment's adoption, education was mostly a local or regional practice. Finally, the Court looks at the established local practices during the time of the amendment's ratification. Although many local municipalities had not embarked on the project to provide comprehensive public education, many families, black and white, sent their kids to local parochial and private schools. These schools were located in segregated black and white churches and single building schoolhouses. Particularly in Washington D.C., many of the those who participated in the adoption of the Fourteenth Amendment sent their own kids to white-only schools. Collectively, all three prescribed steps of initial constitutional procedure (text, intent, and established practices) answered the constitutional question of whether or not educational segregation violated the Fourteenth Amendment's equal protection clause with a clear no. Collectively, the Fourteenth Amendment said nothing about education or segregation, the authors of the amendment surely did not intend for education to be desegregated when they sent their own kids to white-only schools, and established practices at the time did not have a robust public education system.

Warren had a clear answer from the text, intent, and established local practices of the Fourteenth Amendment. If Warren's opinion stayed consistent with the procedural history of the Court, he would have had to uphold *Plessy's* constitutional doctrine of 'separate but equal' preserving racially segregated schools. The late Chief Justice William Rhenquist agreed with this position, writing in a memo in the early stages of *Brown* in 1952 as a Supreme Court law clerk. Rhenquist's memo was written to Justice Robert Jackson, a member of the *Brown* court. Rhenquist stated that although he was excoriated by liberal colleagues for his unpopular and unhumanitarian position, he believed that *Plessy v. Ferguson* should not be overturned.

Chief Justice Warren signaled a shift away from the established traditions and customs of the Court. Warren was deftly strategic in his opinion on the one hand, to acknowledge the historical procedure of the court, while on the other hand, not allowing the substance of his decision to be completely bound by its procedure. That is, the Chief Justice did not step out and directly say his opinion deviated from hundreds of years of established constitutional procedural practice. Nevertheless, he did just that by declaring in the opinion that in looking at the text, intent, and established practices, 'these circumstances provided were at best inconclusive'.[3] Here is where Warren's veering from the Court's tradition is obvious. The text, intent, and established practices of and around the Fourteenth Amendment were clear and conclusive that the equal protection clause was neither written nor intended to apply to segregation in public education.

Chief Justice Warren knew that discarding more than a century's tradition of constitutional jurisprudence in order to avoid the unsavory result of upholding separate but equal would dramatically affect the legitimacy and standing of the Court. Therefore, he had to acknowledge the Court's traditions in style but neglect it in substance. Compared to Supreme Court decisions today (e.g. *Parents Involved* was forty-five pages, not including dissenting opinions), the length of *Brown* is relatively short with only thirteen pages. Warren spent nearly the first eight pages discussing the text, intent, and established practice history of the equal protection clause of the Fourteenth Amendment. Doing so signified that the Court continued to engage in the same constitutional process it had in previous cases. Despite paying careful attention to its traditional process, Warren nevertheless neglected it in order to avoid the obvious conclusion that the Fourteenth Amendment did not address segregation in education. These steps allowed Warren's court to move away from the traditional textual originalism of constitutional jurisprudence that would have all but spelled doom for Marshall and the NAACP. As an alternative, the court utilized what is now commonly called a 'living document' approach in its interpretation. In other words, the Court utilized the spirit of equal protection from the adoption of the Fourteenth, but applied it to a contemporary problem (i.e. segregation in education) that did not exist in kind when equal protection was incepted. Today, the ideological cleavages between liberal and conservative justices rest on whether justices take a living document or originalist approach to constitutional jurisprudence. But as the *Brown* case shows, one of, if not the most, celebrated case in Supreme Court history was not decided on the doctrine of originalism. Rather, *Brown* required the Warren Court to adopt a living document approach precisely because originalism would demand the upholding of *Plessy's* 'separate but equal' constitutional doctrine.

## Structural Versus Individual Harm

By liberating equal protection from the strict constraints of originalism, the Court was able to apply the spirit of equal protection to public education. Although equal protection was originally about citizenship rights for former slaves and their children, freeing equal protection from these original parameters allowed the Fourteenth Amendment to reach across multiple social and civil institutions. With more than half of *Brown's* decision dedicated to addressing procedural matters, the Court carefully positioned itself in order to utilize equal protection in order to overturn *Plessy*. Warren presented the question clearly:

> [D]oes segregation of children in public schools solely on the basis of race, even though the physical facilities and other 'tangible' factors may be equal, deprive the children of the minority group of equal educational opportunities? We believe that it does. . . . Segregation of white and colored children in public schools has a detrimental effect upon the colored children. The impact is greater when it has the sanction of the law, for the policy of separating the races is usually interpreted as denoting the inferiority of the negro group. A sense of inferiority affects the motivation of a child to learn. Segregation with the sanction of law, therefore, has a tendency to [retard] the educational and mental development of negro children and to deprive them of some of the benefits they would receive in a racial[ly] integrated school system.[4]

These famous lines from *Brown* continue to be referenced by academic research and the Court some 60 years after the decision. In specifically studying these famous words, one aspect becomes increasingly clear. The decision focused the harm of segregation on *individual* minority children.

### *The Absence of Structural Harm*

Specific lines such as 'the children of the minority group' or 'affects the motivation of a child to learn' focus the effects of segregation entirely on individual children of color. Although the court did acknowledge that 'separating the races is usually interpreted as denoting the inferiority of the negro group', a reference to group harm, its focus on harm was almost exclusively on individual harm, with the famous inclusion of the Kenneth Clark doll study (see Clark, Chein, & Cook, 1954). Even if individual harm of segregation is important as represented by the Clark doll study, the Court did not need to advance this argument. The Court's understanding that 'separating the races is usually interpreted as denoting the inferiority of the Negro group' is more than enough justification to overturn *Plessy's* separate but equal mandate. This approach would have captured the essence of 'equal protection'. Recalling that the Fourteenth Amendment was originally about protecting the citizenship status of slaves and their children (i.e. a group), expressing the position that segregation thus denotes inferiority of the 'negro group' would likewise confirm the importance of group harm that the Fourteenth Amendment originally sought to protect. However, the Court's opinion neglected the conversation of group harm and instead focused on individual harm.

Although I am highlighting the critical focus of the Court's emphasis on individual harm, I am not suggesting that these individual harms do not represent real harms. In fact, they may be understated. The Court even went so far as to pose the hypothetical of equal physical facilities and other 'tangible factors' to illustrate individual psychological harm. But surely the Court knew that these facilities were neither physically nor tangibly equal, therefore the individual harm for segregated children of color were in fact much more than the Court's rhetoric cared to explicate. However, a shift in focus occurs when the Court highlights individual over group harm. By focusing on the individual, it is easy to sympathize with a specific person. When the Court underscores the psychological harm (e.g. Clark doll test) suffered by an individual, segregation is understood as idiosyncratic. By failing to understand the harm of segregation as suffered by an entire group, the Court fails to understand racism in general, and segregation specifically, as a structural force that affects an entire group, not just individuals. We need to look no further than the specific text the court utilized to overturn 'separate but equal':

> We conclude that, in the field of public education, the doctrine of 'separate but equal' has no place.[5]

A common misconception of *Brown* is that it ended 'separate but equal' in all social and civic institutions. This is simply not true. The Court was careful to minimize the ruling as limited only to the field of public education. As a result, not all forms of separation based on race were outlawed. For instance, anti-miscegenation laws prohibiting interracial marriages were still on the books in Virginia an additional thirteen years after *Brown*.

By focusing the harm of educational segregation on individuals, the Court absolves itself from having to discuss, or address altogether, the ramifications of group harm. That is, if one group or race is subordinated and harmed, would the Court not have to identify the group that is inflicting the harm? Warren avoids this predicament. He ends educational segregation without indicting any groups for said harm. The Court indicates that children of color suffer irreparable harm and 'segregation with the sanction of law, therefore, has a tendency to [retard] the educational and mental development of Negro children.'[6] However, no text can be found that speaks to how white-only schools build positive development of white children. Finally, if segregation generates feelings of inferiority of the 'Negro group', does it likewise generate feelings of superiority for white groups? Obvious in the opinion's text, the Court avoids answering all these questions altogether because its language only focuses on children of color, with a specific emphasis on individual harm so that Whites are absolved of any critical focus as the perpetrators *and*, most importantly, benefactors of racial segregation.

### *The Short, Sweet, and Great Submission*

Thurgood Marshall requested that if the Court ruled in favor of the NAACP against segregation, the Court should order for the immediate desegregation of all public schools. Perhaps this was the most straightforward form of relief for a ruling that clearly stated 'separate but equal has no place in public education'. However, after the Court's famous words overturning *Plessy*, it ruled that due to the varied nature of local conditions affected by the ruling, it would grant local municipalities involved in the case one year to study their options and report back with information as to the most appropriate approaches to achieve desegregation. Perhaps knowing the ominous path of the Court, Marshall chastised jubilant colleagues at the NAACP office knowing that although the Court had favorably ruled against educational segregation, its opinion did not signify an immediate end to educational segregation, thus warning his colleagues: the fight had only begun.

The Court's decision to not immediately order public schools to desegregate is a perplexing result in spite of its powerful language highlighting psychological harm. Although it is regrettable that the Court avoided discussing structural and group subordinating aspects of educational segregation, it nevertheless was correct in asserting the individual harm of racial segregation, underscored by the influential Clark doll experiment. However, in spite of highlighting individual psychological harms, the Court nevertheless accepted the prospects of continuing psychological harm for millions of children of color for at least another year. Furthermore, the Court asked those who had rejected desegregation to fashion approaches toward integration. That is, local municipalities named in the consolidated case by the NAACP had vehemently appealed that segregation did not violate equal protection based on constitutional arguments of originalism (i.e. text, intent, established practices). Following the decisions, the Court entrusted these same segregationists to inform the Court of the difficulties, challenges, and logistical circumstances that, in their opinion, could make for a complicated process of desegregation under local control. In effect, the Court gave segregationists one year to come up with their own plan to effectively slow the process of desegregation as much as possible, or at the very least, present their circumstances as complicated and difficult so that each individual school district could handle its own process of desegregation.

If there was a glimmer of hope despite the great submission by the Court to not immediately desegregate public schools, *Brown II* (1955) essentially eliminated all hope that public schools would systematically be desegregated. *Brown I* established these important facts: racial segregation was unconstitutional, segregation inflicts individual psychological harm, and segregation with the stamp of the law generates feelings of inferiority. The chief focus on *Brown II* was to determine the means necessary to implement the principles announced in *Brown I*. In a similar 9–0 unanimous vote detailing the task of desegregation, the Court answered the two essential enforcement issue of either fast or slow and federal or local with a nod to local courts and school authorities over federal courts and government. The NAACP argued for the immediate desegregation of schools monitored by the federal government and enforced by federal courts. The NAACP did not get its way. The Court unanimously believed that given the diverse nature of racial discrimination in public schools and the diversity through which segregation was practiced across the country, a one-size-fits-all desegregation mandate would not work. As a result, although the Court found that segregation violated the constitution, its *Brown II* opinion understood the constitutional violation as a multifaceted problem that required a variety of local, not federal, solutions. Therefore, the Court conferred desegregation responsibilities and enforcement mechanisms on local school authorities and the lower courts. The ironies were obvious if we keep in mind that White segregationists controlled local governance.

The specific language of desegregation mandated of local school authorities and lower courts were anything but specific. The overall sense of *Brown II* was:

1. Follow the constitutional principles announced in *Brown I*.
2. Local school officials and Courts are *urged* to act on the constitutional principles in a prompt manner and move toward full compliance with principles in 'all deliberate speed'.

Much has been written about the Court's ambiguous language (see Bell, 2004; Ogletree, 2004), but they nevertheless require brief discussion here. The language of 'all deliberate speed' and requirement that local authorities move in a 'prompt manner' definitely sound as if the process of desegregation should be swift. But the Court provided no enforcement mechanisms or metric to determine what would be satisfactory. The Court did not err in noting the varied nature of discrimination and desegregation practiced by local authorities throughout the country. But in prescribing an ambiguous desegregation mandate, the Court furthered, not impeded, the varied nature of racial discrimination by allowing segregationists to find refuge in its ambiguous language.

The result of *Brown II* was absolutely tragic. If prolonging all the harms the Court had compellingly identified in *Brown I* was not enough, *Brown II* perpetuated racial harms indefinitely, as many local school districts interpreted *Brown II*'s ambiguity as legal justification to resist, delay, avoid, and in some cases, altogether reject integration years after 1955. Intended or unintended, the fact remains: in appeasing local school authorities by not issuing an immediate desegregation mandate, the Court built the legal foundations where substantive change to inequality and segregation would be left up to local choice. That is, cities or counties would only see desegregated schools when local officials wanted integration. In some Southern states, segregation continued for years following *Brown II*. In one instance, Prince Edward County in Virginia closed its schools for five years from 1959–1964 to avoid integration and maintain its white schools.

## *Brown's* Reaction

The only possible way for the Court to integrate schools in a meaningful and uniform fashion was to order the immediate desegregation of schools. The Court could have achieved these goals by requiring the immediate desegregation of schools monitored by federal courts. In the circumstances of local school authorities, federal enforcement arms such as the National Guard (who were eventually used in Mississippi) could serve as the monitoring force for the Court's mandate. Instead, the Court fostered an environment of indifference, disdain, and lukewarm attitudes toward the process of desegregation. Although *Brown I*'s proclamation is powerful and memorable, it lacked any authority in terms of enforcement and oversight toward a desegregated public school system. Perhaps controversially, Bell (2004) is accurate with his observation that *Brown* is now nothing more than a hollow victory. Despite the fact that its reference and memory conjure great pride, the case should be judged for what it accomplished, not only for its promise. UCLA's Civil Rights Project/Proyecto Derechos Civiles (see Orfield & Frankenberg, 2014) commemorated the 60th anniversary of *Brown* by issuing a comprehensive report on the current state of segregation in American schools. The report summarized that despite promising progress in the 70s and 80s, the last twenty years have seen a reversal of desegregation and American public schools are now re-segregating.

Showing data collected nation-wide, the racial numbers are unmistakable in underscoring the pervasiveness of segregation. However, we do not need racial data today to know that *Brown* did little to end educational segregation. The issue is not whether we *still* face educational segregation today, but whether segregation ever went away since *Brown*. It is rather a question of what kind or degree of segregation schools suffer today. The issue is steeped in a historical and contextual understanding of *Brown I* and *II* from a perspective of substantive achievement, not simplistically remembered as a canonical case. We only need to look at what local school districts accomplished in terms of desegregation immediately after 1955 to witness *Brown*'s failure to tackle segregation.

## *The Good and the Bad*

Topeka, Kansas was the lead name in the consolidated *Brown* cases. Zelma Henderson, an original plaintiff represented by the NAACP in the Kansas case, recalled in 2004 that Topeka schools desegregated in a peaceful manner with no demonstrations. Answering whether or not Ms. Henderson remembered any significant social unrest after the *Brown* decision, she recalled the decision was accepted and was not long until teachers and principals were also integrated.[7] However, the reception of *Brown's* desegregation mandate was not as smooth in other areas of the country, particularly the South. In Arkansas two years after *Brown II*, Governor Orval Faubus ordered his state's National Guard to block nine African American students (Little Rock Nine) from attending Little Rock Central High School. The plan was to allow only nine black students to attend Little Rock Central High School. Little Rock's superintendent initially drafted a plan to integrate Little Rock Schools at a much faster pace across all grade levels, but this initial plan was forsaken in favor of the State Attorney General's more modest proposal. The new plan called for the integration of only *one* school, Little Rock Central High. Additionally, no other school would integrate until 1960 when a few junior high or middle schools would similarly admit a limited number of black students. Finally, the last phase of the desegregation plan would involve integration of a few elementary schools at an unspecified time.

In response to the State Attorney General's plan to allow the Little Rock Nine to attend Little Rock Central, Governor Faubus summoned his state's national guard to block the nine black students from entering Little Rock Central High. In scenes that captivated and divided the nation, National Guard members physically lined up in front of the schoolhouse doors preventing the black students from entering. In addition to National Guardsmen physically blocking school doors, segregationist groups and protestors verbally abused, assaulted, and spat on the students. Together, the combination of National Guardsmen coupled with the mob mentality of Arkansas segregationists constructed a picture in contrast to *Brown's* racial triumphalism two years prior. The situation was so egregious that President Eisenhower deployed the 101st Airborne Division of the U.S. Army to protect the students. In addition, Eisenhower federalized the entire ten thousand-strong members of the Arkansas National Guard, rendering Governor Faubus powerless against Little Rock Central High's effort to integrate nine black students.

The examples of governors and schools resisting *Brown's* constitutional mandate are numerous and far reaching. In Texas, attorney General John Ben Sheppard created a campaign to establish as many legal obstacles as possible in order for desegregation implementations to fail. In Mississippi at the collegiate level, the most famous example is James Meredith's attempt to attend the University of Mississippi (Ole Miss). Despite being a highly qualified student, Meredith was denied admissions to Ole Miss two consecutive years before petitioning to the Supreme Court on the grounds that he was being denied admissions solely because he was black. The Court agreed and ordered that he be admitted (see *U.S. v. Barnett*, 1964). Reacting to the Court's verdict, Governor Ross Barnett maneuvered to have the state legislature pass a law that was facially race neutral, but directed principally at Meredith. The newly passed law prohibited any person convicted of a state crime from admission to a state school. The law was intended to keep Meredith out of Ole Miss because he was convicted of falsifying his voter registration in an attempt to circumvent the state's racist voter registration rules that disenfranchised black voters. Similar to President Eisenhower's move to bring in the Army to protect nine black students in Little Rock Arkansas, U.S. Attorney General Robert F. Kennedy called in 500 U.S. Marshalls flanked by the Army Engineer Combat Battalion from Kentucky to ensure Meredith's safety. In scenes reminiscent of an active military war zone, tents, kitchens, and military vehicles were set up on the Ole Miss campus.

### *The Ugly*

Although these examples show the extreme nature of resistance from segregationists to keep their schools white-only, none was as extreme and aggressive as the Virginia Prince Edward County School closures from 1959–1964. Following *Brown*, the Byrd Organization led by U.S. Senator Harry F. Byrd, organized a 'Massive Resistance' plan to systematically avoid compliance with the Court's desegregation mandate with help from a network of local politicians, courts, and state lawmakers. Many legal strategies were deployed in order to avoid desegregation under a general course of action known as the Stanley Plan. One strategy in particular established a 'tuition grant' for students to attend private schools, thus establishing *de facto* private pro-segregation academies. Because

*Brown* only applied to public schools, many southern cities began establishing private schools for Whites in order to avoid integration. As a consequence, what were once black and white schools in the public sector became a racial divide through Whites' strategic use of the private sector. Although White flight to the private academies prevented integrated public schools, the possibility remained that, at the very least, Black students in Edward County could attend better schools left empty by their white colleagues. This was not so. After draining its funding coffers by offering tuition grants to white students to attend private schools, the county refused to appropriate any monies to run its public schools, effectively closing all public schools in Prince Edward County. From 1959, the closures lasted five years. During this time, white students exclusively attended private schools established by the 'Prince Edward Foundation', funded and underwritten by public monies.

During this period of public school closures, white students continued their education in *de facto* segregated schools while black students were systematically neglected. Many black students went outside their districts to attend schools with relatives and family, some attended schools set up in basements and offices of local churches, while others were unable to attend school altogether for parts or the entire period of public school closures. Only during May of 1964, a decade after *Brown I*, did the Supreme Court unanimously order public schools to open in Prince Edward county, an immediate ruling that had escaped the Court in *Brown* (see *Griffin v. County school board of Prince Edward County* (1964)). Due to the specific and unequivocal nature of the Court's ruling, state supervisors and local school officials complied by opening its public schools rather than risk prosecution and possible imprisonment. However, the damage was already done. The Court in *Brown* relied on the Clark experiment to highlight individual psychological harm due to educational segregation, but what type of harm results from not having *any* school for up to five years? Some have called black students victimized by Virginia's massive resistance as the 'lost generation' due to the lack of adequate education for five years. School closures in Prince Edward County serve as a reminder that resistance to *Brown* was in some instances much more severe and drastic than its harms pre-desegregation.

## Discussion

It is no wonder that Derrick Bell and other prominent civil rights activist have a lukewarm and disappointing reference of *Brown*. We are now more than sixty years removed from the decision and increasingly its historical reference in civil society is severed from the actual text and resulting political pushback from segregationists who mobilized to keep white schools segregated. In a moment when education continues to struggle with racial segregation, a significant historical moment such as *Brown* must be understood accurately for it to provide any power to improve our current educational problems. There are at least two practical reasons for this. First, the currently constituted conservative Court perpetually cites *Brown* as a legal precedent in striking down nearly all race positive educational policies from public education all the way to graduate and professional school. Second, more and more, *Brown* is revered in civil society and public discourse as a landmark decision, celebrated for what it apparently ended, but never remembered for what it failed to do.

First, although the conservative Court is correct in referencing *Brown* as an important legal precedent, it does so without discussing or considering its nature of white appeasement as an opinion that produced troubling results. For instance, Justice Clarence Thomas routinely cites *Brown* while adding his own statement accompanying his citation. Again, Justice Thomas has routinely stated, often signed on by other conservative Justices, that:

> Indeed, Brown I itself did not need to rely upon any psychological or social-science research in order to announce the simple, yet fundamental truth that the Government cannot discriminate among its citizens on the basis of race.
>
> Segregation was not unconstitutional because it might have caused psychological feelings of inferiority. Public school systems that separated blacks and provided them with superior educational resources making blacks 'feel' superior to whites sent to lesser schools—would violate the Fourteenth Amendment, whether or not the white students felt stigmatized, just as do school systems in which the positions of the races are reversed. Psychological injury or benefit is irrelevant.[8]

According to Justice Thomas, all *Brown* needed to say was that governmental discrimination based on classification is inherently unconstitutional, regardless of any apparent psychological, individual, or group harm. But Justice Thomas commits a fatal revisionist error. Although it would have been significant if *Brown* were decided in accordance with Justice Thomas' rejection of straight-forward racial classifications, the fact of the matter is that it was not. *Brown* was not written with a clear directive that any racial classification amounts to discrimination. Warren's opinion only applied to the field of public education, leaving miscegenation laws and other forms of subordination legal for years after *Brown*. Additionally, the decision itself was incredibly ambiguous as a purposeful appeasement in order to secure a unanimous decision. This ambiguity led to an incredible amount of political and social upheaval that in some instances presented a worse educational reality for Blacks.

When Justice Thomas states that *Brown* did not need to rely on psychological evidence, it signals his inability (purposeful?) to grasp the simple yet undeniable truth that race is not just simple classification, but a form of subordination and oppression based on classification. Today, *Brown* is held aloft severed from its contextual and political history. It is remembered with little historical accuracy either as a legal struggle, compromise, and appeasement or as the beginning of a contentious period in American racial history *after* its decision. When the conservative court references the binding precedent of *Brown*, it does so by writing whatever history and meaning it wants to project onto the case. This is what Justice Thomas accomplishes by neglecting the substantive history of *Brown* by grafting his own anti-classification belief onto its doctrine. This revisionist history has little to do with *Brown* but instead reflects what colorblind conservatives want *Brown* to represent today.

This leads us to the second troubling aspect if *Brown* is not remembered accurately. *Brown's* Holy Grail status is based off a colorblind revisionist fiction while its failure to meaningfully desegregate schools is forgotten. This is troubling in that colorblindness is bolstered by a pivotal moment in American history with limited results. Thus, any critique of colorblindness is seen as an attack on a watershed historical moment that is unfathomably questioned. This is the genius of colorblindness hijacking and rewriting the history of *Brown*. It enjoys the historical capital of *Brown's* legacy while not having to politically own up to it. Rather than challenge the historical revisionist of colorblindness in regard to *Brown*, the colorblind era sees *Brown* as a singular moment ushering in a meritocratic blank slate do-over that absolves our historical racial sins. Troubling facts such as segregated academies, closed schools, National Guard blockades, and a governor's declaration of 'segregation today, segregation tomorrow, segregation forever' are lost products of a cruel racist past, retold by a colorblind revisionist history. The possible response is not to give up on *Brown*. As the colorblind Court continues to cite *Brown* according to its revisionist memory, accurately reclaiming *Brown* both legally and historically presents an opportunity to begin the process to undo the damage of colorblindness. If we remember *Brown* as a constitutional doctrine and historical legacy accurately, colorblindness reveals itself not as a solution, but as a symptom of racism.

## Notes

1. For Instance, in the case that established the requirement of 'Miranda Rights' *Miranda v. State of Arizona* (1966), three other cases were consolidated with *Miranda* (*State of California v. Stewart*, *Vignera v. State of New York*, and *Westover v. United States*). The consolidated action was ultimately called *Miranda v. State of Arizona*, and hence the birth of 'Miranda Rights', because *Miranda* was first alphabetically.
2. *Brown v. Board of Education of Topeka*, 347 U.S. 483 (1954), p. 493.

3. Ibid., p. 489.
4. Ibid., pp. 493–494.
5. Ibid., p. 495.
6. Ibid., p. 494.
7. See Adamson, E. (2003). Breaking barriers: Topekans reflect on the role in desegregating nation's schools. *Topeka Capital Journal*, May 11, 2003.
8. *Missouri v. Jenkins*, 515 U.S. 70 (1995). Thomas, J., concurring, pp. 120–121.

# 5 (Un)Equal Protection and Disproportionate Harm to Minorities

## Introduction

In the context of local school authorities, districts, Courts, and governments pushing back against *Brown's* mandate, there were also examples of social and political movements that continued the Civil Rights struggle for integration and equality. From small to large movements, social activists participated in teach-ins, protests marches, political campaigns, and other activities in order to advance the integrationist goals of *Brown*. For example, after the Supreme Court ordered Prince Edward County to immediately reopen its public schools following a five-year closure, a group of students from Queens College in New York organized the 'Student Help Project' designed to teach, tutor, and prepare black students for the start of the school year. Perhaps the largest and most significant social and political movement immediately after *Brown* was the Civil Rights Movement that culminated in passage of the historic Civil Rights Act of 1964. The Civil Rights Act was a landmark piece of legislation that outlawed discrimination based on race, color, sex, religion, or national origin. In terms of voting rights, the Civil Rights Act ended the unequal application of voter registration requirements that were historically used to disenfranchise Blacks after the reconstruction amendments. In addition, the Act ended racial segregation not only in schools, but also in the workplace and places of 'public accommodation' that served the general public. Continually present with the social and political movements that either worked to stunt or advance the integrative promise of *Brown* and the Civil Rights Act, the Supreme Court continued to play a critical role.

The Court's participation in adjudicating racial disputes was not limited to the field of education. Beyond *Brown*, the court has since adjudicated racial practices in areas of inter-racial marriage, voting and political representation, criminal justice sentencing, and issues of employment discrimination from hiring to the awarding of employment contracts. Through these disputes, the Court was never consistent as to whether or not it favored or rejected racial considerations.

In some instances, the Court allowed social and political policies to use race toward the goals of integration and inclusion. In contrast, the Court also struck down integrative attempts it deemed 'discriminatory' while also refusing to use its authority to stop policies that produced disparate impacts on minority racial groups. That said, the Court's vacillation was not equal. More often than not, the Court struck down affirmative action policies in favor of protecting the racial status quo that favored Whites.

The decade-long resistance to *Brown* effectively stripped the decision of any enforcement authority to secure widespread integration in public education. The Civil Rights Act similarly faced intense opposition. *Brown's* language was notoriously vague and allowed the opposition an arsenal of maneuvers to maintain segregation in education. The Civil Rights Act was clear in the prohibition of discrimination. However, the landmark legislation also ushered in an ironic form of resistance: the emergence of 'race-neutral' policies and practices. Regardless of the appearance of its race neutrality, these new policies and practices continued to subordinate racial minorities. As a result, the Court was asked to confront a new form of racial subordination.

## Resistance: First *Brown*, Now the Civil Rights Act

School districts immediately began to resist the constitutional mandate of integration ordered by *Brown*. However, discrimination in employment, voting, and other civil areas continued until the passage of the Civil Rights legislation. Nevertheless, although opposition to the Civil Rights legislation came some ten years after white uprisings in schools, the motivations from education and employment officials were the same: to prevent integration and maintain the existence of white dominated institutions. The response from businesses to the Civil Rights legislation was not as overtly racist and discriminatory as the educational response to *Brown* due to the clear anti-discriminatory mandate of the Civil Rights Act. Whereas *Brown* was vague in its educational mandate, which allowed for much ambiguity (read: white ambivalence), the Civil Rights Act of 1964 in general, and specifically title VII, was clear in prohibiting discrimination based on race, color, religion, sex, and national origin. In other words, unless places of employment were overtly discriminatory and did not care about violating federal statute and risk imprisonment, any attempt to subvert the Civil Rights Act would be covert in tone and manner compared to Whites' rejection of *Brown's* findings (i.e. school closings, George Wallace's schoolhouse speech). Anti-Civil Rights maneuvers came in the form of prima facie race-neutral changes in employment and workplace policies. Although facially neutral, these maneuvers were enacted with the intent to prevent integration in the workplace.

### *A Glimmer of Hope From the Court*

The Court first addressed so-called race-neutral maneuvers in *Griggs v. Duke Power Co* (1971). The Duke Power Company in North Carolina practiced workplace discrimination and segregation since the early 1950s. Duke power only allowed black workers to work in its labor department where employees were paid the lowest in the entire company. Only white workers were promoted above labor-intensive positions into management. In 1955, Duke required a high school diploma for its higher-paid positions. In response to the Civil Rights Act forbidding racial discrimination in the workplace, Duke dropped its racially discriminatory practice but maintained its high school diploma requirement while adding an IQ test for higher-paid management positions. Because black workers were less likely to hold a high school diploma and scored on average lower on the IQ test, Whites continued to receive promotions and dominate high-paying positions. These 'race-neutral' employment policies represented a novel problem for the Court within the post-*Brown* Civil Rights era. Created from apparently race-neutral requirements and policies, Blacks were harmed at a significantly higher percentage than their white counterparts. This phenomenon became known as adverse/disparate impact, or disproportionate harm litigation.

Although the policy was colorblind and contained no clear racial distinction or classification, the *Griggs* Court unanimously ruled that such requirements were in fact racially motivated. The Court ruled that the high school diploma and IQ test requirement were utilized as a barrier to further restrict black workers from attaining higher-paying positions. Because the requirement of a high school diploma and IQ test disproportionately harmed Blacks compared to their white counterparts, the Court ruled that under title VII of the Civil Rights Act, if employers utilized requirements that disproportionately harmed a class of workers (e.g. sex, race, religion), the employer must show that the requirements (e.g. IQ test) are 'reasonably related' to the employment. In the opinion of the unanimous Court, the Duke power company did not sufficiently demonstrate the necessity for their high school requirement and IQ had little to do with job performance. In fact, clear evidence persuaded the Court that white workers with no high school diploma and who did not take the IQ test performed satisfactory work and made progress in departments that had now instituted the new requirements. The ruling was a significant decision because the Court was not persuaded by supposed race-neutral employment requirements. The Court did not take at face value Duke's argument that it had no intention to discriminate against its black workers through its race-neutral requirements. The judgment did not focus on discriminatory *intent*, but on disproportionate *harm*. In a powerful recognition, the unanimous Court ruled disproportionate harm resulted because Blacks in the company had systematically received inferior education in segregated schools. The opinion cited a previous position where it prohibited the institution of a literacy test for voter registration because of the history of Blacks receiving an inferior education due to segregation. Therefore, *Griggs* established that the imposition of tests and requirements for promotion or employment must show a 'legitimate business interest'.

The unanimous decision first recognized that facially race-neutral requirements and tests were not inherently legal just because they did not overtly discriminate against a class of people based on race. Second, *Griggs* recognized the persistence of racial subordination in society. In other words, so-called race-neutral requirements take advantage of the long history of racism in order to inflict disproportionate harm. Finally, the Court did not focus its analysis on the colorblind requirements and tests, but on outcomes that are the direct result of 'mechanisms that operate as built in headwinds'.[1] In a memorable reflection of its position on the issue, the Court famously proscribed that 'Congress has now provided that tests or criteria for employment or promotion may not provide equality of opportunity merely in the sense of the fabled offer of milk to the stork and the fox'.[2] However, although the ruling was a sweeping win against attempts to subvert integration and the promise of the Civil Rights Act, the case was decided as a statutory decision utilizing the Civil Rights Act. Therefore, the same ruling could not be applied to the constitution, as disproportionate harm under equal protection of the Fourteenth Amendment still had to be settled.

## *The Court Backtracks*

The statutory rule adopted in *Griggs* demanded companies show a legitimate business interest in instituting any mechanisms of hiring or employment promotion if these mechanisms caused disproportionate harm to a targeted class. However, since the case was decided under the Civil Rights Act, it was a statutory opinion that meant the Court's holding does not automatically apply to constitutional equal protection claims. In *Washington v. Davis* (1976), the Court would establish the constitutional rule when it comes to disproportionate harm. *Davis* marked the point when the Fourteenth Amendment's equal protection clause began to constrict against minorities and provide employers with a more favorable constitutional alternative to *Griggs*' Civil Rights statutory standard.

In *Davis*, employment applications to the D.C. police department from two African Americans were rejected due to their performance on a verbal skills exam (test 21). African Americans failed test 21 at a ratio of 4–1 in comparison to white applicants. Encouraged by *Griggs*, the black applicants alleged test 21 violated both the Civil Rights Act and the Fourteenth Amendment's equal protection clause. The case appeared easily resolved through an application of the statutory disproportionate harm tests established under *Griggs*. If *Griggs* were applied, the Court would ask whether or not the hiring mechanism (i.e. the civil service literacy test) constitutes a necessary business interest in relation to the employment. However, in *Davis* the Court augmented and clarified its position in *Griggs*, rather than simply affirming and applying its statutory rule. The Court stated the statutory rule established in *Griggs* did not automatically translate in creating a constitutional rule, and the Court refused to establish such a rule for *Davis*. We must recall that in *Griggs*, Duke Power's supposed colorblind intent requiring a high school diploma and IQ test was not the focus. Instead, the Court emphasized the racially disparate impact of Duke's hiring mechanisms and asked whether or not they constituted a necessary business interest. In *Davis*, the Court shifted from disparate impact and instead focused on intent. The shift from results to intent would make it much more difficult for minorities to affirmatively prove racial discrimination before the Court.

The Court ruled the D.C. Police Department's civil service literacy test was not instituted with a discriminatory purpose. The shift to intent was born out of thin air because in *Griggs*, the Court did not give much attention to intent. Rather, the *Griggs* opinion recognized that even though Duke's requirements were apparently race neutral, the disparate impact was due to institutional manifestations of racism such as poor education and segregated schooling. As a result, the *Griggs* opinion demanded that Duke show a specific relationship between the employment mechanism and a business necessity. In a drastic departure from its statutory rule established only five years earlier, the *Davis* court elevated the importance of intent while diminishing the relevancy of disproportionate harm. *Davis* ruled, 'disproportionate impact is not irrelevant, but it is not the sole touchstone of an invidious racial discrimination forbidden by the constitution'.[3] This is a perplexing straw-man argument. In *Griggs*, disproportionate harm was not the sole touchstone criterion that invalidated Duke's hiring policy. Duke's hiring mechanisms were invalidated because the IQ test and high school diploma requirements showed no specific business necessity to the company other than to serve as a built-in headwind against black applicants. Therefore, the *Davis* court sets up a false binary that did not exist in *Griggs*. *Griggs* was neither about disproportionate harm nor intent, but rather the middle ground of whether or not disproportionate harm was justified under an examination of business necessity. The *Davis* Court abandons this middle ground altogether and establishes the polar extremes of disproportionate harm (which it said was not enough) and intent.

Additionally, by refusing to ask if the D.C. police department's civil service literacy exam constituted a legitimate business necessity, the Court abdicated its authority of judicial review by trusting the D.C. police department that the test 'rationally may be said to serve a purpose the government is constitutionally empowered to pursue'.[4] This standard of review is clearly less stringent than the standard imposed in *Griggs*. The Court in *Griggs* discovered that white workers who did not possess a diploma or take the IQ test had performed in a satisfactory manner compared to those who had taken the tests and completed high school. But in *Davis*, the Court did not ask the D.C. police to prove a business or work necessity. In moving away from enforcing its business necessity standard and retreating to a 'rational basis review' (see the following chart), the Court established a judicial binary that proved impossible for minorities to obtain legal relief from disproportionate harms absent evidence of intentional discrimination or racial bias.

## Standard of Review: Friend *or* Foe

In adjudicating disputes against possible violations of constitutional and statutory rights, the Court utilizes a hierarchy of review standards. Strict scrutiny is the most stringent standard of review followed by intermediate scrutiny and rational basis review.

| | *Rational Basis Review* | *Intermediate Scrutiny* | *Strict Scrutiny* |
|---|---|---|---|
| State/Employer Interest | Legitimate, can be merely conceivable—need not be actual | Must be genuine and important | State interest must be compelling |
| Law's Relation to State/Employer Interest | Must be *rationally* related, or non-arbitrary | Must be substantially related | Must be *necessary to achieve the purpose*, and discriminating policy is 'narrowly tailored' |

Rational basis review simply requires the government to show that the law in question is 'rationally' related to state interests. The Court utilizes this lowest standard of review on benign classifications like prohibiting the sale of alcohol to those under twenty-one. In these instances, the court essentially abdicates its responsibility of review and defers to the justification of the government or private actor. To illustrate further the lax requirement of rational basis review, a law's relation to state interests only needs to be conceivable; whether or not the law is smart or intelligent is of no concern. Therefore, Justice Marshall has often said the constitution does not prohibit legislatures from enacting stupid laws. However, strict scrutiny is a much more difficult standard of review. The Court has consistently ruled that all government classification based on race must apply strict scrutiny as the standard of review. Therefore, strict scrutiny renders all racial classifications constitutionally suspect.

The *Davis* decision represents the historical moment where issues of disproportionate harm and affirmative action (a constitutional issue to come later) would fall under the false binary of Rational Basis (RR) review or Strict Scrutiny (SS). But as the chart and the *Griggs* case showed, there is an intermediate standard of review that requires the Court to find a genuine and important interest that is related to the practice or law in question. The *Griggs* court clearly articulated what constitutes intermediate scrutiny, a standard of review that sits between rational basis and strict scrutiny. The results from this extreme binary have been catastrophic for people of color and can only be understood as a retrenchment of racial inequality while limiting the Court's ability to address the persistence of racial disparity. The Court's false binary is troubling in at least two critical areas: ongoing racial problems cannot be dealt with effectively under rational basis review, while policies and strategies that attempt to address racial problems are struck down by strict scrutiny. In calling the Court's binary false, I am editorializing that the Court's insistence on avoiding intermediate review is a purposeful choice that subjects its methodological review to two extremes. In other words, starting with *Davis*, the Court restricts itself based off its own unwillingness to expand constitutional review. In less than five years, *Davis* simply abandons the intermediate standard of review used in *Griggs*. As a result of the Court's binary imposition neglecting the existence of intermediate review, even though *Griggs* was not overturned explicitly, the Court's elevation of intent in *Davis* all but eliminated the intermediate business necessity test established from *Griggs*.

### *The Elusiveness of Racial 'Intent' in the Colorblind Era*

*Davis* fundamentally altered the methodological focus of how justices would go about determining future statutory and constitutional violations based on race. By elevating intent and diminishing the importance of adverse/disparate impact, the Court utilized the antiquated racial discourse of slavery and Jim Crow racism in order to adjudicate racial problems in the colorblind era. That is, 'slaves as property' in *Dred Scott*, or 'separate but equal' during Jim Crow established in *Plessy* were clear examples of legislative and political *intent* to subordinate Blacks. However, *Brown* and the Civil Rights Acts made overt discriminatory racial intent a thing of the past. In other words, discriminatory racial intent was outlawed and those who wanted to advance racial subordination with intentional acts of discrimination faced arrest and imprisonment in violation of federal law. The changing racial dynamics that made discriminatory intent a thing of the past also spurned an evolved campaign to maintain white privilege in accordance with changing legal and legislative standards. We have already discussed Prince Edward County offering tuition credits for students to attend private, and ultimately white, schools and Duke Power Plant instituting an IQ requirement for promotion. Without contextual consideration, both are race-neutral policies. Nevertheless, these 'race-neutral' policies resulted in racialized results that subordinated Blacks and benefited Whites.

Even though the elevation of intent signaled the diminished importance of disparate impact, the intent test articulated in *Davis* was not impossible. The Court provided several ways to prove discriminatory intent that was, in theory, at least workable. The Court spelled out three approaches in order to infer discriminatory intent:

1. Look at circumstances as a whole, and infer discriminatory purpose.
2. Disproportionate harm so severe that the disparate impact is hard to explain on non-racial grounds.
3. Measure intent from foreseeable outcome.

For these approaches to find discriminatory intent, motive was not a factor, as intent was measured in an inferential way. That is, even in the face of racial motives, intent was not measured by the subjective motives of the actor, but by inferring from the totality of evidence. For instance, if intent was measured by subjective motives, various actors could just deny the existence of discriminatory motives. Therefore, the *Davis* Court's intent test was theoretically workable since it allowed room for intent based on: circumstances as a whole, disproportionate harm, and foreseeable outcome.

This all changed when the Court further elevated and clarified the importance of intent by demanding a show of *purposeful* discrimination. In both *Village of Arlington Heights v. Metropolitan Housing Corp.* (1977) and *Personnel Administrator of Massachusetts v. Feeney* (1979), policies with a clear disparate impact on people of color and women, respectively, were upheld because plaintiffs could not produce evidence of clear intent to discriminate. A suburb of Chicago, Arlington Heights had utilized a zoning ordinance to prohibit the building of multi-family housing facilities in favor of single-family dwellings. As a result, the zoning ordinance barred many minority families and others from low socio-economic backgrounds from living in Arlington Heights. Similarly, in *Feeney*, Massachusetts had a hiring policy that gave preference to veterans over non-veterans. The hiring policy was challenged since less than two percent of all Massachusetts veterans were women, therefore the disproportionate harm for women's hiring prospects in public sector jobs was undeniable. However, in both cases, the Court found the disproportionate harm to racial minorities and women did not violate the constitution because: in *Arlington Heights*, the official action was not found to discriminate *intentionally* against a suspect or protected class, and in *Feeney*, the hiring policy was not found to reflect in any way a *purposeful* discrimination on the basis of sex.

The insistence for minorities to show intentional and purposeful discrimination is perplexing. Again, its understanding of racism in the colorblind era is stuck in racial narratives of the past. The Court essentially asks plaintiffs to prove overt, clear, and direct practices of racial discrimination in order to invalidate a particular policy. With this standard, the only possible way for any policy or practice to be invalidated is a finding of clear bigotry either in the text of policy itself or affirmative words by policy actors. Furthermore, even though the intent standard in *Davis* presented a difficult barrier, proving discriminatory intent was at least theoretically possible through the inference of a totality of consequences. However, *Arlington Heights* and *Feeney* articulated further that 'intent' needed to be intentional and purposeful. The Court wiped out arguments of intent determined by results. Instead, discriminatory intent could only be determined by a showing of purpose and intention independent of result. This means that just because a policy has a disproportionate harm does not necessarily suggest that the policy actors purposefully intended for that disproportionate harm to happen. Here, intent was further clarified to mean malice. Together, *Arlington Heights* and *Feeney* made *Davis'* intent test of inferred circumstances meaningless. The only consideration was whether or not racial minorities can show malicious discriminatory intent.

### *Finding the Unicorn of Malicious Discrimination*

The Court's evolving intent test results in situations where, absent a finding of malicious discrimination, policy practices and laws would survive judicial review even if disproportionate harms to minorities were severe and indisputable. This point was validated in *McCleskey v. Kemp* (1987). The Supreme Court reviewed *McCleskey* concerning the state of Georgia's death penalty sentencing guidelines. Warren McCleskey, an African American, was found guilty of two counts of armed robbery and one count of murder. The jury found two circumstances beyond a reasonable doubt: McCleskey committed a murder during the course of an armed robbery, constituting a felony murder, and McCleskey murdered a police officer while the officer was on duty. According to Georgia's sentencing guidelines, either aggravating circumstance is sufficient to impose the death penalty. The jury recommended the death penalty and the presiding Judge agreed, sentencing McCleskey to death. The Supreme Court's review of *McCleskey* was based on whether or not Georgia's sentencing guidelines violated Title VII of the Civil Rights Act and the Fourteenth Amendment's equal protection clause.

Georgia's sentencing guidelines for murders are divided into three categories

1. Murder convictions with an automatic death sentence.
2. Murder convictions where death penalty option is up to the discretion of the prosecutor.
3. Murder convictions where death penalty is NOT an option.[5]

Georgia's three sentencing categories for murder and the death penalty are rather clear. Category 1 is reserved for murders so heinous the only available sentence is the death penalty. Category 3 is for murders that are not severe enough to merit considerations of the death penalty. Category 2 concerns crimes that are heinous and severe but do not fall within range of category one. Sentencing severity for murder cases that fall within category 2 are left entirely up to the discretion of the prosecutor. Therefore, the prosecutors' office is given discretion as to whether or not the death penalty is an option for murders in category 2. The *McCleskey* case hinged on the constitutionality of prosecutorial discretion for category 2 murders. McCleskey charged that because category 2 death penalty sentencing hinged on the discretion of mostly white prosecutors' offices, Blacks were disproportionately harmed. Category 2 convicted black murderers faced the death penalty at a significantly higher percentage than category 2 convicted white murderers. The Baldus Study clearly supported McCleskey's claim that Georgia's discretionary sentencing guidelines disproportionately harmed Blacks. Law professors David Baldus, Charles Pulsaski, and statistician George Woodworth (1983) studied more than twenty-five hundred murder cases in Georgia and found category 2 discretionary sentencing produced racially disproportionate results on several categories. With the help of the Baldus Study, McCleskey showed that when black defendants were *accused* of murder, they were twenty-two times more likely to face the death penalty when the victim was white than when the victim was black. Second, when black defendants are found *guilty* of murder, the convicted murderer is 4.3 times more likely to receive the death penalty than when the defendant was white.

Despite the findings of overwhelming disproportionate harm against Blacks in Georgia's death penalty sentencing structure, the Court found no constitutional violation. Regarding the Baldus study's findings, the Court did not dispute the validity of its claims. In other words, the Court accepted the validity of the Baldus study and acquiesced to the existence of disparate impact to Blacks as a result of Georgia's discretionary death penalty sentencing. The study clearly showed that race was the biggest factor in the midrange category 2 cases. However, the Court was unmoved absent a finding of purposeful discriminatory intent. Referring to the Georgia state legislature, which instituted the sentencing structure allowing for prosecutorial discretion, the Court reasoned:

> There was no evidence . . . the Georgia legislature enacted the capital punishment statute to further a racially discriminatory purpose.

> Nor has McCleskey demonstrated that the legislature maintains the capital punishment statute because of the racially disproportionate impact suggested by the Baldus Study.[6]

Here, the *McCleskey* Court forcefully differentiates between discriminatory purpose/intent and discriminatory effect. Clearly, disparate impact no longer holds any constitutional importance. This is why despite the incontrovertible evidence from the Baldus Study proving the existence of disproportionate harm, the Court is unmoved because the Baldus Study does not prove discriminatory intent by the Georgia State legislature. McCleskey argued that the state legislature was guilty of equal protection violation because it has adopted a death penalty statue with discriminatory application and continued to utilize it despite evidence of disparate harm to Blacks. Here, McCleskey argues for implied intent by the Georgia legislature because of the overwhelming and consistent frequency in racially disparate death penalty sentencing.

McCleskey argued that for a sentencing program to produce such consistent results, intent and purpose should be implied due to the clear statistical results of the Baldus study. The Court refused to accept McCleskey's argument for implied intent. The opinion explained:

> Discriminatory purpose implies more than intent as volition or intent as awareness of consequences. It implies that the decision maker, in this case a state legislature, selected or reaffirmed a particular course of action at least in part 'because of', not merely 'in spite of' its adverse effects upon an identifiable group.[7]

With this clarification of intent and purpose, the Court articulated that intent would now be further defined by malice. That is, foreseeable consequences and awareness of predicted outcomes is not sufficient to prove intent. McCleskey had to prove that the racially disparate application of Georgia's death penalty sentencing was the intended result when the Georgia state legislature enacted the sentencing guideline. McCleskey would need to produce evidence, such as recordings, legislative memos, or documents that affirmatively prove malicious intent. Absent these types of evidence, the Court argued the discrepancies that correlate with race are 'inevitable part of our criminal justice system'.[8] In essence, the Court is sanctioning *de facto* discrimination so long as no evidence of malice exists. To the Court, disproportionate harm no longer matters. The *McCleskey* majority focused its judicial review entirely on purposeful and intentional acts of legislative practice that are only proven by malicious intent. Because of *McCleskey's* 'malice test', not a single racially disproportionate policy has met the Court's standard of malice.

## Too Much Justice?

Not only was the *McCleskey* Court not swayed by the Baldus Study's statistical evidence to overturn Georgia's death penalty statute, it was also mindful of other social and civil policies that produced racially disproportionate results. Fearing an avalanche of potential lawsuits if the Court were to recognize and affirm the disparate impact of race in sentencing penalty, the majority realized the problem was not only limited to death penalty sentencing. In other words, the Baldus Study could be replicated to prove racially disparate effect in other areas of the criminal justice system. Predicting a 'parade of horribles'[9] the Court warned against an impending avalanche of litigation. Blowing caution to the wind, the Court admitted, '[I]f we accepted McCleskey's claim that racial bias has impermissibly tainted the capital sentencing decision, we could soon be faced with similar claims as to other types of penalty'.[10] As a result, the Court argued the integrity of the entire justice system would be called into question. Interestingly, the 'parade of horribles' argument is utilized as if eradicating racial bias from all areas of the criminal justice system was in fact a horrible thing to do. In other words, the *McCleskey* Court cautioned against too much justice.

Receiving little fanfare (infamy?) within our popular memory of canonical Supreme Court cases, *McCleskey* is nevertheless considered one of the worst Supreme Court decisions since WWII by leading progressive scholars. Some have called *McCleskey* the *Plessy* and *Dred Scott* of our time. Opinions and its place in history aside, *McCleskey* fundamentally changes how discrimination is viewed by the Court in our colorblind era. To the Court, discrimination is no longer measured by the disparate impacts any policy or statute may produce even if the racial disparities were clearly detectable. Discrimination only exists in express acts of purposeful discrimination, measured by malicious intent, not disproportionate impact. The Civil Rights and legal scholar Michele Alexander argued *McCleskey* has essentially inoculated the criminal justice system from legal scrutiny against racial discrimination (see Moyers, 2010). In effect, *McCleskey* has made it virtually impossible to indict any aspect of the criminal justice system absent a showing of intentional discrimination or malicious bias. Alexander pointed out that these types of evidentiary requirements are impossible to produce absent an affirmative admission.

Additionally, because proof of malicious discrimination is nearly impossible to prove, the Supreme Court has substantively closed its doors to claims of racial abuse, thereby turning a blind eye toward racial disparity within the criminal justice system and other civil institutions. With *McCleskey* and the progeny of cases where the Court elevated intent over disparate impact, the Court went from punting, deferring, and finally to abdicating completely its responsibilities of judicial review in cases of disproportionate harm to minorities. As a result, full faith and credit were given to legislatures and other bodies of authority to continue administering policies and practices that have grossly disproportionate impact on minorities without threat of impunity from the courts. Recalling the chart showing the differing levels of judicial scrutiny, disproportionate harm cases are treated with the same judicial rigor as benign issues such as the national drinking age. In shifting its scrutiny away from disproportionate harm and focusing instead on malicious intent, the Court equated the racial disproportionate harm of the death penalty with the 'disproportionate harm' of those affected by the legal drinking age, because under both instances, the Court utilize the same 'rational basis' standard of review.

The Court's judicial trajectory elevating intent, purpose, and malice over evidence of disproportionate harm also signified its approach toward legislative action that expressly utilizes race, such as affirmative action policies in employment and education. It is here where, in the eyes of the Court, issues such as death penalty sentencing distinguish themselves from affirmative action policies because of racial intent. That is, Georgia's death penalty sentencing guidelines were 'race neutral' whereas affirmative action policies are race positive. In the next chapter, I will discuss the Court's procedure in differentiating express uses of race (what it calls 'discrimination') versus so-called race-neutral policies that have a disparate impact.

## Notes

1. *Griggs v. Duke Power Co.*, 401 U.S. 424 (1971), p. 432.
2. Ibid., p. 431.
3. *Washington v. Davis*, 426 U.S. 229 (1976), p. 242.
4. Ibid., p. 246.
5. See Baldus, D. C., Pulaski, C., & Woodworth, G. (1983). Comparative review of death sentences: An empirical study of the Georgia experience. *Journal of Criminal and Criminology*, 74, 661–753.
6. *McCleskey v. Kemp*, 481 U.S. 279 (1987), pp. 298–299.
7. Ibid., p. 298.
8. Ibid., pp. 312–313.
9. The 'Parade of Horribles' is a rhetorical device the Court has routinely used in order to avoid ruling adversely against a law or statute by claiming doing so would usher numerous judicial challenges, real or imagined, before the Court.
10. *McCleskey v. Kemp*, 481 U.S. 279 (1987), p. 315.

# 6 Affirmative Action = Discrimination (to Whites) in the Colorblind Era

## Introduction

In tracing the trajectory of the Court's approach toward 'race-neutral' policies and practices that produce racially disparate impacts, the Court's methodology outlining what it considers discrimination is important. For disproportionate harm cases, discrimination was defined by intent, purpose, and malice. The emphasis on malicious intent over results had a discriminatory effect on individuals or groups' ability to make a compelling claim for equal protection in disparate impact cases. The shift toward malicious intent in disproportionate harm cases signaled the narrowing of 'equal protection'. Disparate impact claims consistently failed because the Court steadily increased the required threshold to prove discriminatory intent. The Court's rigid definition of what constitutes express practices of discrimination established a limiting and restrictive structure to review affirmative action practices. Beginning with issues of disproportionate harm and continuing contemporaneously with affirmative action and race positive policies, the constitutional world on race related issues is sharply divided into two divergent approaches. On one hand, 'race-neutral' practices that produce an immense amount of disproportionate harm almost always survive constitutional review. On the other hand, race positive affirmative action approaches almost never survive because of how the Court approaches and defines 'discrimination'.

In Chapter 5, I discussed the 'built in headwinds' (see *Griggs*) that claims of disproportionate harm face as a result of the Court's focus on malicious intent over disparate impact. In constructing and narrowing the definition of discrimination as only express forms of racial practices, the Court not only constructed its own rules on how to adjudicate 'colorblind' policies, but most importantly, it articulated the parameters for affirmative action cases. By mapping the historical trajectory of race related cases since the era of Jim Crow racism, the Court has exhibited three distinct approaches to race:

1. **Jim Crow Racism:** Enforcement of *Plessy's* 'Separate but equal' constitutional mandate. Express forms of racial discrimination were legal so long as separate accommodations were 'tangibly equal'. Eventually overturned by *Brown.*
2. **Colorblind/Race Neutral Disproportionate Harm:** Express forms of discrimination were no longer legal. Colorblind, facially 'race neutral', practices were utilized but nevertheless maintained racial disparity (see *Griggs*, *Arlington Heights*, & *Feeney*). Here, the court started by looking at disparate impact, but precipitously moved toward intent, purpose, and malice.
3. **Affirmative Action/Race Positive Policies:** policies that purposely and intentionally attempt to address racial disparity. Here, the Court constitutes these policies as 'express discrimination' because the policies use racial classifications, thereby ushering in a completely different standard of review (i.e. strict scrutiny) compared to race-neutral disproportionate harm claims.

Arguably, the various disparate impact claims could be considered as attempts by policy makers and employment authorities to maintain racial stratification and subordination. There were clear examples of 'colorblind' attempts at maintaining a white-dominated racial hierarchy (e.g. *Griggs*), and ones less obvious (e.g. *Washington v. Davis*). Nevertheless, whatever the intent or purpose of policy actors from the progeny of disproportionate harm cases, none was for the express purpose of *promoting* racial justice, diversity, and integration. This changed with the emergence of affirmative action policies practiced at the federal and local level in order to speed up the interests of the Civil Rights movement toward integration, access, and equality for people of color.

If policies that produced disproportionate harm were on one side of the political spectrum, affirmative action policies were on the opposing end. Not surprisingly, there was tremendous opposition to affirmative action policies. The passage of affirmative action laws and policies were immediately contested through the courts. Historically with *Dred Scott*, *Plessy*, and other pre-*Brown* cases, the Court overwhelmingly ruled in the interests of Whites to the detriment of minorities. *Brown* and the Civil Rights legislation were supposed to be a major turning point in the Court's trajectory. The developing 'equal protection' promise that started in *Brown* and continued through anti-miscegenation and discriminatory employment cases initially signaled the Court's developing willingness to understand the pervasiveness of racial practices and subordination. Unfortunately, the promise was short lived. No matter how damaging the Court's impact upholding disproportionate harm policies and practices, its methodological approach in striking down affirmative action policies is at least equally damaging.

## The Disproportionate Constitutional World on Race

As mentioned previously, the Court uses three standards of review in adjudicating laws, policies, and public practices under its power of constitutional and statutory review. Although three distinct approaches are clear, the Court has only utilized intermediate scrutiny in one case: *Griggs*. After establishing a promising standard looking at foreseeable outcome, the Court backtracked on race related cases to a position where it now only utilizes two extreme approaches of rational basis and strict scrutiny.

| | *Rational Basis Review* | *Intermediate Scrutiny* | *Strict Scrutiny* |
|---|---|---|---|
| | After Griggs, applies to all 'race-neutral' disproportionate harm claims | *Grigg's* 'Legitimate business necessity' standard | Any express use of race; applies to *all* affirmative action cases |
| State Interest | Legitimate, can be merely conceivable—need not be actual | Must be genuine and important | State interest must be compelling |
| Law's relation to State Interest | Must be *rationally* related, or non-arbitrary | Must be substantially related | Must be *necessary to achieve the purpose*, and discriminating policy is 'narrowly tailored' |

In early disproportionate harm cases, although the Court initially utilized intermediate scrutiny in *Griggs*, it abandoned intermediate scrutiny in *Washington v. Davis* and regressed to rational basis review. As a result, there are now only two divergent standards of review when it comes to race related cases: rational basis and strict scrutiny. For disproportionate harm claims, the Court has only vacillated between intermediate scrutiny and rational basis review. The Court *never* utilized strict scrutiny for any disproportionate harm claims, no matter how drastic the disparate impact. The Court's most stringent standard of review, strict scrutiny, comes into consideration for affirmative action and race positive policies because the Court treats these policies and practices as express forms of 'discrimination'. Therefore, because affirmative action policies purposefully utilize racial considerations, the Court's 'intent test' is satisfied and must be reviewed under strict scrutiny. That is, affirmative action policies purposefully utilize race and therefore fulfill the 'intent' test.

The chances for any challenged action to survive constitutional review can be predicted with a high probability according to the Court's standard of review. That is, any challenged action reviewed under rational basis is essentially guaranteed to pass. On the other hand, before the emergence of affirmative action claims, only President Roosevelt's Executive Order 9066 interning about one hundred and twenty thousand Americans of Japanese ancestry survived strict scrutiny[1] (see *Korematsu v. United States* [1944]). Strict scrutiny was established in *Korematsu* because Executive Order 9066 expressly and purposefully discriminated against Americans of Japanese ancestry. Nevertheless, the *Korematsu* Court agreed with Roosevelt's argument that Japanese internment was necessary to achieve the compelling interests of 'national security'. The Court's history has produced only two examples where an express use of race has survived strict scrutiny: Japanese internment and diversity in higher education (e.g. *Bakke*, discussed later).

The Court's definition of discrimination constructs a reality where all disproportionate harm practices are left undisturbed while nearly all affirmative action policies are struck down. Here, the constitutional word bifurcates into two polar extremes with an 'anything goes' standard of review on one end, and a 'nothing goes' standard on the other.

- Racial Classification/Express Use of Race?
  - Yes → Strict Scrutiny (Affirmative Action Policies and Practices)
  - No ↓
- 'Race Neutral'/No Express Use of Race? (Results in Disproportionate Harm)
  - Intentional/Purposeful/Malicious?
    - Yes → Strict Scrutiny
    - No → Rational Basis Review

With the Court's rigid review structure when it concerns race related issues, social and political movements that campaign for integration and diversity through race positive practices face a steep legal structure of difficulty. Additionally, if so-called 'race-neutral' policies are challenged, they are all but guaranteed protection due to the soft standard of rational basis review. The totality of these positions by the Court is made possible by its naive, yet devastating, construction of what constitutes racial 'discrimination'. As a consequence, not only is equal protection constricted, but also used as a weapon *against* efforts to speed up integration and achieve racial equality. As the Court's recent history shows, the arc of race positive and affirmative action policies before the Court reflects the same trajectory as that of disproportionate harm cases discussed in the previous chapter: a glimmer of promise early on, followed by extreme constriction and pushback.

### *Affirmative Action: A Glimmer of Hope*

*United Jewish Organization of Williamsburg v. Carey* (1977) (*UJO*) was the first case where the Court adjudicated the constitutionality of race-based affirmative action. In *UJO*, several voting districts in New York City were reapportioned under a 1972 plan with the goal of guaranteeing at least a 65% non-White voting majority. New York's motivation was to prevent racial minorities from being repeatedly outvoted by majority White populations in assembly and senate districts. Under the Voting Rights Act, any redistricting plan had to be submitted to the U.S. attorney general or the district court of D.C. for pre-clearance to satisfy safeguards against racial gerrymandering. Upon review, the U.S. attorney general established for New York a 65% non-White threshold for constitutional and statutory approval. Before the plan was instituted, a community of over thirty thousand Hasidic Jews lived entirely within one assembly and senate district of the Williamsburg area in Brooklyn, New York. Under the 1972 plan after pre-clearance guidance from the U.S. attorney general, New York redrew two adjacent districts. In meeting the minimum 65% non-White majority threshold, the redrawn districts split the Hasidic Jewish community, each belonging to two adjacent senate and assembly districts. As a result, the United Jewish Organization of Williamsburg, representing the Jewish community, petitioned to the Court that their equal protection rights were violated by New York's redistricting plan.

*UJO* is the first instance before the Court where a public authority expressly used race in its policy in order to promote greater minority representation. This was a radical shift from the disproportionate harm cases that at the time were common before the Court. In the disproportionate harm cases, the Court had to *find* intent, purpose, or malice in order to strike down the particular policy practice. In *UJO*, intent and purpose were obvious. New York State sought to increase minority representation by redistricting. If the Court was to follow its own intent test for 'race-neutral' disproportionate harm cases, New York State's redistricting plan would have surely faced the Court's highest standard of review: strict scrutiny. However, similar to its approach in *Griggs v. Duke Power Co.* the *UJO* Court focused on intent *and* harm. In *Griggs*, just because Duke Power utilized a 'race-neutral' policy of requiring a high school diploma and IQ test for promotion, the Court was unmoved that the 'race-neutral' criteria were *not* racially discriminatory practices. Therefore, the Court additionally focused on the discriminatory impact of Duke Power's employment policy. With the same approach, the Court in *UJO* was not immediately moved that New York state's race positive consideration to reapportion senate and assembly districts amounted to racial discrimination. As it did in *Griggs*, the Court wanted to figure out the real or foreseeable impact of the 1972 redistricting plan. In a near unanimous 7–1 decision (Justice Thurgood Marshall did not participate), the Court ruled in favor of New York's apportionment plan. New York's plan to guarantee racial minority representation was approved and the redistricting plan did not violate the Fourteenth or the Fifteenth (right to vote regardless of race, color, or previous condition of servitude) amendments.

In a clear ruling, the Court found that neither amendment prohibited the use of racial factors in districting and apportionment. Additionally, the State's plan to establish a 65% quota of non-White majority does not violate the same amendments. The most compelling part of the Court's opinion stated that although New York was purposeful, intentional, and deliberate in using race as a factor to increase non-White majorities with its redistricting plan, the Court ruled there was no systematic 'fencing out' of the white population in the county from electoral participation. That is, New York's plan did not in any way under-represent Whites in the electoral process relative to their share of the population. It is important to note the inherent racial fallacy that *UJO* utilized to argue against New York's plan. If there is a minimum 65% non-White majority, then there is a maximum 35% white minority. One of the main motivations for New York's plan was to prevent Whites from systematically outvoting minority groups. The establishment of a 65% threshold of non-White voters does not automatically suggest that the entire non-White majority will outvote Whites as one monolithic bloc. The 65% non-White majority is just that: non-White. It surely does not mean all Black, or Latino, or Asian. In fact, due to the city's diverse population encompassing more than just a binary black and white population, the 65% non-White majority goal does not automatically mean that any particular group can outvote a 35% white voting bloc. The *UJO* Court understood this. More importantly, the Court showed a critical understanding of race and what ultimately constitutes an act or practice of racial discrimination.

In *UJO*, the Court understood discrimination as a form of classification *and* subordination. Members of the majority court acknowledged that New York had classified non-White minorities as the target of their apportionment. This was fundamentally an act of classifying non-White and white groups in accordance with a clear racial classification. However, classification was not the only metric the Court used to measure discrimination. With the acknowledgment and discussion of 'electoral participation', being 'fenced out', and 'proportional representation', the Court investigated the reasonable and foreseeable outcome of New York's redistricting plan. The Court's investigation led the justices to conclude that white voter participation and representation would not be 'fenced out' in the same way that literacy tests were once utilized to disenfranchise Blacks from suffrage. The Court concluded that as long as Whites, as a group, were provided fair representation, there was not a 'cognizable discrimination against Whites' (p. 146). This shows the *UJO* Court understood discrimination as a form of classification and subordination.

Furthermore, the Court demonstrated a critical understanding of racialization that begins with an identification of difference, but most importantly, that this classification is then used to subordinate groups.

Express forms of classification and substantive subordination were the *modus operandi* of historical acts of racial subordination (e.g. Jim Crow Segregation). But with *Brown*, *Loving v. Virginia* (striking down anti-miscegenation), and the Civil Rights Act, the focus on classification as the prerequisite and central characteristic of identifying acts of racial discrimination lost its importance because overt forms of discrimination were outlawed. With *Griggs* and *UJO*, the Court at least signaled an understanding of the changing nature of racial practices as a result of the shifting legislative and political landscape. In both cases, the Court placed an enhanced emphasis on impact and foreseeable results underscoring the importance of subordination as the measure of unconstitutional racial discrimination. Unfortunately, the *UJO* Court's nuanced and historically specific understanding of racial discrimination was all but lost in less than a year when affirmative action entered higher education in *Regents of the University of California v. Bakke* (1978).

### *Affirmative Action: Hope Is Lost*

The dispute in *UJO* centered on New York's attempt to ensure and increase non-White political participation in senate and assembly elections. *Bakke* was predicated on the University of California, Davis' attempt to increase minority representation in its medical school. UC Davis' medical school instituted a quota system that set aside 16 out of 100 spots for racial minorities. After two consecutive years of being rejected by U.C. Davis, Allan Bakke sued the University alleging an equal protection violation due to its special quota system. Before Davis twice denied Bakke, twelve other medical schools rejected him, including the University of Southern California and Northwestern University, which expressly said a major reason for his rejection was due to his older age. At the time of his application, Bakke was already thirty-three years old, making his admission into medical school much more difficult since, at the time, many schools openly practiced age discrimination. Bakke's GPA and MCAT scores were both above the average of those admitted during his two unsuccessful years applying to Davis. The admissions committee signaled a hesitation in admitting Bakke because of his age. Most importantly, during an interview with Dr. George Lowry, the chairman of the admissions committee, Lowry gave Bakke an unsavory evaluation, which was the only part of Bakke's application that received a negative evaluation. In his assessment after Bakke's interview, Dr. Lowry reported that Bakke held rigid opinions based more on his own point of view as opposed to larger studies of issues. That is, Dr. Lowry did not think that Bakke was open minded. In comparison with New York State's redistricting plan in *UJO*, both instances were examples of express uses of race with the goal of filling a minimum racial quota of minority access. Like in *UJO*, the *Bakke* Court had the same circumstances and opportunity to utilize *UJO*'s standard of review in looking at the impact and intent of Davis' admissions quota system. However, a divided court split sharply on the preferred standard of review. Rational basis review was automatically out of the question because Davis' quota system contained an express use of race. The standard of review rested on the remaining two possibilities: intermediate review and strict scrutiny.

In a plurality decision, the dissenting liberals argued for intermediate review, suggesting that although Davis' quota system was a clear express use of a racial classification, it was well within reason to satisfy a multitude of state interests presented by the University of California system. The dissenting liberals felt the case should have been decided like *UJO*, with the Court's decision resting on whether or not there is intent *and* disparate impact on Whites generally, and Bakke specifically. If the Court adopted intermediate review and its methodological approach in *UJO*, Davis' quota admissions system would have easily survived review because its admissions number would neither have 'fenced out' Whites from participation nor would sixteen seats set aside for minorities create conditions where Whites would be disproportionately underrepresented at the medical school. In fact, it was due to persistent underrepresentation of minorities that spurned Davis' affirmative action policy to increase minority enrollment, meaning, white students were already well represented. The plurality opinion was tightly contested and the liberals were in the minority on the constitutionality of Davis' quota system. Four conservative justices wrote their own opinions, while Justice Powell authored his own opinion, thus creating some confusion as to the ultimate outcome of the case. In what was ultimately considered a great compromise, Justice Powell sided with the conservatives in striking down Davis' affirmative action quota system, but agreed with the liberals in ruling affirmative action policies constitutional in order to pursue the compelling governmental interest of promoting diversity in higher education.

On the standard of review, Justice Powell sided with the conservatives in imposing strict scrutiny. Following the standard set in *Korematsu*, Davis had to prove a compelling governmental interest to justify its racial classification in the same way that 'national security' was the justification for internment in *Korematsu*. The University of California presented four justifications to satisfy the Court's compelling interests test:

1. Reducing the historic deficit of traditionally disfavored minorities in medical school and the medical profession.
2. Countering the effects of societal discrimination.
3. Increasing the number of doctors to under-served communities.
4. Diversity in the classroom.

Joined by four conservative justices, Justice Powell rejected the first three justifications. In a famous proclamation, Powell declared that the U.S. was 'a nation of minorities'. Therefore, Powell argued Davis' quota system amounted to 'discrimination for its own sake'. Specifically, in response to Davis' argument that its quota system counters the effects of societal discrimination, Justice Powell believed that the reason was too amorphous and imposes a burden on Whites who bear no responsibility for the harm. Regarding the charge that Davis' program will increase the number of minority doctors to under-served communities, the conservative Justices dismissed the claim because Davis had failed to provide any evidence to prove that this will actually happen. In the only position where Justice Powell could agree with the liberal justices, he declared promoting diversity in the classroom *was* a compelling governmental interest. As a result, the plurality opinion recognized diversity in the classroom as a compelling governmental interest, but Davis' usage of a quota system was declared unconstitutional and the Court ordered the medical school to admit Bakke.

## 'A (White) Nation of Minorities'

Although initially hailed as a compromise, the enduring affirmative action landscape established by *Bakke* meant that all future race positive policies in education would be adjudicated within the parameters of *Bakke's* 'diversity' discourse, with strict scrutiny as the mandated standard of review. Powell and the conservatives automatically concluded that the existence of a minority quota system meant that Bakke and other Whites suffer from racial 'discrimination'. By identifying Bakke as a victim of 'discrimination' and declaring the U.S. as a 'nation of minorities', Justice Powell proclaimed that 'equal protection' was about individuals, as opposed to groups. This was a significant move because it allowed Whites to claim 'minority status', thereby making it possible for Whites to be 'victims' of discrimination. More importantly, by defining equal protection as a focus of individuals over groups, group discrimination is discarded as a worthwhile, or even relevant, point of analysis. The ramifications of focusing on individual discrimination over acts of group subordination is far reaching. Justice Powell manages to shift fundamentally the historical understanding of racial subordination of Blacks and minorities toward a racial discourse where *anyone* can be a victim of discrimination, regardless of historical precedents or whether or not they are members of an underrepresented group. This is perhaps the most important legacy of *Bakke*.

*Bakke's* importance does not lie in the forced admission of Bakke, or even in its declaration that diversity is a compelling governmental interest, as the issue would be revisited and narrowed later under the progeny of new affirmative action challenges. *Bakke's* far-reaching significance is located within the shift in the Court's definition of racial discrimination. In *Griggs* and *UJO*, the Court's understanding of racial discrimination was heavily influenced by a historical appreciation of how race was utilized as a stratifying and subordinating principle. As a result of *Bakke's* shifting rhetoric on race, Omi and Winant (2014) observe that the Court's decision amounted to a fundamental pivot signifying a new racial formation. This new racial formation elevated the importance of racial classification of any kind for anyone while discarding any importance of subordination. Taken together, the Court effectively eliminated the significance of historical racism. As a perplexing result, the Court is 'unable' to tell the difference between Jim Crow policies and voluntary affirmative action policies. Additionally, because the Court cannot identify any difference between Jim Crow policies and affirmative action policies, Whites can consider themselves as much a victim of racial discrimination from affirmative action as Blacks did under Jim Crow segregation. With the Court's new definition of 'discrimination', both circumstances are categorically the same. Additionally, because all Jim Crow acts of overt racism are considered prohibitively antiquated, the only explicit practices of racial classification are voluntary affirmative action policies. Through the prism of the Court's *Bakke* decision, Whites become the only members of Justice Powell's 'nation of minorities' who are racially discriminated in the colorblind era. As a result, Whites become the only 'minorities' who are afforded constitutional equal protection under the Fourteenth Amendment in the colorblind era.

If Justice Powell's belief in a 'nation of minorities' is to be taken seriously, the Court's trajectory since *Bakke* appears to overwhelmingly favor White 'minorities' over non-White minorities. First, the *Bakke* decision had the collective effect of expanding the possibility and opportunity for Whites to claim discrimination—all happening in the fledgling Civil Rights Era. Second, by only identifying diversity as a compelling state interest, *Bakke* drastically narrowed the likelihood of success for future affirmative action policies in education to survive strict scrutiny. If the country were indeed a nation of minorities, all policies enacted by government agencies should be treated as products of political struggles between competing minorities and the Court should defer to the political process and utilize rational basis review, as it did in all of the disproportionate harm claims of the 60s and 70s. But this was not the case. The Court viewed Davis' quota system with the same antagonism at par with Roosevelt's Executive Order 9066 that interned Americans of Japanese descent in *Korematsu*. 'National security' in *Korematsu* and 'diversity in higher education' in *Bakke* represent the only two circumstances where a government action has survived strict scrutiny, the Court's highest standard of review.

The reasoning behind strict scrutiny's rigid and difficult standard of review is that the disputed action in question is believed to violate a fundamental right protected by the constitution. For instance, in *Korematsu*, President Roosevelt's executive order violated several constitutional rights, the most obvious of which being freedom, due process, and equal protection. As a result, the Court asked the government to provide a compelling state interest to justify the violation of these fundamental constitutional rights. The U.S. government argued it was in the best interest of 'national security' during a time of war and that the Court should defer to Congress' constitutional enumerated war powers to conduct its business. In other words, the U.S. government argued that the proposed internment was an act under the scope of its war powers. The *Korematsu* Court agreed. Dissenting Justices argued the majority cannot demand a standard of strict scrutiny on one hand while simultaneously deferring to Congress' war powers on the other. The *Korematsu* dissent concluded that deference is antithetical to strict scrutiny. The Court's oxymoronic deployment of strict scrutiny aside, the *Korematsu* case established that 'national security' was a compelling government interest to satisfy strict scrutiny. With *Bakke*, diversity in higher education was added to the list of government interests that could possibly satisfy strict scrutiny. Although Justice Powell's independently authored opinion in *Bakke* endorsed diversity as a compelling government interest, he nevertheless rejected that intermediate review can ever be used in affirmative action cases—examples of what he and conservatives call practices of 'intentional discrimination'.

Along with the conservatives on the Court, Justice Powell's opinion that strict scrutiny is the required standard of review for affirmative action cases was solidified in *City of Richmond v. J.A. Croson Co.* (1989) and *Adarand Constructors, Inc. v. Pena* (1995). These cases involved equal protection disputes of municipal (*Croson*) and federal (*Adarand*) programs designed to award work and construction contracts to minority-owned businesses. Both cases collectively established the structure of strict scrutiny for affirmative action, racial classification, and race positive considerations we see today. Although *Bakke* established that diversity was a compelling interest, it did not concretely provide the structure regarding how state authorities can go about satisfying strict scrutiny. *Croson* and *Adarand* changed this. Even though both cases were sharply divided between conservatives and liberals on the Court, conservatives formed the ruling majority in both disputes. Justice Sandra Day O'Connor was the deciding vote tilting the balance of the Court toward the conservatives. First in *Croson*, the majority ruled it was appropriate to utilize strict scrutiny to review the City of Richmond's usage of a racial quota to award minority construction contractors municipal contracts. Second, the majority Court accepted Richmond's statistical evidence showing inequality in the granting of municipal contracts between white- and minority-owned businesses. However, the Court ruled that Richmond had not investigated any 'race-neutral' alternatives to correct the imbalance before resorting to its racial quota system. As a result, *Croson* established that under strict scrutiny, race positive options could only be used as a last resort.

Six years later in *Adarand*, again with Justice O'Connor's swing vote forming a conservative majority, the Court not only held that strict scrutiny was warranted for state actions that utilize racial considerations, but mandated that all racial classifications imposed by federal, state, or local government actors *must* be analyzed under the standard of strict scrutiny. Most importantly, the challenged affirmative action policy must be narrowly tailored to impact the very racial problem it is designed to address, with Justice O'Connor citing *Croson* declaring that 'Racial classifications are simply too pernicious to permit any but the most exact connection between justification and classification'.[2] Taken together with the precedent in *Croson*, *Adarand* established the structure of strict scrutiny for race positive affirmative action policies.

## '(White) Government Cannot Make Us Equal'

Together, *Croson* and *Adarand* establishes the two-pronged test that all race positive affirmative action policies must satisfy under strict scrutiny:

1. All non-racial alternatives have been exhausted and racial inequality still persists.
    a. Racial consideration is the only remaining option, making the government sponsored policy a last ditch effort, i.e. of last resort.
2. Narrowly tailored to combat the identified problem of racial inequality.
    a. Will not exacerbate other racial problems from proposed action any further than the principal racial problem.

One of the many controversial points of contention to arise out of *Adarand* is the dispute between 'benign' and 'invidious' racial classifications. The dissenting liberals in *Adarand*, led by justice John Paul Stevens, chided conservatives on the Court for their inability (or willingness) to tell the difference between benign and invidious racial classifications, asserting that normal citizens can surely tell the difference between good and bad intentions. Conservatives shot back suggesting that strict scrutiny is too important and stringent a standard of review to rely, i.e. defer, to the supposed 'good' or 'bad' intentions of legislators. Justice Stevens criticized the majority Court because it 'equates remedial preferences with invidious discrimination' and ignores the difference between 'an engine of oppression' and an effort 'to foster equality in society'.[3] In response, the conservatives ignored Justice Steven's assertions by proclaiming an adherence to the principle of constitutional consistency in the application of equal protection. Focusing on individual harm, conservatives argued judicial intervention is required when individuals have 'suffered an injury that falls squarely within the language and spirit of the Constitution's guarantee of equal protection'.[4] The conservative majority's insistence on consistency and its unwillingness to differentiate between benign and invidious acts of racial discrimination is best articulated by Justice Clarence Thomas' concurring opinion.

Justice Thomas agreed with the conservative majority that all governmental racial classifications should be reviewed under strict scrutiny. However, he wrote his own concurring opinion to emphasize his disagreement with the liberal justices arguing 'it is irrelevant whether a government's racial classifications are drawn by those who wish to oppress a race or by those who have a sincere desire to help those thought to be disadvantaged'.[5] In Justice Thomas' opinion, the single most important factor in deciding the constitutionality of racial considerations is in the existence of a classification, regardless of whether there is a history of 'racial paternalism'. To articulate further his disagreement with Justice Stevens, Justice Thomas declared:

> I believe that there is a moral and constitutional equivalence between laws designed to subjugate a race and those that distribute benefits on the basis of race in order to foster some current notion of equality. *Government cannot make us equal*; it can only recognize, respect, and protect us as equal before the law.[6]

Justice Thomas' assertion of moral and constitutional equivalency between invidious acts of racism, such as Jim Crow legislation, and benign or race positive attempts to promote racial equality goes even further than the O'Connor-led majority opinion. Justice O'Connor focused on the consistency of applying strict scrutiny, thus underscoring the importance of constitutional jurisprudence to the majority. However, in utilizing a moral, albeit rhetorical, equivalence between benign and invidious racial practices, Justice Thomas collectively compares hundreds of years of systematic institutional racism with half-hearted and feeble affirmative action attempts, attempts that Zeus Leonardo (2007) has called 'ambivalent action'. I use half-hearted and feeble to describe the limited effectiveness of affirmative action policies, not as a criticism of the arduous and careful campaigning required to bring these policies to fruition. In remembering the legacy of Jim Crow racism, 'separate but equal' policies are historicized today not only for their passage as legislation, but for the deleterious material effects of stratifying Blacks and non-Whites for nearly a hundred years. As a result, for Justice Thomas to compare and equivocate peace-meal affirmative action policies that were barely getting off the ground as morally equal to systematic practices of

Jim Crow racism reveals at best a negligent ignorance of history, and at worst, a willful act to prevent the Court from substantive and meaningful racial remediation.

How else can we understand Justice Thomas' assertion that 'government cannot make us equal'? If the moral equivalency of Justice Thomas is in fact negligently ignorant, then perhaps there is a glimmer of hope that affirmative action policies can be disengaged from being equated with historical legacies of institutional racism. Negligence and ignorance suggest an innocence, of not knowing, and preserves a degree of unintentional culpability. Therefore, if Justice Thomas' moral equivalence was evidence of definitional ignorance, then his may be overcome by understanding and engaging Justice Stevens' race positive position. Nevertheless, Justice Thomas and the other conservatives on the Court are members of the nation's highest Court, recognized, nominated, and approved by a political process as the best and brightest legal minds in the country. This leads Justice Stevens to scold the conservative Justices for their inability (unwillingness?) to tell the difference between benign and invidious usages of race. However, the more we investigate Justice Thomas' logic of equivalence between benign and invidious usages of race, his opinion is clearly an example of willful volition meant to establish a racial *tabula rasa*. In Justice Thomas' view, this racial blank slate will respect and treat us as equals before the law. Equality before the law is a noble goal for the function and limits of the law, but this goal is entirely subject to the validity of Justice Thomas' initial premise: that government cannot make us equal.

If it is true that government cannot make us equal, then perhaps the next best thing is for all of us to be treated equally before the law. This is the overall sentiment of Justice Thomas' opinion in *Adarand*. The position is built on the neoliberal colorblind view that society is inherently unequal because we are born into unequal lots in life. As a result, neoliberalism argues a government that attempts to equalize an inherently 'natural' organizing principle would only amount to an exercise in social engineering (see Friedman, 1990; Hayek, 2007). However, Justice Thomas' premise that 'government cannot make us equal' is a perplexing premise that inverts and forgets what government has already been guilty of for hundreds of years. That is, perhaps it is true that government cannot and will not make us equal, but the Court's racial history has clearly shown that government has time and time again made us unequal.

I have already analyzed in detail the many examples of the Court inventing, reproducing, and articulating various positions of racial significance that privileged Whites over non-Whites (e.g. *Dred Scott*, *Plessy*, *Korematsu*, etc.). As an officer of the Court, Justice Thomas is well aware of these cases and how they represent canonical examples of instances where the Court, one of three branches of the government, has perpetuated racial subordination. In affirmative action cases where Justice Thomas has authored his own concurring or dissenting opinions, he has routinely cited Justice Harlan's famous dissenting words in *Plessy*. Although Justice Harlan acknowledged the supremacy of the white race 'in prestige, in achievements, in education, in wealth, and in power',[7] he believed that:

> in the eye of the law, there is in this country no superior, dominant, ruling class of citizens. There is no caste here. Our constitution is color-blind and neither knows nor tolerates classes among citizens.[8]

Justice Harlan's famous words have been repeatedly referenced as a justification for a colorblind reading of the constitution and the outright rejection of race conscious affirmative action. However, in his repeated citation of Justice Harlan, Justice Thomas and other opponents of affirmative action have rarely ever mentioned that Justice Harlan's famous words came in a dissenting opinion, therefore it did nothing to change the material ramifications for Homer Plessy, who, along with all other non-Whites, continued to be segregated and subordinated under Jim Crow laws. As a result, not only did the majority *Plessy* Court not agree with Justice Harlan's colorblind view of the constitution, the majority opinion legitimized a subordinating racial practice for nearly a hundred years. Clearly, rather than attempt to treat people as equals before the law, *Plessy* is only one in many examples where the law solidified the status of Whites and non-Whites as unequal. The fact that Justice Thomas and his supporters reject affirmative action policies by referencing a case that clearly made us unequal reveals the fallacy of colorblindness when it concerns racial equality. As a result, reflecting Justice Thomas' own words, the law will never make us equal if it does not atone for treating us unequally.

The process of judicial atonement has never come. In *Brown*, the Court reversed *Plessy's* 'separate but equal' constitutional doctrine and desegregated schools. Similarly in *Loving*, the Court struck down one of the main pillars of whiteness by outlawing once and for all anti-miscegenation laws. But these canonical cases are not acts of atonement; they are merely admissions of wrongdoing. Atonement is to make whole what has been fragmented or harmed. Admissions of wrongdoing do not repair injury from harm. In the case of civil law and criminal law, justice is served not only by convictions or admissions of guilt, but by serving a sentence or paying a civil judgment as punishment or atonement for the harm done. The Court has never atoned or 'paid' a punishment for its past racial harms; in fact, it has collected interest on its wrongdoings. It has only begrudgingly admitted to embarrassing mistakes only to respond by constitutionalizing a colorblind racial discourse that commits new forms of racial subordination. Justice Thomas and opponents of race conscious affirmative action policies are skipping steps in the process of racial atonement, if indeed it is atonement that is their ultimate goal, which seems doubtful.

## Discussion

Since *Brown*, the Court has at times shown a willingness to admit its past racial wrongdoings, but has done little to fix them. Of course, it is not up to the Court as an arm of the government to 'make us equal', but surely the Court can do more in its role not to block and strike down legislative actions designed to make us a little less unequal. This is the most destructive role the Court has played concerning the disproportionate harm and affirmative action cases. The trajectory of the Court since *Brown* via its interpretation of constitutional equal protection and Title VII of the Civil Rights Act has perverted Justice Thomas' goal for the law to 'treat us as equals'. In reality, the bifurcation of race related equal protection claims has flipped Justice Thomas' initial standpoint that 'the law cannot make us equal' on its head. With the Court unwilling to advance its initial commitment toward racial atonement shown in *Griggs* and *UJO*, equality was off the table and any glimmer of hope for authentic affirmative action was essentially lost. As a result, it is not that 'the law cannot make us equal'; the Court has simply refused even to try. As a consequence of its refusal, there is no escaping the apparent permanence of racism. The Court's structure of review offers unconditional protection and survival for all so-called 'race-neutral' practices with no regard for the predictable and foreseeable amount of disproportionate harm. On the other hand, race-based affirmative action policies are now automatically reviewed with strict scrutiny, the same standard of review that was supposed to be used, but which failed, during the Japanese American Internment of WWII.

This is where the Court's colorblind trajectory on racial disputes has taken us. Its methodology of judicial review views the disproportionate harm of death penalty sentencing with the same vigor as the national smoking age. Similarly, a university's attempt to diversify its student body is as serious as Congress and the President interning one hundred and twenty thousand Americans of Japanese ancestry without due process. This is the result of a fundamental perversion of clarity around race and subordination. Time and time again, the Court's colorblind tendencies have shown a willful rejection and dismissal of arguments from dissenting justices imploring the Court to recognize the effects of racial subordination. In this rejection, the Court as a whole continues to abide by a strict scrutiny constitutional standard that all but guarantees the perpetuity of racial subordination in the colorblind era.

## Notes

1. Although scholars have located *Korematsu* as the standard cite where the Court established strict scrutiny as the highest standard of review, the majority opinion did not in fact apply strict scrutiny in *Korematsu*. Rather, scholars point to the Courts' deference to Congress' enumerated 'war powers' as a sign that strict scrutiny was in fact not followed. This was a point contested in

Justice Frank Murphy's dissent, pointing to the fact that although the Court lays out the initial structures of strict scrutiny, it substantively defers to Congress' 'war powers', resulting in a judicial approach more akin to deference, as opposed to 'strict'.

2. *City of Richmond v. J.A. Croson Co.*, 488 U.S. 469 (1989), pp. 516–517.
3. *Adarand Constructors, Inc. v. Pena*, 515 U.S. 200 (1995), p. 28.
4. Ibid.
5. Ibid. Thomas Concurring Opinion, p. 1.
6. Ibid. Italics mine.
7. *Plessy v. Ferguson*, 163 U.S. 537 (1896). Harlan Dissenting Opinion, p. 559.
8. Ibid.

# Section III

# Critical Contemporary Perspectives

# 7 After *Fisher v. University of Texas*

## Racial Justice or Whiteness Rising?

### Introduction

This chapter critically examines the significance of the *Fisher v. University of Texas, Austin* (2016) affirmative action decision. I consider *Fisher's* importance within a larger constellation of Civil Rights battles from the Supreme Court. By affirming the use of racial considerations in college admissions, I ask whether or not this fundamentally harms whiteness and white privilege in and beyond the institution of education. Although the decision was mildly unexpected and fortuitous, the election of Donald Trump makes future favorable race positive decisions less likely. Justice Anthony Kennedy was the key swing vote that affirmed the constitutionality of limited racial considerations in college admissions. Since the *Fisher* decision, he has retired and been replaced by Justice Brett Kavanaugh, considered to be much more conservative than Kennedy. Therefore, substantive change in racial progress is doubtful across multiple institutions of public life beyond the narrow confines of selective college admissions. *Fisher's* real 'value', if we can even call it that, is that it reminds racial justice advocates of the evolving and adaptability of institutional practices that maintain whiteness. In looking at the Court's current racial discourse, this chapter suggests we have taken a massive step backwards in our racial understanding, despite the tenuous victory in *Fisher*.

First, I give a brief history and forecast the significance of *Fisher* for affirmative action practices moving forward. In addition, I locate *Fisher* within a broad historical trajectory of affirmative action policies since its initial implementation in the 1970s. Second, I analyze *Fisher* not simplistically as an insulated college admissions dispute, but within a regime of political maneuvers intended to defeat advances in racial justice and sustain whiteness in the colorblind era. Third, I argue for educational studies to practice what Zeus Leonardo (2016) might call a form of 'educational criticism' in order to forge a more just racial world by considering the very legal apparatuses that severely impinges justice. Finally, the chapter discusses two significant legal disputes that should be considered in conjunction with *Fisher*. Separated by sixty years, the two cases show the legal discourse on race has truly gone backwards, thereby all but guaranteeing the perpetuity of whiteness.

## *Fisher v. University of Texas* and Affirmative Action

After nearly eight years, the affirmative action odyssey known as *Fisher v. University of Texas* finally ended in the Spring of 2016. Through several maneuvers between lower courts and the Supreme Court, we are precisely where we were in 2008 when the case initiated as Abigail Fisher applied to, and was subsequently denied from, the University of Texas at Austin. That is, nothing much has changed other than millions of dollars in legal fees only to maintain the status quo of minimal racial considerations in college admissions. The first affirmative action dispute in education occurred in 1978 involving UC Davis' medical school and Alan Bakke. The UC Davis medical school utilized a quota system designed to ensure a minimum of sixteen minority students out of a class totaling one hundred medical students. In a compromised plurality decision, a fractured Court struck down the constitutionality of racial quotas, but nevertheless affirmed the permissibility of utilizing racial considerations for the benefits of diversity in education. Although diversity was constitutionality recognized, the justices did not explain nor establish the accepted race positive practices that schools could adopt to achieve diversity—the opinion simply ruled racial quotas unconstitutional and recognized diversity in education as a compelling governmental interest. It took the Court nearly twenty-five years to further clarify the specifics of acceptable affirmative action practice to achieve the benefits of educational diversity.

In 2003, the Supreme Court issued dual rulings on the University of Michigan's race positive admissions practices. In *Gratz v. Bollinger* (2003), Michigan's undergraduate admissions practice was struck down because the review process automatically assigned twenty points to minority applicants. In a wide-ranging review process where applicants who accumulated 100–150 points were automatically admitted, the Court ruled race was determinative and therefore unconstitutional. In *Grutter* (2003), the Court ruled Michigan's law school admissions program did not violate 'equal protection' because race was used only as a factor of consideration without a predetermined value. That is, minority applicants to Michigan's law school did not receive any fixed points and race was no more determinative toward admissions than a white applicants' desire to practice *pro bono* law. A clearer picture of constitutional and unconstitutional affirmative action practices emerged after *Gratz* and *Grutter*. Racial considerations in admissions are acceptable only when race is utilized as a plus factor—not unlike other facially 'colorblind' considerations such as community service and non-academic interests. Alternatively, if race is utilized in a 'mechanized' way through fixed awarding of points or non-individualized group evaluations, the practice is prohibitively unconstitutional.

Fisher and her legal team wanted to do away with racial considerations altogether—regardless of whether or not race was modestly utilized as a plus factor. As a direct response to the legal parameters set forth from the twin Michigan decisions, the University of Texas tailored its undergraduate admissions policy to weigh racial considerations—without any fixed values—among a plethora of other factors such as family socioeconomic status and high school location. Therefore, the *Fisher* case was not an attempt to further restrict race positive admissions practices, but an outright attempt to once and for all end affirmative action in education. Perhaps *this* is the legacy of *Fisher*. A decision that merely affirmed the status quo of modest racial considerations in admissions will be a footnote to *Grutter*—the case that established the current precedent for race positive college admissions. Unless prohibited by their respective states (e.g. Prop 209 in California) colleges and universities will continue to consider an applicant's race as one factor in a wide-ranging holistic review process. However, considering the trajectory of challenged race positive policy practices before the Court since the Civil Rights era, perhaps an as-you-were decision is in fact a victory. Before *Fisher* with few exceptions, nearly all other race related or affirmative action decisions in education, employment, contracting, and criminal justice have been decidedly against the interests of racial justice, expanding legal protections for minorities, and integration.

*Fisher* tempts us with the appearance of an accelerated march toward justice. Whereas the Court waited some thirty years between *Bakke* and *Grutter*, the permissibility of racial considerations affirmed in *Fisher* arrived in less than half that time. However, educational problems do not exist in a vacuum independent of other social problems and political institutions. The permissibility of racial considerations in education has at best received inconsistent results. In areas such as voting, employment, and political participation, the suppression of minority rights has been consistent and devastating. Time and time again when given an opportunity to step in to trigger equal protection for minorities, the Supreme Court has consistently avoided judicial intervention to only further racial subordination. Taken together, the vitality of racial considerations in education is at best a flickering light in an otherwise defeated trajectory of social and political policies intended to bring about racial change. Tempting as it is to read *Fisher* in its own historical echo chamber, it also maintains a connected significance within a broader legal and political campaign specifically designed to sustain whiteness in undermining Civil Rights Era legislation. In fact, we need only to look at those behind the *Fisher* legislation to reveal an unapologetic anti-Civil Rights agenda.

## Fisher as Part of an Anti-Civil Rights Movement

*Fisher's* costly near decade-long legal dispute was entirely bankrolled by the curiously named Project on Fair Representation (POFR). The non-profit legal defense fund supports litigation that challenges racial and ethnic classification and preferences in federal and local courts. The Project's goal is not only to eliminate racial considerations from educational policy, but *all* governmental policies. The Project is quite specific about its goals. On the front page of its website, its mission is clear: to challenge public policy distinctions and preferences made on the basis of race and ethnicity. POFR identifies four arenas where it will work to influence jurisprudence, public policy, and public attitudes:

1. Voting: Reforming those provisions of the Voting Rights Act and other laws that encourage and mandate the creation of racially gerrymandered voting districts.
2. Education: Ending the use of race-based affirmative action in college admissions and k–12 student assignments, as well as racial considerations in awarding scholarships, fellowships, and academic enrichment programs.
3. Contracting: Challenging the courts' municipal, state, and federal programs that award fixed percentages of contracts to individuals and firms based upon race, gender, and ethnicity.
4. Employment: Representing individuals who have been victims of racial discrimination in hiring, firing, and promotion.

If the Project on Fair Representation existed during the Jim Crow era, the likes of Homer Plessy, Takao Ozawa, Bhagat Singh Thind, and Herman Sweatt would have benefited greatly from its resources and mission. Because of their status as racial minorities, all of these men suffered from discrimination in areas of education, civil society, and land ownership. In every instance, the Supreme Court sanctioned their racial subordination. Additionally, as lead counselor for the NAACP during the consolidated *Brown v. Board of Education* case, Thurgood Marshall would surely accept the Project's mission to eliminate racial distinctions in the areas of voting, education, contracting, and employment in public policy. In the *Brown* case, Marshall demanded the Courts not only find that segregation was unconstitutional, but also as a form of relief, order the schools to immediately desegregate. With the hindsight of history, we know the political nature of the Court and the resulting political pushback all but stunted the integrative promise of *Brown*. Nevertheless, Marshall's demand to immediately end practices of racial distinction in education can be conceived as similar to the Project on Fair Representation's current demand for the Court to end race positive considerations in education and other areas of public policy. In fact, conservative Justices (e.g.

Clarence Thomas) routinely cite *Brown* as a justification to reject contemporary practices of race positive considerations. Conservatives reject proponents of affirmative action by equating them with Jim Crow segregation alleging that both wish to use race in educational policy.

Is the Project on Fair Representation continuing to wave the flag of the NAACP, which flew during the Civil Rights Era? Conservatives and those who oppose race positive policy considerations indeed think so, as they routinely utilize the famous words of the most prominent figure from the Civil Rights Era, Dr. Martin Luther King Jr. However, criticisms that colorblind conservatives gratuitously quote Dr. King equally apply here when the Project on Fair Representation attempts to associate itself with *Brown's* legacy. Both pick and choose convenient moments of importance while purposely refusing to acknowledge the nature of systematic and structural racial subordination. In other words, conservatives who claim to carry the flag of the Civil Rights Era and *Brown's* legacy are able to sever the subordinating practices of race from the benign use of race in order to locate inequality. Colorblind adherents claim that race positive policies and systematic segregation during Jim Crow are one and the same because they both utilize a classifying mechanism to identity different people based on race. Or to repeat Chief Justice Roberts, they both 'discriminate' based on race. But the similarities end there. It is this strategic end where the campaign against race positive policies masks itself as a 'post-racial' campaign while maintaining race as a subordinating concept in policy and practice. By attempting to sever the subordinating elements of race and only talk about race in terms of classification, the 'post-racial' campaign reveals itself as a discourse of whiteness and white privilege.

### *White Privilege via Post-Race Discourse*

When Peggy McIntosh (1990) reflected on the invisible knapsack of white privilege, it represented a fascinating take on the taken-for-granted privileges and advantages that are practiced and enjoyed by Whites. Building off the momentum created by critically engaging with white privilege and whiteness in the colorblind era, multiple interventions have identified the ways that race advantage continues to manifest in the colorblind era. Particularly, Zeus Leonardo (2009) argues that one cannot talk about white privilege without identifying the structures of white supremacy that make white privilege possible. In other words, white privilege, or a state of being, owes itself to a structure that recognizes and sanctions it. In the colorblind era, white supremacy goes beyond the KKK, racial riots, lynching, *de jure* segregated schools, or segregation. In the colorblind era, whiteness manifests itself through institutions, the political process, and the ways that racial privilege is woven through the various participatory and subject-making avenues of political and social life. In short, white privilege is structured into common sense. Michael Omi and Howard Winant (1994) argue the meaning of race is historically in flux and always constructed and contested throughout society. Additionally, this historical process occurs through collective struggles and individual action. As a result of this multidimensional and layered process, racial categories are constantly unstable, formed, re-formed, and often destroyed. Omi and Winant use the term 'racial formation' to refer to the historical process where multiple social, cultural, economic, and political forces construct and determine the substance of racial meaning. Finally, foundational to the racial formations thesis is the uptake of race operating as what they call a 'central axis' of social relations, and ultimately, social problems.

Although Omi and Winant were not specifically talking of whiteness in their description of racial formations, Charles Gallagher (1997) identifies a white racial formation, a practice of white racial identity based off both past and *future* formations. Gallagher argues past and future white racial formations are dependent on the political, social, and institutional engagement of other racial groups in the public arena and the perceived threat of material deprivation as a product of a diversified public arena. The focus on the future continuation of white privilege is perhaps the most important and sheds light on the costly and enduring campaign against race positive policies. Goodwin Liu (2002) has called the threat felt by Whites in race positive college admissions as a white anxiety against impending minority competition, and the perceived threat that racial minorities receive an advantage via race positive admissions. Here, George Lipsitz's (1998) contribution in identifying the possessive investment of whiteness is germane. As an identity politics with material and structural consequences, white interests are observed by investing valuable resources and time via the political process with the hope of a return on investment in the form of 'colorblind' admissions policies that ultimately benefit Whites. As a result, Whites are the biggest users of the so-called 'race card'.

The campaign against race positive considerations in public policy is not just about the simplistic goal of removing racial considerations from governmental policy. Removing race positive considerations in public policy in our current racial climate would, summarizing Lipsitz, widen the deficit between material resources available to Whites and those unavailable to underserved communities. This is what Lipsitz calls the possessive investment in whiteness. Beyond Bakke, Grutter, Gratz, Fisher, or yet to be identified Asian American students from the Harvard and University of North Carolina at Chapel Hill cases, the anti-affirmative action campaign is fundamentally about maintaining white spaces and guaranteeing that whiteness and its ability to recruit allies sustain privilege across various institutions. When universities utilize race positive admissions, the educational return on investment for whiteness loses value because race positive policy is specifically designed and implemented with the goal of ameliorating racism—even though deployed through the more socially palatable diversity discourse. White privilege is the ability to attend white majority schools funded by advantageous tax laws like California's Proposition 13, exacerbated by residential segregation. This racial privilege is further enhanced when college admissions standards do not do enough to recognize the inherent inequality of under-resourced and segregated schools. As the majority of Whites increasingly attend white majority schools, particularly in the suburbs, a legal standard that forbids all institutions of higher education from considering racial inequality not only rewards Whites, but legitimizes segregation under the banner of a 'colorblind' and 'race-less' social discourse.

The only thing 'blind' about the colorblind racial discourse is that it no longer cares (has it ever?) for a Civil Rights racial discourse that focused on classification *and* subordination. Like neoliberalism in economics, which restores class power in the hands of the bourgeoisie, colorblindness in the law represents the white gambit to restore race power. Whereas it shows at best an indifference to issues of subordination and structural racism, at worst, colorblindness shows a downright disdain for any mentions of race, believing that racism will go away when the U.S. stops talking about race. Colorblindness champions a race-less individualism. In this way, achievement and access to desirable privileges in life are allegedly earned and accrued through hard work and stick-to-itiveness. But Cheryl Harris (1995) has portrayed that these white privileges do not simply drop out of the sky only to be picked up by the fittest, or in the case of education, the children of the fittest. As Zeus Leonardo (2004) has recounted, it is akin to someone walking down the street while random and unidentified persons repeatedly place money in their pockets. In the end, this person enjoys the newly acquired cash and believes that his industry of walking down the road is responsible for the newly accrued money. In the same scenario, minorities can exercise the same industry and effort in walking down the street while having their pockets picked by whiteness. This is an appropriate illustration depicting the current state of racial accumulation and its mystification, helped along by the continued judicial assault on affirmative action education policy.

If we only focus on the end and inspect who has the most accolades in order to reward privileges (e.g. college admissions), the privileged will perpetually be rewarded. However, if we not only inspect the end product but also observe the entire process of how candidates accumulate their accolades, our ideas around meritocracy will have to change as a response to the arbitrary and discriminate manner in which resources and opportunities are distributed. In fact, Leonardo argues that not only are Whites advantaged, minorities oftentimes have their precious few resources taken away in the form of new policies, laws, and practices. Observed in the race related constitutional disputes, the Supreme Court has played a discriminatory and arbitrary role in awarding privileges to

Whites at the expense of minorities. In conjunction, the Court has also acted as an impenetrable safety net sanctioning white privilege by prohibiting any substantive attempts at racial redress. In this way, not only is our minority pedestrian unable to accrue any amount of money in comparison to his counterpart who enjoys institutional white privilege, he is dismissed at the end when he points out that his fellow white pedestrian enjoyed privileges along the way, no thanks to his own industry. As simplistic as this allegoric exercise is, it is unfortunately not far from describing the current state of affair in race, law, and education.

## *Whiteness Rising: An Assist From the Court*

It is imperative to grasp fully the current legal climate for race positive educational and public policies. In education, the *Fisher* decision simply affirmed the status quo for race positive holistic admissions. Although diversity was not overturned as a compelling governmental interest, the *Fisher* Court reaffirmed its standard of strict scrutiny pertaining to race positive disputes. Historically, strict scrutiny has been fatal to race positive policies. Additionally, strict scrutiny leaves open the possibility that a future conservative Court could find that colleges and universities can achieve diversity with alleged 'colorblind' alternatives such as high school percentage plans. Because 'strict scrutiny' demands that racial considerations be used as a last resort, it goes to reason that a future Court still retains the ability to strike down the constitutionality of race positive considerations if it determines other race-neutral alternatives were not exhausted before the exercise of racial considerations. In fact, this is precisely the legal strategy adopted by POFR in the anti-affirmative action lawsuit against the University of Carolina at Chapel Hill. Although *Fisher* maintained the status quo of racial considerations in college admissions, the long-term vitality of race positive policies looks increasingly bleak.

True to the mission statement of the Project on Fair Representation, education policy is not the only area of public policy being attacked. In the 70s, the Court ruled in several cases that disproportionate harm to minorities does not automatically equate to an act of 'intentional' discrimination. As a result, the Court allowed many 'race-neutral' policy practices to continue despite persistent disparate impact to racial minorities. Today, the Court has gone even further to ensure that policy practices that produce disparate impacts will face no legal threat. This is a significant escalation in protecting whiteness. In *Ricci v. DeStefano* (2009), the city of New Haven was not allowed to invalidate, and therefore forced to reinstate, a civil service examination even though the test disproportionately impacted minorities. Originally, New Haven elected not to utilize the civil service test out of fear against potential disproportionate harm litigation. One hundred eighteen New Haven firefighters took the promotion exam for fifteen captain and lieutenant positions. Out of one hundred eighteen firefighters, fifty were minorities. From the fifty minority firefighters, only two had scores that qualified them for promotion. The case exemplifies the viciousness of whiteness. In other words, the City of New Haven recognized its promotion exam disproportionately disqualified minority firefighters from promotion. Therefore, the city went about finding a new method of promotion consideration that would provide more equitable results. The Court revealed its indifference toward disparate impact against minorities and demanded New Haven reinstate and utilize the test results.

Voting rights and housing policies are also under attack. In another 5–4 vote (see *Shelby County v. Holder*, 2013), the conservative majority all but guts the important Voting Rights Act of 1965. The Court invalidated two of the most important sections of the Voting Rights Act:

1. Section 5: Requires that certain state and local governments must obtain federal preclearance before implementing any changes to their voting practices and laws.
2. Section 4(b): Contains formula of preclearance determination of which voting jurisdictions are subjected to the preclearance requirement based on their histories of discrimination in the voting process.

The elimination of these two provisions effectively allows jurisdictions carte blanche to gerrymander and implement voting laws according to their politics. Shortly after the Court's announcement, the state of Texas immediately implemented a previously blocked voter identification law. Donald Trump's presidential victory is the first presidential election in the post-*Shelby* era. The Voting Rights Act is not the only 60s era Civil Rights legislation that may be gutted by the Court. The Court has also placed limitations on whether or not 'disparate impact' can continue as justifiable evidence for federal lawsuits against lenders and housing authorities under the Fair Housing Act of 1968 (see *Inclusive Communities*, 2015). Historically, disparate impact has been the *modus operandi* for plaintiffs under the FHA and did not require evidence of purposeful discrimination. Now, the Court has moved to demand a more robust causal connection between challenged practices and alleged disparities. The move paves way for the *laissez-faire* form of residential racial segregation that Chief Justice John Roberts has dismissed as a product of 'benign' personal choice.

Taken together, these recent changes in the law signal a concerted effort not only to preclude future race related litigation, but also to challenge Civil Rights legislation. It is not enough only to say that race positive policies are being stunted from future implementations. Rather, the future vitality of race positive policies is being wiped out while incremental Civil Rights advances are systematically drawn back. In this climate, disparate impact to minorities in and beyond education will continue to increase without fear of litigation. As Leonardo (2007) highlighted, the colorblind discourse of whiteness within No Child Left Behind Act amounts to an act of whiteness. Likewise, the Court's current trajectory in gutting any and all regimes of racial consideration is similarly an instantiation of the strident march toward whiteness. The Court has systematically guaranteed the possessive investment of whiteness in areas of education, employment, and housing.

## The Response in Education

In 2016, Zeus Leonardo (2016) proposed a fledgling new direction in educational scholarship termed 'educational criticism'. Utilizing existing fields of critique from other disciplines, e.g. literary criticism, Leonardo imagines educational criticism as a point of departure that serve as witness to historical experiences that intersect each other at meaningful tangents. In education, we should be engaged in ways proponents of race positive policies can meaningfully make sense of the Court's legal trajectory. Therefore, engaging in a criticism of the law and education allows us to advocate for a world beyond whiteness as active subjects or agents intertwined in historical processes of difference. Education must continue to emphasize the significance of race in educational policy, governance, practice, and results. It is by no coincidence that as the Court's colorblind trajectory continues to make a mockery out of the relationship between racial subordination and its so-called colorblind jurisprudence, education continues to face difficulty trying to address racial problems via 'race-neutral' policies. The fundamental problem lies in whether or not the Court and various neoliberal educational forces truly desire to confront racial problems. With the Court's history as an indicator, the answer is an unequivocal no. Not only is the Court negligent, or squeamish at best, in addressing the issues of race, it participates in prolonging racial subordination, a reality much worse that just simply not doing anything.

Our colorblind era is not post or *sans* race. It is the next installment, chapter, phase, or the next formation in the long and unfortunate history of racial subordination in the U.S. During the slave era, the institution of slavery, colonialism, the slave trade, state-sponsored violence, and dehumanization of transplanted African bodies contributed to the discourse of white superiority and black inferiority. As a result of the changing landscape in acceptability of racial practices after the Civil War and constitutional amendments during Reconstruction, racial practices shifted pragmatically toward segregation between Blacks and Whites in accordance with *Plessy's* (1896) 'separate but equal' legal doctrine. *Brown*, the Civil Rights Era, and the tense geopolitical climate of the Cold war (see Bell, 2004 and discussion on interest convergence) enveloped what were becoming increasingly outdated racial practices in the U.S. In response to these national and geo-political developments, the U.S. again shifted its racial discourse away from 'separate but equal' toward a colorblind model of 'race-neutral' governance—maintaining racial stratification, but under a new discourse. As a consequence, our colorblind era has witnessed ample examples of institutions, forces, and political movements that have utilized so-called 'race-neutral' mechanisms to sustain and advance racial subordination.

Gary Orfield and Erica Frankenberg's (2014) report measures the improvements and retreats in school desegregation, and forecasts the long road ahead for racial equality for integration in U.S. public schools. Progress was clear during the 70s and early 80s, which produced the highest ratio of minority students attending integrated schools. This was a drastic improvement in comparison to the ten years immediately after *Brown II* where schools were slow to integrate due to large and wide-ranging white campaigns against desegregation. The rate of integration in the decade following the *Brown* decision was modest at best. The progress witnessed in the 80s has nearly been cut down to half and the downward trend shows little signs of abating. The long road ahead is dependent on a collective commitment to reverse the troubling downward spiral of (re)segregation. The road toward increased integration does not need to be paved anew, but renewed with the hard-fought commitments established previously by activists and scholars during *Brown* and the Civil Rights era.

The clichéd undertaking of race as a social construction is repeated often in discussions on race. The problem does not revolve specifically around the number of times this particular undertaking of race is mentioned, but because it is often done without critically considering for what purpose race socially is constructed. The early Critical Race Theorist in legal studies exposed Civil Rights Era legal practices that continued to subordinate racial minorities. CRT scholars did not simplistically understand race as a concept of classification, but as an entire discursive regime of difference utilized to distribute tangible material resources. Their work radically implicated the law and its governing apparatuses as a conspirator in social and institutional processes of subordination based on the concept of race. Hence, not only did CRT fundamentally identify that America had a race problem, but that the current climate of supposed legal progress spurned by *Brown* and the Civil Rights Era did little to confront directly issues that contributed to racial inequality.

Today, America's race problem continues to be ignored. The pink elephant in the room has become the wooly mammoth. The Civil Rights Era fought tooth and nail for incremental progress in areas of education, employment, criminal justice, and housing. However, these incremental positive changes are being rolled back by a colorblind jurisprudence hell bent on eliminating the modest built-in mechanisms of racial protection gained from the Civil Rights Era. The institution of education is currently on the front lines and taking the heaviest blows. As the Court continues to chip away at the permissible use of race in education policy and governance, democratic educational institutions are struggling to adjust their policies, forced at times to craft the kernel of racial arguments within the shell of race-neutral logics. Schools must both meet their desire to diversify while also remain legally palatable to outside forces who are all too eager to pursue costly litigation as an oversight mechanism. However, we must take a step back from this tit-for-tat game of policy practice and governance oversight. Education's current trajectory of using 'race-less' or quasi-race positive holistic admissions while having to simultaneously remain 'colorblind' is in no way the most effective strategy dealing with persistent segregation in education. Education cannot effectively take up America's race problem when the Supreme Court and other governing apparatuses forbid education from recognizing the significance and continuing salience of racial subordination in the first place.

Pioneering research on race and education has identified many facets such as curriculum, teacher workforce, resources, and cultural capital that require careful attention toward the ways in which these issues may singularly or collectively compound racial disparities in education. In our current historical conjuncture when colorblind sensibilities are hegemonic, it is time educational research turns its critical eye toward the law. The legal institution, as represented by the Supreme Court and its Justices, must be stripped of its veneer of impartiality and supposed objectivity. Specifically, the conservative wing's church of 'originalism' must be tackled and laid bare in educational discourse as nothing more than a mechanism of whiteness that conceals, sustains, and advances racial subordination.

## A Refreshing Yet Sobering Reminder of Where We Are on Race

### *When the Court Truly Understood Race*

*Brown* is popularly remembered as one of the most significant race cases, but it is also infamous for allowing prolonged resistance to desegregation via *Brown II*. In terms of a Supreme Court case that meaningfully understands the nature of race and racial subordination in a majority opinion, perhaps no case achieves these elements quite like *Hernandez v. State of Texas* (1954). Decided earlier, but in the same year as *Brown*, *Hernandez* hinged on whether or not a history of systematic exclusion of Mexican Americans from serving in juries is unconstitutional. Pete Hernandez was convicted of murder and sentenced to life in prison. His legal team did not appeal the murder conviction, but alleged equal protection violation on the basis that the convicting jury was all White. All-white juries in Texas were a product of systematic exclusions of Mexican Americans. This was not unique in Texas and Jackson County, the site of the trial. Both sides acknowledge that no Mexican American or persons with Latino last names had served on a jury for twenty-five years, a time span that totaled more than six thousand jury members in a county with a fifteen percent Mexican American population. As Haney López (2005) points out, the case is unique because *Hernandez* is not expressly a race case. This is because both sides acknowledged Mexican Americans were legally considered 'white' in the state of Texas. Texas simply argued no equal protection violation exists because since Mexican Americans were widely considered white (i.e. not black), Mexican Americans were not racially and systematically excluded from participating in juries. In response, Hernandez's team argued that even though the state of Texas considered Mexican Americans white, they were subordinated as a distinct sub-*class* of white.

Chief Justice Earl Warren was faced with a tricky case alleging systematic discrimination and exclusion even though both parties agreed that Mexican Americans were white. In other words, *Hernandez* was not expressly a case about race as both sides acceded to the simplistic notion that race was a black and white issue. However, Warren was not persuaded by an understanding of discrimination and exclusion based solely on race or color but instead asked whether or not a class of people was subordinated. Warren's emphasis focusing on group subordination as the basis for determining whether or not certain groups require constitutional protection is worth repeating in full. Warren wrote for the unanimous court:

> Throughout our history, differences in race and color have defined easily identifiable groups which have at times required the aid of the courts in securing equal treatment under the laws. *But community prejudices are not static, and, from time to time, other differences from the community norm may define other groups which need the same protection.* Whether such a group exists within a community is a question in fact. When the existence of a distinct class is demonstrated, and it is further shown that the laws, as written or as applied, single out that class for difference treatment not based on some reasonable classification, the guarantees of the Constitution have been violated.[1]

Whether or not the Warren Court knew, it was expressing a profound understanding that race is based on community norms and practices and whether or not these social practices subordinate groups based upon ideas of differences. To determine if Mexican Americans in Jackson County were indeed treated as a subordinated class, the Court simply looked at social practices that clearly distinguished Whites from Mexican Americans. The Court noted that in education, Mexican Americans were segregated up until the fourth grade. Restaurants in town prominently displayed signs that read 'No Mexicans Served' or 'We Serve Whites Only, No Spanish or Mexicans'. Even at the time of the case's hearing in Texas' courthouse, there were two men's bathrooms, one unmarked and the other marked 'Colored Men' and 'Hombres Aqui'. The collective evidence was clear to the Court: social practices in Texas and Jackson county distinguished Mexican Americans as a different group from Whites. Consequently, the systematic exclusion of Mexican Americans from serving in juries was not unlike other institutional practices of group subordination and, as a result, required the court to guarantee Mexican Americans, and Hernandez specifically, equal protection.

As Haney-López points out, despite the fact that the case is not expressly a race case, it is ironically perhaps the only Supreme Court majority opinion to understand fully that race is a social construction. Haney López observed that despite *Hernandez* not being expressly a race case, the case's holding perhaps stands alone as the most insightful Supreme Court opinion ever on the constructivist nature of race. That is, even serendipitously, Warren emanated a racial understanding that focused on social practices and material life. Furthermore, the opinion was not persuaded that there existed no legal classification of Mexican Americans as a sub-group—since Mexican Americans were considered 'white'—but focused on the community norms and practices that so clearly subordinated Mexican Americans as non-White.

### *How Does the Court Understand Race Now?*

In 2014, Justice Sonia Sotomayor wrote an impassioned opinion in *Schuette v. Coalition to Defend Affirmative Action (BAMN)* (2014). In 2006, Michigan voters approved Proposal 2 that amended the state constitution. Proposal 2 enshrined a ban on race and sex-based preferences in employment, contracting, and public education. The campaign was a direct response to the 2003 *Grutter* decision affirming the permissibility of race positive considerations at the University of Michigan Law School. It was essentially Michigan's equivalent of California's Proposition 209. Like 209 in California, Proposal 2 effectively ended affirmative action in Michigan after it passed by a margin of 58%–42%. The case is unique in the sense that the traditional plaintiffs in race related cases during the colorblind era have usually been white individuals who alleged reverse racism as a result of race positive policies (e.g. Bakke, Grutter, Gratz, Fisher). However, in this case, Michiganders voted to outlaw completely all affirmative action considerations from public policy, and those in favor of affirmative action were now alleging discrimination. This claim is entirely of a different nature than reverse-discrimination claims. Reverse discrimination claims appeal on an individual basis. The Coalition to Defend Affirmative Action made a group claim, arguing that Proposal 2 puts those in favor of affirmative action at a permanent disadvantage against a majority that opposes affirmative action.

In a 6–2 verdict with the recusal of Justice Elena Kagan, the majority comprising of the conservative bloc plus liberal Justice Breyer ruled that Proposal 2 did not violate equal protection. However, in a dissenting opinion joined by Justice Ginsburg, Sonia Sotomayor disagreed with the majority and accused it of continuing to ignore the country's 'long and lamentable record of stymieing the right of racial minorities to participate in the political process'.[2] Sotomayor charged that Proposal 2 had fundamentally changed the political landscape by prohibiting racial consideration and favoring its outright ban. She went further and argued the measure amounts to a mechanism that fences off proponents of affirmative action from the political process altogether because it was now enshrined permanently in the Constitution and any reactionary campaign to repeal Proposal 2 would practically be impossible. Sotomayor argued the democratic process in and of itself does not sufficiently provide protection for insular minority groups against oppression, which is why the equal protection clause is needed. Sotomayor stressed that without judicial checks on democratic processes, majorities can subordinate minority groups via the democratic process. In speaking of the guarantees of equal protection granted by the Constitution, Sotomayor writes:

> Although the guarantee is traditionally understood to prohibit intentional discrimination under existing laws, equal protection does not end there. Another fundamental strand of our equal protection jurisprudence focuses on process, securing to all citizens the right to participate meaningfully and equally in self—government. That right is the bedrock of our democracy.[3]

She suggests that if Michiganders opposed race positive considerations, they can elect school officials to change the policy of the university through the political process, a process that would also be available to those in favor of race conscious admissions. This participatory process guarantees that those in favor of race-based preferences can in the future elect and campaign for representatives who may implement policies constitutive of their politics. Sotomayor argues that legacy and athletic admits can participate politically to influence school admissions policies, but Proposal 2 bans such political activity on the basis of race. In this case, majority voters who opposed affirmative action elected to change the political process altogether by enacting a state constitutional provision that locked out their opponents. To Sotomayor, this is fundamentally unconstitutional and violates equal protection. She concludes her impassioned dissent, arguing 'the constitution does not protect racial minorities from political defeat. But neither does it give the majority free rein to erect selective barriers against racial minorities.'[4]

Sotomayor's dissent is noteworthy because her focus on the political process, results, and substance is similar to the understanding of racial subordination as socially constructed exhibited in *Hernandez* more than sixty years before *Schuette v. BAMN*. In both instances, race was not about black, white, or any other identifiable racial signifier, but hinged fundamentally on community norms and practices. Most importantly, both opinions focused on whether or not social practices subordinated insular minority groups. Even though both sides vehemently denied the case was about race, the Court in *Hernandez* nevertheless identified Mexican Americans as an oppressed class in the political process because they were systematically denied the opportunity to serve on juries. In the same way, Sotomayor did not identify any particular racial group suffering from racial discrimination, but identified a class of the political process who were effectively shut out by their political adversaries with the passage of Proposal 2.

## *A Flickering Hope for Educators*

Unfortunately, Sotomayor's opinion holds absolutely no legal weight in terms of reversing the implementation of Proposal 2 because it was a dissenting opinion. But it is still historically meaningful as a champion of a more expansive interpretation of equal protection and critical understanding of race. This fact notwithstanding, the arc of the Court's trajectory on race is distressingly clear. Ian Haney López rightly states that the Court's equal protection jurisprudence in the colorblind era is an absolute tragedy that works directly against the interests of integration and anti-subordination. There are few alternatives available to reverse the tide of racial subordination in society, but the few alternatives are nevertheless our only hope. As a form of social understanding, race cannot be abandoned. The political processes that continue to fence off insular minority groups must be targeted via the original language of racism that focuses on oppression, exploitation, and subordination. Without doing so, education specifically, and civil society as a whole, will continue speeding down the downward spiral of increasing racial subordination under the 'race-less' sensibilities of colorblindness.

As educators, we can be mindful to connect our classroom race talk to consequences of the political process. During one of Donald Trump's many bombastic election rallies, he addressed his historic unpopularity amongst conservatives by suggesting that conservative voters have to vote for him anyways. The then presidential candidate quipped that despite his unpopularity to some conservatives, he would get their vote anyways because of the Supreme Court. From afar, it may appear we have little hope to make an impact in the outcome of the Courts because justices hold lifetime appointments. This would be wrong. Though true that justices hold lifetime appointments, the persons who appoint and confirm them are elected politicians. In the years forward when the words Trump and Clinton begin to subside from our collective consciousness, perhaps one remaining name we can remind our students of is Scalia.

Here, I refer not specifically to the conservative Supreme Court justice who passed away in the spring of 2016, but at the lost opportunity to shift the ideological balance of the Supreme Court toward justice and humanity. But as Stuart Hall (1996) reminds us, social and political forces that lose out in a historical conjuncture do not necessarily disappear from the terrain of struggle; nor is struggle in such moments suspended. In this historical conjuncture, it is ever more imperative for educators to sustain, perhaps transform, the discourse on race, whiteness, and subordination in public policy. The lost opportunity that was Scalia will come again in a future historical moment. We can ensure that when this opportunity comes again, we have fought enough to tilt the tendential balance in the discursive forces against whiteness. A democratic society where Sotomayor's famous words in *Schuette v. BAMN* forms a majority opinion would truly be remarkable and filled with hope—an authentic promise toward racial justice.

## Discussion

The analysis I offer in this chapter is intended to situate the fortuitous *Fisher* decision within a larger discussion of whiteness that indicts other political maneuvers against the interests of racial justice and civil rights. Read singularly as a legal decision on the permissibility of racial considerations in college admissions, *Fisher* is a victory in the interests of diversity, albeit limited. However, against a backdrop of entrenched political maneuvers intended to undermine modest racial remediation since the civil rights movement, *Fisher* is little more than a small speed bump on the road toward maintaining whiteness. I propose for educational criticism to keep a conscious focus on the law and its role in adjudicating educational discourse so that we are able to function as active subjects and agents in naming our own political processes of difference.

By revisiting a contemporary and historical example on how the law once understood and now understands race, it is clear that from the perspective of the Court, we have in fact gone backwards. Through various institutional manifestations, colorblind sensibilities have functioned to delegitimize the social constructivist understanding of race. As such, Sotomayor's impassioned opinion imploring for an understanding of race as institutional and located in considerations of subordination has been relegated to the powerless pages of a dissenting opinion. Therefore, a critical analysis on the current state of race, law, and education not only suggests that racial justice is in steep decline, but that whiteness is rising. Therefore, our historical conjuncture requires a continued commitment to speaking and addressing the issues of racial subordination in public policy. Doing so with ardor and devotion rejects whiteness and signals our intentions toward achieving meaningful forms of civil rights, democracy, and humanity.

## Notes

1. *Hernandez v. Texas*, 347 U.S. 475, p. 478. Italics mine.
2. *Schuette v. COALITION TO DEFEND AFFIRMATIVE*, 134 S. CT. 1623 (2014). Sotomayor Dissenting Opinion, p. 1.
3. Ibid.
4. Ibid., p. 57.

# 8 Diversity Trending Up, Affirmative Action on Life Support, and the Perilous Status of Asian Americans

## Introduction

In 2013, the *Fisher v. University of Texas at Austin* case had yet to be legally settled and two more lawsuits were already filed against holistic admissions at Harvard and the University of North Carolina at Chapel Hill. The Project on Fair Representation, a right-wing legal defense fund, is behind the *Fisher* case and the newly filed challenges. In *Fisher*, the alleged 'victim' of reverse-racism was a white student. The new Harvard and UNC cases strategically recruit Asian Americans as 'victims' of race positive holistic admission while establishing a tenuous racial alliance. The new lawsuits, on their face, appear to dramatically shift the anti-affirmative action narrative away from Whites and place the scrutinizing spotlight squarely on the efficacy of affirmative action projects because they argue that a sub-minority group is harmed. The responses from proponents of holistic admissions have been focused primarily on the centrality of the lawsuits' argument. Critics argue that pinpointing Asian American student achievement, as measured by GPA and test scores, is too narrow a focus in determining admissions to selective universities. Additionally, the suit also forgets the impact of legacy admits whose candidacy often times are buoyed anywhere from 20–50% depending on the relationship to a family alumnus of the University. However, the arguments highlighting the excellence in diversity and the varied processes in which universities make their admissions decisions become more and more repetitive.

These arguments have already been made. They were made in *Fisher* years ago (2012), and clearly laid out in *Bakke* some four decades ago (1978). These arguments seem to fall on intentionally deaf ears. No amount of reason, statistical data, or well-intentioned arguments in favor of affirmative action seems to derail the single-minded campaign and its goal of dismantling the apparatus of civil rights and anti-subordination legislation. This myopic project is product of the racial discourse that many scholars have called whiteness, and this latest attack on holistic admissions in the name of Asian Americans as the proxy victim of reverse-racism is an act of whiteness. This contemporary maneuver to dismantle the political and institutional apparatuses intended to ensure minority participation in public and civic life cannot be dismembered from the trajectory of previous historical attempts toward maintaining white privilege. To take up these anti-affirmative action cases without connecting them to past trajectories would foolishly accept the premise that racial subordination was eviscerated as a result of *Brown* and the Civil Rights legislation.

Education has been at the forefront of the Supreme Court's conversations on race and public policy. The Harvard and UNC litigation, *Fisher*, *Parents Involved*, *Grutter*, and *Gratz* have all pivoted around the institution of education from grade school to higher education. However, although race-based education policy has suffered the brunt of colorblind attacks, the concerted colorblind campaign against race-based considerations is not limited to education. Education is only one target in a multitude of public policy arenas currently targeted by the Project on Fair Representation and other political non-profits. Its collective goals are to roll back the enforcement mechanisms of Civil Rights legislation and prevent any possibility that equal protection can be adjudicated with an anti-subordination understanding. The attack on education is merely a contemporary fulcrum, but not the only site of contestation against racial consideration in public policy. As a result, although we start with education, the institution of education must be located as part of an entire set of race positive public policies currently under attack.

## The Current (Sad) State of Education

With *Brown*, the NAACP had crafted together four consolidated cases that addressed educational segregation as a broad American practice. However, as the concerted and prolonged pushback from segregationists prevented any substantive desegregation of public schools, black students did not have any access to white schools until the late 1960s when the Court finally and forcibly mandated desegregation in *Green v. Kent County* (1968).[1] With the Court taking a much more active role in enforcing desegregation, the percentage of black students in majority white schools peaked in the 70s and 80s. With the peak of 44.5% of black students in majority white schools occurring in 1988, the upward trend from the mid-1960s to its peak in 1988 has since reversed. As Gary Orfield and Erica Frankenberg's (2014) report commemorating the 60th anniversary of the *Brown* decision showed, the peak of 44.5% of black students attending majority white schools has almost been cut in half to 23.2% by 2011. The 2011 percentage mirrors the percentage that existed in 1968 and the downward trend shows no signs of reversing. The report is unequivocal about one fact: sixty years after *Brown*, more than 75% of Black students in American public schools attend majority-minority schools.

As the U.S. becomes increasingly more than just black and white with growing Asian and Latino American populations, the problem of segregation is creeping into the suburbs. Highlighting Orfield and Frankenberg's UCLA Civil Rights Project report, *USA Today* noted that although black educational segregation concentrates in urban centers, Latino students are significantly more segregated in suburbia (see Lee, 2014). The *USA Today* report quoted University of Kansas education professor John Rury, who argued that part of the reason for continued segregation was due to racism, but also due to the choice movements of economically advantaged families to better school districts. The article commemorates the 60th anniversary of *Brown* by pointing out that segregation continues to be widespread in American communities and public schools. However, it is perplexing for the article to feature a blurb that believes the continued segregation of American public schools is due to anything other than racial discrimination. The sentiment falls in line with the colorblind discourse of what constitutes discrimination and racism. As a result, the 'movement' of families seeking better-resourced and reputable districts are simply non-racial choices that somehow less affluent families do not also make. John Roberts, the Court's current Chief Justice, has also made these claims. In *Parents Involved*, Roberts wrote that the movement of families according to residential 'choices' is a benign contribution to racial segregation, articulated in a majority opinion signed on by all of the Court's conservative justices.

### *White Flight as Non-racial?*

Better-resourced and reputable schools do not just exist in a vacuum. The existence of desirable and undesirable public schools is undeniably indebted to the Court. In the early 70s, as black students began to make headway into historically white-only schools, the Supreme Court ruled in two cases that any amount of income disparity and racial segregation *across* district lines did not violate equal protection. To the Court, as long as there were no official state policies of racial segregation and income discrimination, it would do nothing to prevent segregation by white flight. The combination of *San Antonio Independent School District v. Rodriguez* (1973) and *Milliken v. Bradley* (1974) construct a nationwide trend where income disparity and racial segregation are only problems if they happen intra-district.

In the *Rodriguez* case, a consortium of minority families from the Edgewood school district in San Antonio filed a suit charging that Texas' local property tax school financing system violated equal protection. The suit alleged that because some districts were much more affluent than other minority-majority school districts, the availability of resources to school districts adversely discriminated against minority communities in districts with a much lower tax base. Edgewood families pointed to nearby Alamo Heights school district, where per pupil expenditure nearly doubled Edgewood's. During the years the case went through the legal system, the disparity actually increased from $310 in 1968 to $389 in 1972. Unequal resources produced predictable difficulties for Edgewood and equally predictable advantages for Alamo Heights. Compared with Alamo Heights, Edgewood could not hire sufficiently qualified personnel and suffered from disadvantages in physical facilities, supplies, equipment, and books. In comparison, Alamo Heights enjoyed advantages in classroom size, student to teacher ratio, student to counselor ratio, and a four times lower dropout rate of 8% to Edgewood's 32%.

Decided the following year after *Rodriguez*, *Milliken v. Bradley* hinged on whether or not segregation across district lines in Detroit violated *Brown v. Board of Education*. Due in part to the Great Migration, Detroit's black population increased dramatically. As thousands of African Americans migrated from the south to Detroit, they were systematically excluded from white neighborhoods via institutional methods of segregation such as residential redlining, or subjected to discriminatory practices such as threats of violence, bombings, arson, and mob attacks. These are well known. By the early 1970s, many urban Detroit school districts had black super majorities while white communities expedited their flight out of urban areas into the suburbs. The NAACP brought suit against Michigan State officials, including its governor, William Milliken. The suit alleged that although Detroit did not have an official policy of forced segregation à la *Plessy's* 'separate but equal' doctrine, the city had practiced other policies that led to *de facto* educational segregation, such as redlining. The lower courts agreed with the NAACP and ruled that all levels of government in Michigan were accountable for segregation in education and it was the state's responsibility to integrate the heavily segregated Detroit metropolitan area. The lower and district court's ruling was an encouraging sign for the NAACP's campaign to address continued segregation in the post-*Brown* era. As a result of the decision, Detroit began a busing program of inter-district integration across all fifty-three districts.

Local and state governments were not satisfied with the court's desegregation mandate and appealed to the Supreme Court. Led by the same conservative majority a year prior in *Rodriguez*, the Supreme Court reversed the lower district court. It clarified the distinction between *de jure* and *de facto* educational segregation. In the majority's opinion, neither state nor local governments in Detroit practiced an explicit policy of forced segregation and therefore *Brown* was not applicable. The Court attributed the ongoing persistence of racial segregation in Detroit to arbitrarily drawn district lines. A remedy of forced busing to desegregate Detroit public schools would only be appropriate if it could be proven that district lines were drawn with 'racist intent' for the specific reason to segregate public schools. Of course, no such evidence was produced to prove 'racist intent'. The Court concluded that just because arbitrary district lines produced segregation, it did not mean district lines constitute a form of *de jure* segregation. The Court's opinion established the legal foundation for any amount of racial segregation to persist so long as it occurs across district lines absent evidence of racist intent. As a result of the *Milliken* decision, Detroit public schools reached a black super majority of 90% by 1987.

### *Cementing the Urban/Suburban Divide*

*Rodriguez* and *Milliken* collectively put a halt to any projects designed to address educational inequality and segregation across district lines. As a result, the specter of addressing education inequality and racial segregation was reduced to intra-district politics, made even more impossible and fruitless by systematic white flight out of urban metropolitan areas into the suburbs. In both cases, the same Court provided the legal foundation for continued segregation and inequality in post-*Brown* America. Even more destructive, its differentiation between *de jure* and *de facto* forms of segregation further relegated *Brown's* relevance only to instances where explicit state policies of segregation were still practiced, turning *Brown* into nothing more than a passing fad a mere twenty years after its passage. Professor Rury's sentiment in *USA Today* that more reputable and better-resourced schools are not products of racial discrimination comes as no surprise when we consider the impact of *Rodriguez* and *Milliken*. As a matter of legal discourse, both have effectively severed the conversation of inequality and segregation in public schools from any considerations of race. Here, the Court's bifurcated approach to 'express' usages of race versus 'race-neutral' policies that produce disparate impact maintained income inequality and racial segregation across district lines.

In its jurisprudence adjudicating the issues of unequal funding and segregation across district lines, the Court looked specifically at whether or not an expressed use of race was involved in the language or implementation of both cases. None could be found. Twenty years after the *Brown* decision, the only policies that had an express use of racial considerations were affirmative action policies designed to promote racial integration. Other than affirmative action cases, the last policy that utilized an express mention of race was the remaining anti-miscegenation law in Virginia during the 1960s, ultimately struck down in *Loving v. Virginia*. Under the Court's evolved racial discourse post-*Brown*, Edgewood parents and the NAACP stood little to no chance before the Supreme Court. The legacy of the Court's posture toward racially disparate impact claims reaches far beyond the immediate consequence for Edgewood and Detroit. Because any amount of inequality and disparity was allowed as long as it happened across district lines, the Court had cemented the permissible structure of racial inequality in public education throughout the country. Even more damaging, the Court's judicial approach refusing to use strict scrutiny also meant that although these cases had racial consequences, the disputed policies were effectively treated as non-racial, where race was an effect rather than a cause. Therefore, similar to disputes in employment law and criminal law, the Court's decision followed the bifurcated trajectory of affirmative action and disparate impact claims. All affirmative action (i.e. express usages of race) would face strict scrutiny, whereas all disparate impact claims (i.e. facially race neutral) survive constitutional review.

## The Diversity Response

The Supreme Court plays an important role as an institutional referee who legitimizes our historical and contemporary racial discourse. By legitimacy and recognition, I mean that the Court acts as a referee in selecting the legally acceptable discourse on race while also identifying those to be treated as faddish, passé, extreme or marginal. The Court's response also has the power to drive public policy according to its racial sensibility, or in its current trajectory, toward a colorblind sensibility *sans* race. The Court's posture and its continued trajectory of both striking down affirmative action policies while upholding disproportionately harmful 'race-neutral' practices has fundamentally changed the current climate in public policy. That is, policy makers must attempt to address racial subordination by paradoxically utilizing non-racial tactics. For example, some readily accept explanations of white flight for better reputed and resource schools as a product of personal choice. The 'personal choice' explanation leaves little room to discuss the subordinating history of case law that created the legal foundation for financially unequal schools across district lines. With the Court as a principal actor, we are now in a twilight zone of double talk full of dog whistle race politics from both sides of the affirmative action debate. For conservatives, the discursive approach mirrors the posture of the conservative Court. The racial rhetoric appears to be post-racial (or even non-racial) even though material circumstances produce incredible racial disparity. On the other hand, proponents of affirmative action and race positive policies must craft policy that is non-racial in appearance but racial in substance, amounting to discursive summersaults. These circumstances, thanks in large part to the colorblind Court, contribute to a public racial discourse that often makes no material sense and borders on absurdity.

### *The Proponents*

It is worth recognizing that in the face of increasing racial segregation in society, many American institutions of higher education affirmatively work to provide racial minorities and other historically disadvantaged groups greater access. As colorblindness turns the screw a half turn tighter, reputable institutions, like the University of California, struggle to maintain their commitment to diversity. In California, Proposition 209's ratification, which strikes a blow to affirmative action, makes sticking the landing of diversity somersaults even more difficult. In undergraduate admissions, due to the passing of propositions or laws that all but prohibit the express use race in admissions policy, many states have adopted holistic admissions plans to maintain minority representation while adhering to colorblind mandates, or whiteness turned into a veritable law. These dynamics make holistic policies difficult to understand, let alone implement, as an admissions policy. The issue comes down to whether or not an admissions policy intended to increase racial representation can really be non-racial. The short and simple answer is no. However, this confusion is not of any school's doing, but exists as a historically specific response to the Court's mandates on the permissible use of race in education policy since *Brown*.

- *Regents of the University of California v. Bakke* (1978): Affirmative action constitutional, class diversity is a compelling governmental interest. However, UC Davis cannot use a quota system. Race can be a factor, but cannot be a decisive factor.
- *Hopwood v. Texas* (1996): Four white students successfully challenged affirmative action at the University of Texas School. The Fifth Circuit ruled the university may *not* use race as a factor in admissions. The university appealed to the Supreme Court but was denied review. *Hopwood* would later be abrogated with *Grutter* in 2003 as a Supreme Court case. As a result, for a period of seven years, affirmative action was banned in Louisiana, Mississippi, and Texas, the three states within the Firth Circuit's jurisdiction.
- *Grutter v. Bollinger* (2003): Class diversity is a compelling governmental interest, thus usage of race is constitutional to achieve class diversity. But policy to achieve class diversity must be narrowly tailored and of last resort to survive strict scrutiny.
- *Gratz v. Bollinger* (2003): University of Michigan's point system awarding automatic points to racial minorities in undergraduate admissions ruled unconstitutional because point system is not narrowly tailored in accordance with strict scrutiny. By automatically awarding minority applicants twenty points, Michigan treated race as a decisive factor and violates Justice Powell's opinion in *Bakke*.

Together, this bundle of cases establishes the permissible usage of race in higher education policy. Schools are allowed to consider race in admissions policy, but cannot treat race as a decisive factor (e.g. given a fixed value). In accordance with *Bakke*, race can be considered as one factor among a number of salient factors. However, consistent with *Bakke*, race must be utilized to meet a university's desire for a diverse learning environment. The diverse learning environment has to be specific, such as the value of a diverse learning environment in a law school where students are exposed to a diversity of opinions that reflect the legal world. Finally, racial considerations must be of last resort and narrowly tailored for the specific purpose of achieving the benefits of a diverse learning environment. In other words, the Court allows for the usage of racial consideration when it is the only remaining option available to schools in the pursuit of racial diversity. If in some way schools can achieve racial diversity without racial considerations, the Court can be expected to strike down the usage of race.

Due to these legal mandates, many U.S. universities have widely adopted the practice of holistic admissions in the pursuit of racial diversity. In addition to class rank, academic background, SAT/ACT, essays, honors, and awards, the University of Texas, for example, considers[2]:

- Special accomplishments, work, and service both in and out of school.
- Special circumstances that put the applicant's academic achievements into context, including his or her socioeconomic status, experience in a single parent home, family responsibilities, experience overcoming adversity, cultural background, *race and ethnicity*, the language spoken in the applicant's home, and other information in the applicant's file.

In states where there are prohibitive bans on any usage of race (see California prop 209 and Michigan voting to ban affirmative action in 2006), holistic admission policies are still used while the express criterion of race or ethnicity is eliminated. However, express racial considerations are replaced by benign sounding criteria that essentially substitute for racial considerations. The University of California's holistic admissions procedure, called comprehensive review, uses criteria such as:

- Quality of a student's academic performance relative to the educational opportunities available in their high school.
- Location of a student's secondary school and residence.

Together, these criteria read a lot like the UC is considering whether or not students attend underfunded schools and/or whether or not their high schools are segregated due to residential segregation, issues exacerbated by the Court's previous intervention in *Rodriguez* and *Milliken*. As a nod to the legal climate in which the UC must fashion its admissions policy, specific language states that 'no pre-assigned weights' (i.e. points) are given to any criterion while considerations based on race and ethnicity are excluded. Except for the express mention of race, both holistic admissions policies at the University of Texas and the University of California are essentially the same. Even if the specific considerations do not match word for word, both universities share the common goal of attaining a diverse student body for their campuses. The Court's confounding trajectory forces both schools to tweak their admissions policy for it to satisfy national and local law even though they engage in very similar tactics to achieve diversity. It is no wonder that Justice Ginsburg believes 'those that candidly disclose their consideration of race are preferable to those that conceal it'.[3] But in our current constitutional world set forth by the Court's decisions, it is the University of Texas, candid about its usage of race, which faces costly litigation whereas the University of California, which conceals its intentions through 'non-racial' considerations, escapes costly and time consuming legal scrutiny.

### *The Antagonist*

In a quintessential example of dog whistle politics, the *Fisher* case features racial double-talk from opponents of racial preferences. Abigail Fisher's claim of victimhood from the UT's holistic admissions policy is a fallacy when looking at the admissions data. In a YouTube video produced by her legal representatives, Fisher argued:

> There were people in my class with lower grades who weren't in all the activities I was in, who were being accepted into UT, and the only other difference between us was the color of our skin. I was taught from the time I was a little girl that any kind of discrimination was wrong. And for an institution of higher learning to act this way makes no sense to me. What kind of example does it set for others?[4]

This is a common talking point from the reverse-racism discourse. It comes with two related assumptions. First, lesser-qualified minority students are admitted only because of their race. Second, more qualified white applicants are denied admissions because they are white. Looking closely at UT's admissions data for 2008, neither the talking point nor the two related assumptions have any basis in fact. For the 2008 admissions year, UT accepted forty-seven students with lower GPA and SAT scores than Fisher, of which forty-two were white. In undermining the second assumption, one hundred sixty-eight students with as good as or better GPA and SAT scores than Fisher were rejected; all were students of color. Students of color with similar or better SAT and GPA were not the only ones rejected. Other white students with better scores than Fisher were also denied admission. However, the story of admissions remains the same. As was the case in *Bakke*, GPA, SAT, or MCAT scores do not make up the totality of the admissions criteria.

Fisher and a host of other conservative organizations that filed Amicus briefs encouraged the UT and all of its sister campuses to abandon its holistic admissions criteria in favor of a strict merit-based standard, or expand its current Top-Ten Percent program. Enacted in 1997, the Top-Ten admissions program guaranteed admission to any UT institution if a student finished in the top-ten percent of their high school class. For instance, various[5] libertarian and conservative foundations advocated for the 'race-neutral' Top-Ten Percent program as preferable to the 'constitutionally suspect' race positive holistic admissions program. For all students admitted in 2008 at UT, the Top-Ten admissions program accounted for 92% of admitted students. Therefore, the race positive holistic program only accounted for 8%. Conservative justices sided with Fisher, arguing the university should get rid of holistic admissions altogether since it only accounted for 8%. The argument believed, rightly, that if Texas wanted a diverse, critical mass of students, a significant percentage would come from the Top-Ten program, not holistic admissions. This argument is correct, since statistically, even if 100% of admitted students from holistic admissions were students of color (they were not), it would only make up 8% of admitted students in 2008.

However, Fisher and her proponents never care to mention why the Top-Ten percent produces diversity. In her dissent to the 2013 procedural opinion reverting the decision back to the lower courts, Justice Ruth Bader Ginsburg provides a stinging, yet appropriate, criticism of the Court's conservatives, Fisher, and her proponents. Referring to Fisher's advocacy of so-called race-blind merit review and Texas' Top-Ten Percent program, Justice Ginsburg quipped that 'only an ostrich could regard the supposedly neutral alternatives as race unconscious'.[6] Justice Ginsburg refers to the House Research Organization Bill Analysis of the Top-Ten Percent program from the Texas legislature:

> Many regions of the state, school districts, and high schools in Texas are still predominantly composed of people from a single racial or ethnic group. Because of the persistence of this segregation, admitting the top 10 percent of all high school students would provide a diverse population and ensure that a large, well qualified pool of minority students was admitted to Texas Universities.[7]

Clearly, race consciousness drives the Top-Ten Percent plan, not race blindness. It is only appropriate that Justice Ginsburg quipped that only an ostrich with its head in the sand can believe that a plan explicitly designed to produce racial diversity is in any way not race conscious. But here is where the nature of colorblindness reveals itself. First, conservatives and Fisher reject any consideration of race in admissions processes. Second, in rejecting race positive practices, so-called 'race-neutral' alternatives like Texas' Top-Ten program are favored. But clearly, the Texas legislature confirms that race is a fundamental component that allows the Top-Ten program to produce a diverse student population for public Texas Universities. If conservatives and Justices are at all principled and committed to their rejection of race positive admissions policies, Texas' Top Ten Percent should get the most constitutional scrutiny and rejection, not holistic admissions. The reason is rather simple and a basic exercise in arithmetic. Holistic admissions accounted for only 8% of admitted students in 2008, whereas 92% came from Top-Ten Percent. It is clear that race is a central factor in the Top-Ten Percent program, but in holistic admissions, race is only one factor among other factors.

### *Who Are the 'Victims' of Race Positive Policies?*

Fisher's reverse discrimination claim and its inability to hold up against empirical scrutiny should not be surprising. Occurring nearly forty years before *Fisher*, Allan Bakke similarly claimed victimhood due to the medical school's affirmative action quota system. Upon empirical scrutiny, not only did Bakke have higher GPA and MCAT scores than admitted minority students, he fared better than most of the admitted white students. Looking at evaluative metrics, Bakke should have been admitted because he was a top candidate regardless of the school's quota system. However, in the same way that Texas' holistic admission policy takes into account a multitude of factors in determining admissions, UC Davis' medical school similarly accounted for factors beyond the MCAT and GPA scores. Discussed in greater detail in the preceding chapter, Bakke had two factors that negatively affected his candidacy: his advanced age as a 33-year-old and a poor interview evaluation. Interviewers evaluated Bakke as someone who was combative, opinionated, and not open minded toward different perspectives. Surely, these are not the characteristics that bode well for a potential physician. Nevertheless, despite careful scrutiny that revealed race had little to do with Bakke's rejection to the medical school, the *Bakke* court nevertheless accepted his reverse-discrimination claim in the same way that a lack of empirical evidence did little to dissuade the *Fisher* Court.

This presents a peculiar problem because conservatives and colorblind adherents must find a victim of 'discrimination'. Although Whites claim 'reverse-racism', careful analysis reveals white victimhood to be a red herring playing off a possessive investment in white privilege and xenophobic fears of impending minority competition. Missing any real white victims of subordination, conservatives revert to a tried and true method of painting minority students as the unintended yet 'real' victims of race positive admissions policy, exposing the splendor of its paternalistic attitude toward students of color. Referencing Thernstrom and Thernstrom (1999), Justice Thomas uses research data to show that an achievement gap persists between students of color and their white and Asian American counterparts at elite universities because so-called 'under-qualified' students (read: African Americans and Latinos) are not prepared to handle highly competitive academic environments. To bolster his claim,

Justice Thomas also cites Sander and Taylor's (2012) mismatch theory, whose advocates believe minority students will be better served if they attend less competitive schools where they are in environments that better suit or match their educational 'abilities'. Finally, conservatives believe the ultimate harm for minority students is that they wear a badge of inferiority at elite schools, since minority students have no idea whether or not their admissions are based entirely on their 'race-neutral' qualifications like SAT or GPA, or if race played a role in their admissions.

The achievement gap, mismatch theory, and badge of inferiority line of arguments presumes that by getting rid of racial considerations, so-called merit-based GPA and SAT admissions criteria have nothing to do with race. This assumption is wishful thinking. If a school like UT were only to make admissions considerations based on GPA, does it then regard all GPA scores equally? This would be impossible when the Texas legislature clearly admits that a majority of its schools are severely segregated based on race. Therefore, if the quality of education at white majority schools is the same as that found in minority majority schools, we would never have the problem of white school districts taking so-called district hoppers to court. For instance, there have been numerous examples of white majority school districts litigating against those they accuse of 'stealing' an education via district hopping. Even Justice Thomas has criticized allegedly merit-based tests like the Law School Admissions Test because they are measures influenced by factors such as wealth, educational access, and cultural capital. These factors have been shown again and again to be racial along the lines of segregation, discrimination, and disparity.

## The Perilous Status of Asian Americans

Against this backdrop of colorblind repertoire, the Project for Fair Representation's suit against Harvard and UNC at Chapel Hill has the potential to dramatically shift the affirmative action narrative. Locating high achieving Asian Americans who are 'unfairly' rejected by Harvard and UNC Chapel Hill, the suit alleges the schools' holistic admission policies amount to a campaign of impermissible discrimination by engaging in racial balancing (i.e. *de facto* quota) by limiting the number of admitted Asian American applicants. In other words, the Harvard suit specifically alleges the *de facto* imposition of a racial quota against Asian Americans. Specifically, in the lawsuit against UNC Chapel Hill, the Project for Fair Representation opportunistically takes advantage of an *Amicus Curiae* brief previously filled by UNC in the *Fisher* case. In the brief, UNC hinted that the school could possibly maintain racial diversity through 'race-neutral' practices such as automatic admissions percentage plans if the Court were to end race-based admissions policies. However, UNC argued this was an undesirable alternative because race-neutral policies like a top-ten percent program would limit the type of students it can admit. In addition, racial compositions of states are not always the same. Therefore, if a program produced a critical mass of racial diversity in one state, the same practice will not automatically work for another state if there are differing racial compositions of public high school students. These cases have the potential to eliminate all racial considerations from education policy. If the Supreme Court hears these cases and rules that so-called 'race-neutral' policies can achieve the same amount of numerical diversity as race positive admissions, the Court will surely ban all race positive admissions because strict scrutiny demands schools use racial considerations as a last resort.

The UNC Chapel Hill and specifically the Harvard complaint on behalf of Asian Americans is hardly about Asian Americans. Indeed, the Harvard case is the first of its kind brought on behalf of Asian Americans against race positive public policy. However, these cases are by no means unique concerning Asian Americans being used as a wedge against other racial minorities. Claire Jean Kim's (1999) influential racial triangulation theory chronicles several historical epochs where Asian Americans have been ostracized while also utilized as a 'model minority' to subordinate other racial minorities. Additionally, Kim argues Asian Americans are also simultaneously used to protect the racial privileges of Whites against claims of structural subordination. Particularly, Kim's identification of the second wave of 'model minority' victimizing started under Reagan applies to the UNC and Harvard legal battle. These legal battles fall lock step in line with vigorous 80s era conservative campaigns to eliminate all vestiges of Civil Rights and affirmative action programs in public policy.

Additionally, the 'model minority' trope not only disciplines other racial minorities, it fundamentally also subordinates Asian Americans as perpetually foreign. For instance, in his book extolling the virtues of so-called 'Confucian-Americans', Lawrence Harrison (1992) argues that Asian Americans exemplified a strong work ethic, value for education, and pro-merit ideas to the melting pot at a time when those values are much in need of revival—reflexively illuminating stereotypes of black and brown communities who ostensibly do not value these ideas. Interestingly, Harrison's attempted valorization of Asian American values for America's melting pot does not include ideals such as civic participation and citizenship. Kim's significant work chronicling the history of Asian American racial positioning as middlemen suggests not an intrinsic cultural value system that Harrison promotes, but confirms Stanley Sue and Sumie Okazaki's (1990) concept of 'relative functionalism' in that Asian Americans perceive and experience restrictions in upward mobility in areas unrelated to education. As a result, gravitating toward and holding onto the promise of education is the only acceptable choice for Asian Americans in search of social mobility. In short, Asian American educational ascendancy is less about culture, let alone cultural superiority, and equally about responses to racialized structures.

It is from this racial vantage point that the Asian American Harvard dispute comes into historical focus. To read the Project for Fair Representation's suit challenging Harvard's practice of holistic admissions as only about the alleged Asian American students it represents is historically myopic. I do not doubt that the many students who volunteered to have their names included to form an aggrieved class suffered from visceral emotions of unfairness and disappointment—which I attempted to capture in the preface with Andrew's story. The lawsuit, no matter its outcome, does little to directly alleviate these disappointments. For instance, the *Fisher* case was an eight-year legal odyssey. When the case ended with the Supreme Court's final verdict in 2016, Abigail Fisher was already a four-year alum of Louisiana State University working in Houston, Texas. An argument could be made that eliminating racial considerations will eliminate future disappointments from those who may feel aggrieved by so-called discriminatory admissions processes. This position is likewise shortsighted and shows further a limited understanding of exactly how selective colleges and universities compose its student body. It is true that many selective private and public colleges utilize racial considerations. Many more admit students based on legacy connections, significant parental donations, and athletic contributions. Getting rid of race positive considerations will not only fail to alleviate any potential disappointment and unfairness from admissions rejections, but will more than likely heighten disappointment and unfairness from other practices of preferential admissions which have been shown to overwhelmingly favor Whites.

These dynamics reveal an uncomfortable racial truth. Somehow as a society, we are infinitely more offended at the idea of racial considerations than wealth discrimination. Revealed during the legal discovery process in the Harvard litigation, Harvard reserves admissions considerations specifically for students whose family made or will potentially make significant donations to the university. These special admissions list, known specifically at Harvard as the 'Dean's Interested List' and 'Director's List' are available only to the wealthy, no matter how accomplished and unique a poor black or brown applicant may be. The difference in admissions rate success for students on these lists compared to all students is staggering. Depending on the year, Harvard's admissions rate for all applicants vacillate between 5–7%; for students on these special lists, the admissions rate rises above 40%. These spots are a clear quota that discriminates based on wealth. Students are unable to access these specific slots unless their family possesses an economic status that has little to do with the student's own admissions profile—unless one considers parental wealth to be a product of the students' hard work and industry. When schools utilize admissions lists for children of significant donors or give preferential treatment to legacies of alumni, they are by definition fencing out non-affluent students whose parents are not alumni. Therefore, the elimination of racial considerations in higher education admissions destroys a democratizing mechanism for students and families who simply are unable to access the entrenched institutional markers of wealth and privilege. Additionally, the end of racial considerations ushers in a veil of meritocracy under the fog of colorblindness even though reserved quotas based on significant financial donations and legacy admissions will surely continue to be practiced undisturbed.

This will result in a perilous status for Asian American racial positionality as a result of the Harvard suit. The allure is strong for those who feel particularly aggrieved to think that any current or future student will have an increased chance of admissions if racial considerations are ruled unconstitutional. As schools have always done during the long history of anti-affirmative action challenges, they adapt their policies and practices to remain legally tenantable, but always with an eye toward maintaining racial diversity, even through so-called race-neutral mechanisms similar to those practiced by the University of California. The more significant consequence is that Asian Americans will once again be utilized as a racial wedge against the interests of all racial minorities—only this time as willing participants.

My colleague Jocyl Sacramento and I have named this racialization 'polarized positionality'. One the one hand, the Harvard case elevates the academic stories and admissions disappointments of incredibly accomplished and hardworking students. These Asian American students are propped up as irrefutable examples that race positive considerations hurt other minorities, and the case is designed to be even more damming when it hurts the most hard working and accomplished students. But to what extent does it 'hurt' these students beyond their feelings of disappointments and frustration? Students who feel they have a legitimate chance of getting into some of our nation's most selective schools *will* be admitted somewhere else similarly prestigious, elite, and exclusive. Perhaps not the exact school they wanted, but there was never going to be a guarantee. However, the elevation of a small group of Asian American students as high achieving 'victims' of race positive admissions does not tell the story of many more Asian Americans, and other minority students, who are beneficiaries of racial considerations. This is what we mean by polarized positionality. Whereas Chinese men suffered oppression in bachelor societies due to immigrant restrictions and hundreds of thousands of Japanese American citizens were interned, Asian Americans now occupy the racial status of the preferred other, the Asian American model minority, elevated even above Whites in terms of academic achievement. There is no middle ground, or even left of middle or right of middle.

The history of Asian American racial positionality is one of extremes, of polarization. In a little more than half a century's time, the public discourse on Asian Americans has completely flipped from what Edward Said (1977) once named the exotic oriental to the preferred minority placed on an educational pedestal in the colorblind era. Most importantly, racial positionality does not happen in an ahistorical vacuum severed from the racialization of other groups. Omi and Winant's racial formations thesis suggests that Asian American positionality is as much about Asian Americans as it is about the racial formations of other minorities, and most importantly, Whites. During Japanese internment, a discourse of disloyalty, perpetual foreignness, and untrustworthiness plagued Japanese Americans as thousands were forced to endure humiliating 'loyalty' hearings to declare their fidelity to the U.S.—as opposed to the emperor of Japan. Of course, no such requirements were demanded of the hundreds of thousands of ethnic German Americans living in the midwest and east coast at the same time. In other words, whiteness took on the form of national sovereignty. Contemporaneously while black Tuskegee Airmen were risking their lives flying combat missions in Europe, millions of fellow black Americans back home were still subjected to Jim Crow laws and disenfranchisement that defined blacks as no more than second class citizens. For Asian and black Americans during this period, a web of laws, policies, and executive orders formed a white racial formation that clearly defined who did and did not belong to the proverbial white house.

The white house has now expanded with the addition of a guest house for preferred (read: model) minorities. Once on the outside looking in, Asian Americans are now occupying the white house's guest house. Unfortunately, this invitation comes at a significant cost. The small group of Asian Americans aligning with anti-Affirmative Action forces not only signals a realignment of white racial interests, it also marks an explicit formation to methodically destroy Civil Rights Era protections for all subordinated classes, Asian Americans included. The invitation is a best perilous, and at worst, fatal. For the false promise of college admissions meritocracy, this new white racial formation will do away with Civil Rights Era legal protections in housing, voting, and employment. The old and new white racial formations are true to form with Gramscian hegemony theory.

Jim Crow laws and Japanese internment are militaristic maneuvers that were clear and unflinching examples of white racial power. However, these militaristic maneuvers are time limited and unsustainable in the long run. They are unsustainable not only as an exertion of physical violence, but most importantly unsustainable as an inhabitant of white psyche. We no longer have Jim Crow laws not because they were overturned by people of color, but by Whites, even if begrudgingly. In addition, interned Japanese Americans received reparations and an official apology from the Reagan administration during the 1980s. White racial formations must constantly remake themselves. The infusion of a minute amount of elite Asian American interests in college admissions under an all-encompassing anti-Civil Rights umbrella forms a strategic alliance that sustains a neo-hegemonic white racial formation. This new alliance is not brand new, but new to the extent that the same old master has a new partner dancing to a slightly different tune. White interests are no longer clearly recognizable by simply identifying the likes of Allan Bakke or Abigail Fisher. Rather, the new tune is composed of intersecting interests of relatable Asian American students who have done nothing more than be studious model minorities in chasing their educational American dreams. It is to be determined whether or not Asian American students, families, and communities will see a substantive return in being willing accomplices of this new white racial formation. One thing is clear, this perilous alliance that is unapologetic concerning its anti-Civil Rights goal will make all racial minorities worse off.

## Notes

1. In *Green v. County School Board of New Kent County*, the Court ruled so-called 'freedom of choice' plans unconstitutional and in violation of *Brown's* desegregation mandate. Under these plans, white and black families almost uniformly chose schools identified with their own race. Additionally, students were automatically assigned to the school previously attended unless they applied for a different school that was determined according to a state board. These provisions collectively maintained *de facto* racial segregation.
2. These admissions considerations were ultimately taken down from the University of Texas' admissions webpage while the *Fisher* case was in limbo on the Supreme Court.
3. *Gratz v. Bollinger*, 539 U.S. 244 (2003), p. 301.
4. www.youtube.com/watch?v=sXSpx9PZZj4.
5. These organizations and foundations are: Pacific Legal Foundation, The American Civil Rights Institute, The Center for Equal Opportunity, Individual Rights Foundation, Reason Foundation, Project 21, and The National Association of Scholars.
6. *Fisher v. University of Texas*, 570 U.S. ___ (2013). Ginsburg Dissenting Opinion, p. 2433.
7. Ibid.

# 9 Future Directions

Our conversation now ends where it began with the stories of Andrew and Jesse. Their educational experiences are replicated year after year by high school students from all corners of the United States. However, the numbers of students with educational trajectories similar to Jesse's dwarfs that of students similar to Andrew's. For instance, we should consider this revealing fact: The University of California, Berkeley enrolls more low-income students, a great number being students of color, than the eight Ivy League institutions—combined.[1] This fact is not to promote a rush to judgment on the admissions and enrolling practices of Ivy League schools. More importantly, the fact should allow us an opportunity to recalibrate our conversation on affirmative action, racism, and education. If elite schools such as Harvard were to do away with racial considerations, it would make a drop in the bucket difference for low-income and minority students in terms of diminishing educational opportunities. In fact, a public institution like Berkeley enrolls more low-income students even while being prohibited from using explicit racial considerations. Pressing questions remain that both sides of the debate must address: why are racial considerations so offensive/worthwhile when its impact is negligible? Furthermore, is the legal battle to save racial considerations necessary when schools like the University of California can use supposedly 'race-neutral' considerations such as socio-economic status and automatic admissions percentage plans?

First, the 'race neutrality' of socio-economic status (SES) and percentage plans: together, SES and percentage plans provide a high degree of racial diversity *because* of race. Residential redlining, racial covenants, and the arbitrary creation of school district lines have all compounded to collectively act as built in social headwinds for many people of color. The history of these practices need not be repeated here to suggests that measures of SES center race and racism. Therefore, the argument that utilizing SES amounts to 'race neutrality' is an attempt to enter the white house through the back door to avoid being seen cavorting with race. Additionally, percentage plans that automatically admit high school students to state colleges and universities have been universally championed by conservatives as preferable 'race-neutral' alternatives to affirmative action practices. The alleged race neutrality of percentage plans is at best willful ignorance and at worst, an instantiation of colorblind racism. Again, responding to Fisher's claims that the University of Texas' percentage admissions plan is race neutral, Justice Ginsburg quipped 'I have said before and reiterate here that only an ostrich could regard the supposedly neutral alternatives as race unconscious'.[2] Justice Ginsburg's take is not only a product of her broader conviction in the fallacy of race neutrality in our racialized world, but a direct assessment of the Texas legislative process centering racial segregation when the percentage plan was deliberated in the state legislature.

The 1996 *Hopwood v. Texas* decision by the Fifth Circuit Court of Appeals in New Orleans had at the time halted affirmative action practices for all jurisdictions under the Firth Circuit, which included the state of Texas. In response to the legal mandate, the Texas state legislature was required to enact a new admissions practice that, on the one hand, needed to be compliant with the new legal mandate, but also continue admitting a diverse student body representative of Texas' growing racial diversity. The state legislature adopted an automatic admissions plan for Texas students based on where they ranked academically from their graduating high school class. High school percentage plans are favored by conservatives because facially, the policy itself is race neutral—there is no mention of race in the actual policy. However, the policies' effectiveness toward producing the desired racial diversity fundamentally centered race. For proof, we need to look no further than texts during the deliberative process from the Texas state legislature mentioned in the previous chapter where the state legislature explicitly referenced the racial segregation of Texas schools. That is, Texas' percentage plans produce racial diversity because Texas high schools are racially segregated. This is Justice Ginsburg's criticism of those who advocate for percentage plans based on some fairy tale notion of race neutrality. Arguments that percentage plans are in any way race neutral is based solely on the wording of the policy, as opposed to the racialized reality and material history that gives life to the policy's implementation. Even more curious is that the adoption of percentage plans means that conservatives would be in favor of a plan that critically relies on race for its effectiveness, even though it does not facially mention race. Conversely, conservatives will deploy millions of dollars and an unlimited amount of political capital to defeat affirmative action policies that only minimally rely on race. Is the answer to this peculiar reality entirely because conservatives wish to eliminate the *word* race from all public policy? History tells us that this is an obtuse observation.

In *Griggs*, the Duke Power company did not focus on preserving the word race or racial signifiers in adopting allegedly race-neutral employment requirements; its singular goal was to keep blacks from reaching management positions. Duke Power was operating in a new racial formation ushered in by a Civil Rights legislative mandate that prohibited discrimination on race. This facially colorblind ethos undergirds anti-affirmative action movements today. However, the policy makers and advocates who now use the word race and other racial signifiers do so not to debase people, but as an attempt to ameliorate racism and uplift society from racial debasement. As a sad, but predictable response, anti-affirmative action advocates rely on an increasingly favorable conservative legal landscape needing simply to not talk about race—or more specifically, eliminate the word race. Like *Griggs*, the importance is not whether the word race is used or mentioned, but to ask what material realities and racial manifestations are being preserved. As mentioned, the Project on Fair Representation is fairly straightforward, stating its mission is to challenge race positive public policies in voting, education, contracting, and employment. Therefore, anti-affirmative action cases like *Fisher* or against Harvard is not myopically only about eliminating modest racial considerations in elite college admissions. Anti-affirmative action cases in college admissions is simply a contemporaneous act in the broader historical show—a Greek tragedy portraying the demise of Civil Rights promises.

As a response, it is absolutely necessary to fight any and all attempts to do away with affirmative action in college admissions. Anti-affirmative action cases are spokes in a larger wheel constructed to run roughshod over the entire edifice of Civil Rights protections. Therefore, questions about whether it is worthwhile to maintain the limited constitutionality of race positive admissions misrecognizes the struggle's place within the broader trajectory of Civil Rights history. Central to this struggle is the problem of racial inequality and the role of democratic public policy. The contemporary multipronged attack on democratic attempts to ameliorate racial inequality slowly peels back—one policy and legal mechanism at a time—the hard-fought institutional protections for subordinated communities. The direct consequence is that the relationship between public policy and law as it relates to the problem of race is now utterly upside down—what Ian Haney López (2005) calls a disaster. The trajectory of the conservative Court on race has essentially condemned democratic attempts toward greater racial justice while condoning colorblind manifestations of racism.

These are the broader colorblind parameters that frame Jesse and Andrew's educational experiences. For Jesse, a seemingly endless loop of social and institutional forces collectively coalesces to shape his educational future. From housing segregation, underfunded schools based on arbitrary district lines, to racial isolation brought on by 'benign' choices, Jesse's educational achievements are not *because* of his educational environment, but *in spite* of it. A short drive away, Andrew's educational world is an ecology of the best opportunities from both the public and private sectors seamlessly woven together to provide an invaluable platform for Andrew to regard all of his accomplishments as uniquely his own. From afar, reasonable observers can compare these students' educational worlds and conclude that available educational opportunities for Andrew, and lack thereof for Jesse, played a significant role toward their educational paths. I am confident this observation is uncontroversial. However, conservative constitutional race law—even more conservative since President Trump—feels compelled to provide Andrew with even more institutional privilege while simultaneously fencing out Jesse even further. Colorblindness and the conservative Court do so by keeping the doors of equal protection open, perhaps even inviting, for students like Andrew to utilize the Court to solidify their educational privilege. Andrew does not have to prove any tangible racial harm or injury, merely that he perceives discrimination from affirmative action practices. On the other hand, Jesse can present undisputed data on funding disparity, racial isolation and segregation, or tangible and intangible differences in educational opportunities. But Jesse's claims will fall on deaf ears because, as Michelle Alexander has observed, the doors of equal protection have been closed on racial problems like Jesse's. I agree with Ian Haney López's observation that constitutional race law is a disaster. In fact, the disaster might only be getting worse. However, reflecting the observations of Stuart Hall (1996) on the hegemonic process and civil society, the struggle for Civil Rights protections and Affirmative Action policies are not suspended nor does it disappear despite the contemporary hegemony of colorblindness. Indeed, the struggle continues, and I observe it must continue on at least two fronts: in law, and in education.

## Directions in Law

This book is not principally focused on the developments of constitutional law from a doctrinal perspective. Nevertheless, my analysis significantly referenced developments in doctrinal law to make racial analyses that, I argue, significantly maintained social stratification and white racial structures via a colorblind discourse. Therefore, I would be remiss to not consider future legal directions in the struggle against colorblind jurisprudence and its dangerous impact in a racialized society.

First, jurisprudence as it relates to interpretation and the promise of equal protection must move past the conservative threshold of procedural equality toward the more expansive doctrine of substantive equality. That is, the mere provision of equal processes does not equate that the quality and substance of those processes are comparable. For instance, one of the foundational legal protections for Americans during encounters with the law is that we must all be read 'Miranda Rights' when arrested or taken into custody (i.e. '*You have the right to remain silent, anything you say . . .* '). Central to Miranda Rights is the right to an attorney. Miranda satisfies equal protection from a procedural standpoint because everyone has the right to legal representation by an attorney, even if one is unable to afford one. However, Miranda falls short of substantive equality because not all attorneys are equal. Those who are unable to afford an experienced and high-priced attorney will be assigned a public defender, who more often than not is less experienced and burdened with a heavy case load from other public defender cases. Criticisms of the doctrine of substantive equality suggests that an equality of result cannot be achieved, with intangible circumstances that significantly contribute to the outcomes of legal processes. These arguments are valid if substantive equality was in fact advocating for equal outcomes. However, substantive equality advocates for greater parity in the process. That is, procedural equality should not just be treated as a threshold, but more an actual process. Substantive equality does not so much demand absolute equality, but spotlights the gross injustice that occurs when equal protection jurisprudence is limited by a threshold imposition of procedural equality.

In the affirmative action cases, the divergence in how conservatives enforce strict scrutiny as a procedural and substantive process is striking. For instance, when democratic institutions wish to practice affirmative action policies, they are made to satisfy a strict standard of review where multiple points of evaluation must be met (e.g. narrowly tailored and of last resort). For example, when Harvard or the University of Texas argue that their race positive admissions practices are necessary to admit and enroll a diverse student body, the Court has, and will continue to, investigate whether or not these claims are actually true. That is, conservatives view race positive diversity arguments as inherently suspect and democratic actors must prove otherwise to satisfy the Court's own judgement. According to conservatives, they will never defer to the so-called benevolent and well-intentioned motivations of actors when racial classifications are utilized. Both Harvard and the University of Texas have had to turn over years of admissions data, documents, and deliberative notes from admissions officers to satisfy the exacting examination of 'strict scrutiny'. No such requirements have *ever* been required from those who claim 'reverse racism'. That is, the likes of Alan Bakke and Abigail Fisher have never been asked to prove that they would have been admitted but for affirmative action practices. For those claiming to be victims of affirmative action, conservatives have without exception deferred to their claimed status of victimhood without a semblance of exacting scrutiny or critical investigation. For proponents of affirmative action, 'strict scrutiny' is indeed strict in theory and fatal in practice. However, for those who claim to be victims of affirmative action, 'strict scrutiny' is in fact strict in theory and absent in practice.

Second, elections matter. Even if we are not lawyers or have formal training, we can impact how the law is adjudicated, enforced, or interpreted through our ability to vote. I illustrated this point briefly at the end of Chapter 7 regarding the death of conservative justice Antonin Scalia. Never mind that republicans in the Senate blocked President Obama's nomination of Merrick Garland; a Hillary Clinton victory over then candidate Donald Trump after the republican's obstruction would have likely replaced Scalia with a justice perhaps more sympathetic toward a more expansive reading of equal protection and substantive equality. Additionally, the retirement of conservative Anthony Kennedy would have further contributed to an ideological shift in the court from conservative to solidly liberal. The value of a majority Supreme Court more sympathetic to an equal protection jurisprudence based on an expansive vision of substantive equality would be immense. At the very least, endemic racial disparities in voting, housing, education, criminal justice, and employment would once again feel the promise of equal protection, not its wrath. Hypotheticals aside, Hillary Clinton did not win. The Supreme Court, and entire federal judiciary, is even more conservative since the Trump presidency than before even while Scalia was alive. Although Supreme Court and Federal Judiciary appoints are lifetime positions, the presidents who make the nominations and senators who confirm the appointments are subject to us: the voters.

## Directions in Education

Most importantly, the struggle for civil rights and racial justice is not limited to the law. The broader, more consequential struggle is whether or not the ideals of racial justice, Civil Rights, and the necessity for affirmative actions can find hospitable space in our hearts and minds. In the colorblind era, our public discourse is one that is at best lukewarm, and at worst, inhospitable to Cornel West's (1994) contention that race still matters. The struggle for our hearts and minds is not led by high-priced lawyers or happens in the chambers of the Supreme Court, but is conducted, formed, and cemented in our school classrooms. Here, we must take a hard look at how we teach Civil Rights, racism, and the perpetuity of racial stratification in the colorblind era. As a result, our entire educational edifice requires critical evaluation to account for what Du Bois (1903) so profoundly proclaimed more than a hundred years ago as the problem of the color line. Or more appropriately for our contemporaneous time, what Zeus Leonardo (2002) calls the problem of the colorblind line. Perhaps more important than settling on an exact name for the problem is finding a commitment to address the problem of race and the fact of racism in our colorblind era. The paradigmatic commitments required in education are too numerous to adequately cover here. However, when we speak of education, we think of schools, and schools begin with a conversation on curriculum—that is, what do we teach and what do students learn?

Today, affirmative action talk in grade school or college classrooms are fraught with stereotyped caricatures of so-called 'undeserving' minorities and white and Asian victims of reverse discrimination in a zero-sum game. If affirmative action conversations start with these points of departures, we have utterly failed as educators to properly provide our students with even a kernel of historical truth pertaining to Civil Rights, racism, and the necessity for affirmative action. As I have showed in Section II of the book, affirmative action was and should never be regarded as only a selective college admissions issue. Even in a hypothetical where elite colleges around the country are given carte blanche to practice full-blown affirmative action in the form of quota-set-aside, the impact would at best be marginal against other forms of racial discrimination in housing, employment, criminal justice sentencing, and *de facto* educational segregation. Therefore, the impetus is for educators to wrestle the affirmative action discourse away from the narrow confines of college admissions toward a language that fundamentally centers the persistence of racism.

In response, we should never begin our conversation with whether or not a student agrees with affirmative action or specific iterations of race positive practices. Rather, we should agree on whether institutionalized racial disparities still persist in our colorblind era. For instance, discussions on race and affirmative action with my college students always begin with an exploration into the type of high schools my students attended. Here, they themselves provide personal illustrations of the institutional disparities that are endemic in our public schools due to, among other factors, the local tax funding structure and housing segregation. Despite reservations, most students eventually acquiesce to the notion of institutionalized disparity along racial lines. As a result, our conversation turns toward a discussion of how to best address racism, as opposed to reductive and outright rejections of affirmative action policies grounded in the dogma that racism does not exist.

The history of anti-affirmative action challenges in education has, without exception, all centered around the opposition to specific mechanisms of race positive decision making. *Bakke* was the quota-set-a-side, *Gratz* was the point system, and *Parents Involved* was the racial tie breaker. One could read all these cases as individual and unrelated opposition to specific mechanism of affirmative action, not affirmative action itself. This would be wrong. Every case has been filled with the goal of eliminating affirmative action once and for all. Not a single case has represented a discursive ethos that says 'yes, we believe racism exists, we just object to this specific practice to ameliorate racism'. At best, the colorblind narrative has always been toward the declining significance of race, and at worst, outright disdain projecting the culpability of institutionalized racial disparities on personal choice—that is, a culture of poverty. As educators, we can push back against this colorblind allusion by ushering in a discourse grounded in material history not only from the law, but more crucially, within our classrooms.

## Closing

More than sixty years ago, the Civil Rights Act ushered in an era of hope and promise for meaningful racial equity across a broad spectrum of public life. In *Brown v. Board of Education*, Chief Justice Earl Warren's unanimous court signaled an expansive horizon for the Fourteenth Amendment's equal protection clause. Within the span of ten years, all three branches of government exemplified a commitment to addressing the problem of racial disparity and subordination. Unfortunately, this commitment is now at best unfulfilled and at worst abandoned. In education, schools are re-segregating at rates not witnessed since *de jure* segregation before *Brown*. Major provisions of the Voting Rights and Civil Rights Acts have been gutted by a constant stream of legislative and judicial attacks deployed almost immediately since its passage. This book may be considered as an attempt to synthesize the multiple prongs of legal maneuvers utilized to undermine and peel back the modest Civil Rights Era protections for insular groups from institutional forms of subordination.

If one were to keep score, the colorblind movement's legal and political interventions have been a resounding success. In law, *Brown's* significance is no longer hallowed, but hollowed—reduced to little more than a symbolic footnote of history. Democratic affirmative action policies in and beyond education have all been defeated, or at least severely stripped of any consequential mechanism for meaningful impact. Politically, the colorblind movement has been able to craft a racial discourse that simultaneously denies the persistence of racism while further perpetuating and entrenching its subordinating impact on some of our most vulnerable communities. These perilous times do not require a new catchy mantra or vanguard to address the fact of racism in the colorblind era. In conversation with Jonathan Kozol (2005), Gary Orfield argued the 'outside the box' thinking simply requires us to recommit to Civil Rights Era promises that were prematurely abandoned. Indeed, it is odd to think that reverting back to past moments in history can be considered 'outside the box'. To the extent that the Civil Rights commitments fundamentally recognized the centrality of race and racism in civic life, this discursive shift would in fact be an escape from our contemporaneous colorblind box. Above all else, this book promotes a renewed effort to Civil Rights, substantive equality, and racial justice.

## Notes

1. See Eaton, C. (2017). How elite colleges hide their cash. *New York Times*, November 10, 2017. www.nytimes.com/2017/11/10/opinion/ivy-league-offshore-tax-stanford.html.
2. *Fisher v. University of Texas*, 570 U.S. ___ (2013). Ginsburg Dissenting Opinion, p. 2433.

# Selected Readings List

## Preface

### *Introduction*

Brown v. Board of Education of Topeka, 347 U.S. 483 (1954).
Fisher v. University of Texas, 579 US_ (2016).
López, I. H. (2006). *White by Law: The legal construction of race*. New York, NY: NYU Press.
Takao Ozawa v. U S, 260 U.S. 178 (1922).
U.S. v. Bhagat Singh Thind, 261 U.S. 204 (1923).

### *Chapter 1*

Balkin, J. M., & Siegel, R. B. (2004). The American civil rights tradition: Anticlassification or antisubordination? In *Issues in legal scholarship, the origins and fate of antisubordination theory: A symposium on Owen Fiss's "Groups and The Equal Protection Clause,"* reprinted in 58 U. Miami L. Rev. 9.
Bell, D. (1995). Brown v. Board of Education and the interest convergence dilemma. In K. Crenshaw, N. Gotanda, G. Peller, & K. Thomas (Eds.), *Critical race theory* (pp. 20–29). New York: The New Press.
Bobo, L., & Smith, R. A. (1998). From Jim Crow racism to laissez-faire racism: An essay on the transformation of racial attitudes in American. In W. F. Katkin, N. Landsman, & A. Tyree (Eds.), *Beyond pluralism: The conceptions of groups and group identities in America* (pp. 182–220). Urbana: University of Illinois Press.
Bonilla-Silva, E. (2001). *White supremacy and racism in the post-civil rights era*. Boulder, CO: Lynne Rienner Publishers.
Brown v. Board of Education of Topeka, 347 U.S. 483 (1954).
Dred Scott v. Sandford, 60 U.S. 393 (1857).
Fiss, O. M. (1976). Groups and the equal protection clause. *Philosophy and Public Affairs*, 5(2), 107–177.
Grutter v. Bollinger, 539 U.S. 306 (2003).
Leonardo, Z. (2007). The war on schools: NCLB, nation creation and the educational construction of whiteness. *Race Ethnicity and Education*, 10(3), 261–278.
Marshall, T. (1987). We the people: A celebration of the bicentennial of the United States Constitution: The constitution: A living document. *Howard Law Journal*, 623.

Parents Involved in Community Schools v. Seattle Sch. Dist. No. 1, 551 U.S. 701 (U.S. 2007).

Plessy v. Ferguson 163 U.S. 537 (1896).

Regents of the University of California v. Bakke, 438 U.S. 265 (1978).

Siegel, R. B. (2004). Equality talk: Antisubordination and anticlassification values in constitutional struggles over brown. *Harvard Law Review*, 117, 1470–1547.

West, C. (1994). *Race matters*. New York: Vintage Books.

*Chapter 2*

Anderson, P. (1976). The antinomies of Antonio Gramsci. *New Left Review*, 100, 7–78.

Bell, D. (1992). *Faces at the bottom of the well: The permanence of racism*. New York: Basic Books.

Bell, D. (2004). *Silent covenants*. New York: Oxford University Press.

Farber, D. A., & Sherry, S. (1997). *Beyond all reason: The radical assault on truth in American law*. New York: Oxford University Press.

Kozinski, A. (1997). Bending the law: Are radical multiculturalists poisoning young legal minds? *New York Times*, November 2, 1997. www.nytimes.com/books/97/11/02/reviews/971102.02kosinst.html.

Leonardo, Z. (2003). Interpretation and the problem of domination: Paul Ricoeur's hermeneutics. *Studies in Philosophy and Education*, 22, 329–350.

Leonardo, Z., & Allen, R. (2008). Ideology. In L. Given (Ed.), *The Sage encyclopedia of qualitative research methods* (pp. 416–421). Thousand Oaks, CA: SAGE.

Leonardo, Z., & Porter, R. (2010). Pedagogy of fear: Toward a Fanonian theory of "safety" in race dialogue. *Race Ethnicity and Education*, 13(2), 139–157.

Linn, R. L., & Welner, K. G. (2007). *Race-conscious policies for assigning students to schools: Social science research and the Supreme Court cases*. National Academy of Education: Committee on Social Science Research Evidence on Racial Diversity in Schools.

Omi, M., & Winant, H. (2014). *Racial formations in the United States* (3rd ed.). New York: Routledge.

Parents Involved in Community Schools v. Seattle Sch. Dist. No. 1, 551 U.S. 701 (U.S. 2007).

Posner, R. A. (1997). The skin trade: New republic at 40. *Book Review*, 40–42.

Ricoeur, P. (1976). *Interpretation theory: Discourse and the surplus of meaning*. Texas: Texas Christian University Press.

Sander, R., & Taylor, S. (2012). *Mismatch: How affirmative action hurts students it's intended to help, and why universities won't admit it*. New York: Basic Books.

Solorzano, D., & Yosso, T. (2002). A critical race counterstory of affirmative action in higher education. *Equity and Excellence in Education*, 35, 155–168.

Sowell, T. (1981). *Ethnic America: A history*. New York: Basic Books Inc. Publishers.

Tatum, B. (1997). *Why are all the black kids sitting together in the Cafeteria? And other conversations about race*. New York: Basic Books.

*Chapter 3*

Althusser, L. (1971). Ideology and ideological state apparatuses. In L. Althusser (Ed.), *Lenin and philosophy and other essays*. New York: Monthly Review Press.
Anderson, P. (1976). The antinomies of Antonio Gramsci. *New Left Review*, 100, 7–78.
Bell, D. (1980a). Brown v. Board of Education and the interest-convergence dilemma. *Harvard Law Review*, 93, 518.
Dred Scott v. Sandford, 60 U.S. 393 (1857).
Du Bois, W. E. B. (1903). *The souls of black folk*. New York: Bantam Classic.
Frankenberg, R. (1993). *White women, race matters: The social construction of whiteness*. Minneapolis, MN: University of Minnesota Press.
Giroux, H. A. (1997). Rewriting the discourse of racial identity: Towards a pedagogy and politics of whiteness. *Harvard Educational Review*, 67(2), 285–320.
Gramsci, A. (1971). *Selections from the prison notebooks*. Ed. & Trans. Q. Hoare & G. Nowell-Smith. New York: International Publishers.
Hall, S. (2006). Gramsci's relevance for the study of race and ethnicity. In D. Morley & D. K. Chen (Eds.), *Stuart Hall: Critical dialogues in cultural studies*. London: Routledge.
Howard, G. (1999). *We can't teach what we don't know: White teachers, multiracial schools*. New York: Teachers College Press.
Ignatiev, N. (1997). The point is not to interpret whiteness but to abolish it. Talk given at the Making and Unmaking of Whiteness Conference, University of California, Berkeley, 11–13 April. www.postfun.com/racetraitor.
Kozol, J. (1991). *Savage inequalities: Children in America's schools*. New York: Crown.
Ladson-Billings, G., & Tate, W. (1995). Toward a critical race theory of education. *Teachers College Record*, 97(1), 47–68.
Leonardo, Z. (2004). The color of supremacy: Beyond the discourse of "white privilege". *Educational Philosophy and Theory*, 36(2), 137–152.
Leonardo, Z. (2007). The war on schools: NCLB, nation creation and the educational construction of whiteness. *Race Ethnicity and Education*, 10(3), 261–278.
Loving v. Virginia 388 U.S. 1 (1967).
Matsuda, M. (1991). Voices of America: Accent, antidiscrimination law, and a jurisprudence for the last reconstruction. *Yale Law Journal*, 100, 1329–1407.
McIntosh, P. (1990). White privilege: Unpacking the invisible knapsack. *Independent School*, 49(2), 31–36.
McIntyre, A. (1997). *Making meaning of whiteness: Exploring racial identity with white teachers*. Albany, NY: Suny Press.
Mills, C. (1997). *The racial contract*. Ithaca, NY: Cornell University Press.
Orfield, G., & Frankenberg, E. (2013). *Educational delusions? Why choice can deepen inequality and how to make it fair*. Berkeley: University of California Press.
Plessy v. Ferguson, 163 U.S. 537 (1896).
Roediger, D. R. (1994). *Towards the abolition of whiteness: Essays on race, politics, and working class history*. New York: Verso.
Sleeter, C. (1993). How white teachers construct race. In C. McCarthy & W. Crichlow (Eds.), *Race, identity and representation in education* (pp. 157–171). New York: Routledge.

Solorzano, D., & Yosso, T. (2001). From racial stereotyping and deficit discourse toward a critical race theory in teacher education. *Multicultural Education*, 9, 2–8.
Wallerstein, I. (1975). Class-formation in the capitalist world-economy. *Politics and Society*, 5, 367–75.
Winant, H. (2000). Race and race theory. *Annual Review of Sociology*, 26, 169–85.

### *Chapter 4*

Bell, D. (2004). *Silent covenants*. New York: Oxford University Press.
Bolling v. Sharpe, 347 U.S. 497 (1954).
Brown v. Board of Education of Topeka, 347 U.S. 483 (1954).
Brown v. Board of Education of Topeka, 349 U.S. 294 (1955).
Clark, K., Chein, I., & Cook, S. (1954). The effects of segregation and the consequences of desegregation. A (September 1952) Social Science Statement in the Brown v. Board of Education of Topeka Supreme Court Case. *American Psychologist*, 59, 495–501.
McIntosh, P. (1990). White privilege: Unpacking the invisible knapsack. *Independent School*, 49(2), 31–36.
Missouri v. Jenkins, 515 U.S. 70 (1995), (Thomas, J., concurring).
Ogletree, C. J., Jr. (2004). *All deliberate speed: Reflections on the first half century of Brown v. Board of Education*. New York: W.W. Norton.
Orfield, G., & Frankenberg, E. (2014). *Brown at 60: Great progress, a long retreat and an uncertain future*. Los Angeles, CA: Civil Rights Project/Proyecto Derechos Civiles.
Patterson, J. T. (2001). *Brown v. Board of Education: A Civil Rights milestone and its troubled legacy*. Oxford: Oxford University Press.
Stern, R. L., Gressman, E., Shapiro, S. M., & Geller, K. S. (2002). *Supreme Court practice: For practice in the Supreme Court of the United States* (8th ed.). Washington, DC: Bureau of National Affairs.
United States v. Barnett, 376 U.S. 681 (1964).

### *Chapter 5*

Baldus, D. C., Pulaski, C., & Woodworth, G. (1983). Comparative review of death sentences: An empirical study of the Georgia experience. *Journal of Criminal and Criminology*, 74, 661–753.
Griggs v. Duke Power Co., 401 U.S. 424 (1971).
McCleskey v. Kemp, 481 U.S. 279 (1987).
Moyers, B. (2010). *Bill Moyers Journal*, April 2, 2010. www.pbs.org/moyers/journal/04022010/transcript1.html.
Personnel Administrator of Massachusetts v. Feeney, 442 U.S. 256 (1979).
Village of Arlington Heights v. Metropolitan Housing Development Corp, 429 U.S. 252 (1977).
Washington v. Davis, 426 U.S. 229 (1976).

### *Chapter 6*

Adarand Constructors, Inc. v. Pena, 515 U.S. 200 (1995).
City of Richmond v. J.A. Croson Co., 488 U.S. 469 (1989).

Friedman, M. (1990). *Capitalism and freedom*. Chicago, IL: University of Chicago Press.
Hayek, F. A. (2007). *The road to serfdom*. Chicago: University of Chicago Press.
Korematsu v. United States, 323 U.S. 214 (1944).
Leonardo, Z. (2007). The war on schools: NCLB, nation creation and the educational construction of whiteness. *Race Ethnicity and Education*, 10(3), 261–278.
Loving v. Virginia 388 U.S. 1 (1967).
Omi, M., & Winant, H. (2014). *Racial formations in the United States* (3rd ed.). New York: Routledge.
Regents of the University of California v. Bakke, 438 U.S. 265 (1978).
United Jewish Organizations v. Carey, 430 U.S. 144 (1977).

### *Chapter 7*

Bell, D. (2004). *Silent covenants*. New York, NY: Oxford University Press.
Fisher v. University of Texas at Austin, 132 S. Ct. 1536 (2016).
Gallagher, C. A. (1997). White racial formation in the twenty-first century. In R. Delgado & J. Stefancic (Eds.), *Critical White studies: Looking behind the mirror*. Philadelphia: Temple University Press.
Gratz v. Bollinger, 539 U.S. 244 (2003).
Grutter v. Bollinger, 539 U.S. 306 (2003).
Hall, S. (1996). Gramsci's relevance for the study of race and ethnicity. In D. Morley & K. Chen (Eds.), *Stuart Hall* (pp. 411–440). London: Routledge.
Harris, C. I. (1995). Whiteness as property. In K. W. Crenshaw, N. Gotanda, G. Peller, & K. Thomas (Eds.), *Critical race theory: The key writings that formed a movement* (pp. 276–291). New York: The New Press.
Hernandez v. Texas, 347 U.S. 475 (1954).
Leonardo, Z. (2004). The color of supremacy: Beyond the discourse of "white privilege". *Educational Philosophy and Theory*, 36(2), 137–152.
Leonardo, Z. (2007). The war on schools: NCLB, nation creation and the educational construction of whiteness. *Race Ethnicity and Education*, 10(3), 261–278.
Leonardo, Z. (2009). *Race, whiteness, and education*. New York: Routledge.
Leonardo, Z. (2016). Education criticism as a new specialization. *Research in Education*, 1(1), 1–6.
Lipsitz, G. (1998). *The possessive investment in whiteness: How white people profit from identity politics*. Philadelphia: Temple University Press.
Liu, G. (2002). The myth and math of affirmative action. *The Washington Post*, April 14, 2002.
López, I. H. (2005). Race and colorblindness after Hernandez and Brown. *Chicano-Latino Law Review*, 25, 61.
McIntosh, P. (1990). White privilege: Unpacking the invisible knapsack. *Independent School*, 49(2), 31–36.
Omi, M., & Winant, H. (1994). *Racial formation in the United States: From the 1960s to the 1990s*. New York: Routledge.
Orfield, G., & Frankenberg, E. (2014). *Brown at 60: Great progress, a long retreat and an uncertain future*. Los Angeles, CA: Civil Rights Project/Proyecto Derechos Civiles.
Plessy V. Ferguson, 163 U.S. 537 (1896).

Ricci v. DeStefano, 557 U.S. 557 (2009).
Schuette v. COALITION TO DEFEND AFFIRMATIVE, 134 S. CT. 1623 (2014).
Shelby County, Ala. v. Holder, 133 S. Ct. 2612 (2013).
Texas Dept. of Housing and Community Affairs v. Inclusive Communities Project, Inc., 576, U.S. ___ (2015).

### *Chapter 8*

Fisher v. University of Texas at Austin, 132 S. Ct. 1536 (2012).
Green v. County School Board of New Kent County, 391 U.S. 430 (1968).
Harrison, L. E. (1992). *Who prospers? How cultural values shape economic and political success*. New York: Harper Collins, Basic Books.
Hopwood v. Texas, 78 F. 3d 932 (5th Cir. 1996).
Kim, C. J. (1999). The racial triangulation of Asian Americans. *Politics & Society*, 27(1), 105–138.
Lee, J. (2014). Still apart: Map shows states with most-segregated schools. *USA Today Network*, May 15, 2014.
Milliken v. Bradley, 418 U.S. 717 (1974).
Orfield, G., & Frankenberg, E. (2014). *Brown at 60: Great progress, a long retreat and an uncertain future*. Los Angeles, CA: Civil Rights Project/Proyecto Derechos Civiles.
Said, E. (1977). *Orientalism*. London: Penguin.
San Antonio Independent School District v. Rodriguez, 411 U.S. 1 (1973).
Sander, R., & Taylor, S. (2012). *Mismatch: How affirmative action hurts students it's intended to help, and why universities won't admit it*. New York: Basic Books.
Sue, S., & Okazaki, S. (1990). Asian-American educational achievements: A phenomenon in search of an explanation. *American Psychologist*, 45(8), 913–920.
Thernstrom, S., & Thernstrom, A. (1999). *America in black and white: One nation, indivisible*. New York: Basic Books.

### *Chapter 9*

Du Bois, W. E. B. (1903). *The souls of black folk*. New York: Bantam Classic.
Hall, S. (1996). Gramsci's relevance for the study of race and ethnicity. In D. Morley & K. Chen (Eds.), *Stuart Hall* (pp. 411–440). London: Routledge.
Kozol, J. (2005). *The shame of the nation: The restoration of apartheid schooling in America*. New York: Crown Publishers.
Leonardo, Z. (2002). The souls of white folk: Critical pedagogy, whiteness studies, and globalization discourse. *Race Ethnicity & Education*, 5(1), 29–50.
López, I. H. (2005). Race and colorblindness after Hernandez and Brown. *Chicano-Latino Law Review*, 25, 61.
West, C. (1994). *Race matters*. New York: Vintage Books.

# Index


abolition of whiteness 41–42
*Adarand Constructors, Inc. v. Pena* 95–96, 98
adverse/disparate impact 74–75
affirmative action 14–16; disproportionate harm cases and 87–93; *Fisher v. University of Texas* and 106–107; as glimmer of hope 89–91; '(white) government cannot make us equal' and 96–99; hope lost despite 91–93; introduction to 85–86; '(white) nation of minorities' and 93–96; proponents of 128–131; as race positive policies 86; stereotyped caricatures of 145–146
Alexander, Michelle 143
Alito, Samuel 49, 50
Allen, R. 31
Althusser, Louis 48
American Council on Education 23
American Education Research Association 23
American Psychological Association 23
*Amicus Curiae* briefs 22–23, 134
Anderson, Perry 45, 46–47, 52
anti-civil rights movement, *Fisher* as part of 108–114
anticlassification 14, 16–17
anti-majoritarian storytelling 26–28, 39; formation of counter narratives and 28–30
anti-miscegenation laws 37
antisubordination 14, 16–17
Arkansas, Little Rock Nine in 66–67
Asian Americans 32, 123–124, 125; history of racial positionality of 137–138; 'model minority' trope and 135, 138; perilous status of 134–139

Bakke, Allan 91–93, 139; *see also Regents of the University of California v. Bakke*
Baldus, David 81
Baldus Study 81–82, 83
Baldwin, James 41
Balkin, Jack 14, 16–17
Barnett, Ross 67
Bell, Derrick 28, 29–30, 38, 40, 68; on *Brown* as hollow victory 18, 65; on property rights 43
Blackmun, Harry 20
Bobo, L. 11
*Bolling v. Sharpe* 57
Bonilla-Silva, Eduardo 5, 18
Breyer, Steven 119
*Briggs v. Elliot* 57–58
*Brown I* 55, 64–65, 68
*Brown II* 55, 64–65, 66, 115, 116
*Brown v. Board of Education* 2, 4–5, 11, 52, 108, 126, 147; antisubordination and 16–17; Byrd Organization's 'Massive Resistance' plan in response to 67–68; as consolidation of four related cases 57–58, 124; counter narratives to 29–30; critical hermeneutics and 30–31; desegregation not ordered immediately after 36–37; as hollow symbolic victory 18–19, 65; legacy of 68–70; Little Rock Nine and 66–67; modern Civil Rights movement sparked by 55–56; overall outcome of 58–61; politics

of 56–61; reaction to 65–68; structural versus individual harm and 61–65
Bush, George W. 49
Byrd, Harry F. 67
Byrd Organization 67–68

Chicago School 37
*City of Richmond v. J.A. Croson Co.* 95–96
civil institutions and the state 45–51
Civil Rights Act of 1964 4, 11, 13, 72–73, 99; *Griggs v. Duke Power Company* and 74–77; resistance to 73–77; *Washington v. Davis* and 75–77
Civil Rights Era 4–5, 109; anti-subordination and 14; slow pace of racial progress following 38, 115–116, 146–147; sparked by *Brown v. Board of Education* 55–56
Clark, Kenneth 62
class formation theory 38
Clinton, Hillary 50, 120, 145
colorblindness, judicial 21–22; as 'act of whiteness' 4–5; antisubordination and anticlassification in 14, 16–17; burden of strict scrutiny and 14–16; consequence of 22–23, 31–32; critical analysis of race and law and 17–20; critical hermenutics and 22, 25–31; elusiveness of racial 'intent' in era of 78–80; future directions in law and 143–145; hermeneutics and interpretation in 22, 23–25; launch of era of 4–5; legal terms and concepts in 5–8; strict constructionism and 13–14; *see also* Supreme Court decisions
Constitution, U.S.: viewed as 'living document' 6, 12; viewed in 'strict constructionist' approach 12–14; *see also* Fifteenth Amendment; Fourteenth Amendment; Nineteenth Amendment; Supreme Court decisions; Thirteenth Amendment
counter narratives 26–28; formation of 28–30
Crenshaw, Kimberle 38
critical analysis of race and law, importance of 17–20
critical hermeneutics 22, 25–31; formation of counter narratives and 28–30; role of 30–31
Critical Race Theory (CRT) 21–22; anti-majoritarian storytelling and 26–28; on continued subordination of racial minorities in the Civil Rights Era 115; critical hermeneutics, storytelling, and 25–31; four central methodological characteristics of 38–39; origins of 38–39; whiteness, education, and 36–42; and whiteness studies in education 42–45
*Croson see City of Richmond v. J.A. Croson Co.*

*Davis v. County School Board of Prince Edward County* 57, 78, 79
Delgado, Richard 38
disproportionate harm litigation 74–75, 85–86, 87–93
diversity response in public racial discourse 128–134
*Dred Scott v. Sanford* 18–19, 20, 33–35, 86; Thirteenth Amendment and 35–36
Du Bois, W. E. B. 37, 41, 145
Duke, David 38
Duke Power Company 74–76

education: current (sad) state of 124–128; flickering hope for 120–121; future directions for 145–146; No Child Left Behind (NCLB) Act and 44–45, 114; proponents of usage of race in policies of higher 128–131; race, hegemonic process, and 47–51; race positive policies in 110–111; response to colorblind era in 114–116; reverse-racism discourse in 32, 118, 123–124, 131–133; socio-economic status (SES) and percentage plans and 140–141; theory of hegemony and 45–47; white flight and 125–127; whiteness studies in 42–45; *see also Brown v. Board of Education*
educational criticism 105, 114
Eisenhower, Dwight D. 67

employment, race neutral policies in 74–77, 78, 89, 90–91, 141–142
equal protection clause 13

*Faces at the Bottom of the Well* 28
Fair Housing Act of 1968 113
Fifteenth Amendment 35
Fifth Amendment 34, 57
Fisher, Abigail 1–2, 17, 19–20, 107, 139
*Fisher v. University of Texas* 1–2, 17, 19–20, 123, 131–133; affirmative action and 106–107; introduction to 105–106; as part of anti-civil rights movement 108–114
Fiss, Owen 14
Fourteenth Amendment 1, 13, 35, 59–60
Frankenberg, Erica 115, 124, 125
Frankenberg, Ruth 40–41

Gallagher, Charles 110
Garland, Merrick 50, 145
*Gebhart v. Belton* 57
Ginsburg, Ruth Bader 119, 131, 132, 141
Giroux, Henry 42
Gorsuch, Neil 49, 50
Gramsci, Antonio 38, 45–47, 51, 52
*Gratz v. Bollinger* 106, 129
*Green v. County School Board of New Kent County* 124, 139n1
*Griffin v. County school board of Prince Edward County* 68
*Griggs v. Duke Power Co.* 74–77, 78, 89, 90–91, 141–142
*Grutter v. Bollinger* 17–18, 106–107, 129

Hall, Stuart 49, 50–51, 52, 121, 143
Haney López, Ian 3, 4, 12, 57, 58, 117, 120, 142
Harlan, John Marshall 17, 99
Harris, Cheryl 111
Harrison, Lawrence 135
Harvard University 32, 123, 135–137, 144
hegemony 38, 45; Gramsci's theory of 45–47; race, education and process of 47–51
Henderson, Zelma 66
hermeneutics: critical 22, 25–31; interpretation and 23–25
*Hernandez v. State of Texas* 116–118
holistic admissions process 1–2, 19–20, 123; *see also* race positive policies
*Hopwood v. Texas* 129, 141
Howard, Gary 43–44

Ideological State Apparatuses (ISAs) 48
Ignatiev, Noel 40, 41–42
instantiation of whiteness 5
interest convergence thesis 39
intermediate scrutiny 87–93
*Invisible Knapsack* 40
invisible knapsack of white privilege 40, 109

Jackson, Robert 60
Jim Crow laws 11, 24–25, 35–36, 85–86, 94, 97–98; Asian Americans and 138–139

Kagan, Elena 50, 119
Kavanaugh, Brett 49, 50, 105
Kennedy, Anthony 1, 49, 50, 105, 145
Kennedy, Robert F. 67
King, Martin Luther, Jr. 21, 109
KKK 38
*Korematsu v. United States* 92, 95
Kozinski, Alex 28
Kozol, Jonathan 43, 147

Ladson-Billings, Gloria 42–43
laissez-faire racism 11–12
Latino Americans 116–118, 125
Leonardo, Zeus 5, 22, 25, 28, 31, 42, 145; on ambivalent action 97; on educational criticism 105, 114; on No Child Left Behind 44–45, 114; on white privilege 109, 111
Lipsitz, George 40, 110
Little Rock Nine 66–67
Liu, Goodwin 110
living document view of the U.S. Constitution 6, 12
Louisiana Purchase 34
*Loving v. Virginia* 91, 99, 127
Lowry, George 91–92

majoritarian stories 26–27, 32
malicious discrimination, findings of 80–82

Marshall, Thurgood 12, 15, 37, 56, 58, 60, 90, 108; on ordering immediate desegregation of schools 63; on stupid laws enacted by legislatures 77
Marxist tradition 45, 47
master narratives 26
Matsuda, Mari 38
McCleskey, Warren 80
*McCleskey v. Kemp* 80–82, 83
McConnell, Mitch 50
McIntosh, Peggy 40–41
McIntyre, Alice 44
Meredith, James 67
Milliken, William 126–127, 130
Mills, Charles 36
mismatch theory 134
'mismatch theory' 26–27
Missouri Compromise 34

NAACP 37, 60, 63–64, 108, 109, 124, 126, 127
'nation of minorities' 93–96
neoliberalism 48–49
Nineteenth Amendment 35
No Child Left Behind (NCLB) Act 44–45, 114

Obama, Barack 49, 50, 144–145
O'Connor, Sandra Day 18, 49, 50, 95–96
Okazaki, Sumie 135
Omi, Michael 21, 37, 45, 51, 94, 110, 138
Orfield, Gary 115, 124, 125, 147
originalism 12–13, 61
Ozawa, Takao 108
*Ozawa v. United States* 3–4

'parade of horribles' 83–84
*Parents Involved in Community Schools v. Seattle School District No. 1* 14, 22–23, 125, 146
Parent Teacher Associations 48
*Personnel Administrator of Massachusetts v. Feeney* 79–80
Phillips, Wendell 41
Plessy, Homer 99, 108
*Plessy v. Ferguson* 17, 18–19, 20, 57, 61, 99, 126; counter narratives to 29–30; structural versus individual harm and 62
polarized positionality 137
Porter, Ronald 28
Posner, Richard 28
Powell, Lewis F. 15, 92–93, 94, 129
*Prison Notebooks* 45, 47
problem of domination 22
Project on Fair Representation 32, 112, 123–124, 134
Project on Fair Representation (POFR) 108–109
property rights 42–43
Pulasaki, Charles 81

race neutral policies: disproportionate harm and 74–75, 85–86, 87–93; diversity response to 128–134; in employment 74–77, 78, 89, 90–91, 141–142; reverse racism discourse and 32, 118, 123–124, 131–133; socio-economic status (SES) and percentage plans and 140–141
race positive policies 1–2, 5, 12, 18, 32, 69, 84, 85–89, 96, 110–111; *Bakke* decision effects on 93; *Fisher* decision effects on 106–109, 112; proponents of 128–131; quasi- 116; recent challenges to 113–114; reverse racism discourse and 32, 118, 123–124, 131–133; storytelling and 25–26; strict scrutiny of 96–98; 'victims' of 133–134; *see also* holistic admissions process
racial biologism 37–38
racial formation theory 38, 110
racial subordination 11, 33, 39–40; employment policies and 74–77, 78, 89, 90–91, 141–142; Jim Crow 11, 24–25, 35–36, 85–86, 94, 97–98, 138–139; residential segregation and (*see* residential segregation); 'separate but equal' 35–36, 61, 62; slavery 33–35, 37
rational basis review 77–78, 87–93
reconstruction of whiteness 42
*Regents of the University of California v. Bakke* 14–16, 20, 91–93, 123, 129, 146; legacy of 93–96
Rehnquist, William 49, 50, 60
residential segregation 125, 142–143, 146; cementing the urban/suburban divide and 127–128; white flight and 125–127

reverse-racism discourse 32, 118, 123–124, 131–133
*Ricci v. DeStefano* 112–113
Ricoeur, Paul 22, 24
Roberts, John 14, 50, 113, 125
*Rodriguez, Milliken v. Bradley* 126–127, 130
Roediger, David 40, 41
Roosevelt, Franklin D. 95
Rury, John 125, 127

Sacramento, Jocyl 137
Said, Edward 137
Sander, Richard 26–27, 134
Scalia, Antonin 13, 49, 50, 121, 145
*Schuette v. Coalition to Defend Affirmative Action (BAMN)* 118–120
'separate but equal' 35–36, 61, 62
Sheppard, John Ben 67
Siegel, Riva 14, 16
slavery 33–35, 37
Sleeter, Christine 44
Smith, R. A. 11
socio-economic status (SES) and percentage plans 140–141
Solorzano, Daniel 26, 27
Sotomayor, Sonia 50, 118–120
Souter, David 49, 50
Sowell, Thomas 27
state and civil institutions, the 45–51
Stevens, John Paul 49, 50, 96–97, 98
storytelling, anti-majoritarian 26–28, 39; formation of counter narratives and 28–30
strict constructionist view of the U.S. Constitution 12–14
strict scrutiny 14–16, 78, 87–93; of race positive policies 96–98; two-pronged test under 96–97
structural versus individual harm 61–65
Supreme Court decisions 2–4, 72–73; *Amicus Curiae* briefs 22–23, 134; beginning of colorblind jurisprudence era of 4–5; *Brown v. Board of Education* (*see Brown v. Board of Education*); current understanding of race and 118–120; *Davis v. County School Board of Prince Edward County* 57, 78, 79; distinct approaches to race in 85–86; diversity response to 128–134; *Dred Scott v. Sanford* 18–19, 20, 33–36, 86; findings of malicious discrimination in 80–82; *Fisher v. University of Texas* 1–2, 17, 19–20, 131–133; *Gratz v. Bollinger* 106, 129; *Green v. County School Board of New Kent County* 124, 139n1; *Griggs v. Duke Power Company* 74–77, 78, 89, 90–91, 141–142; *Grutter v. Bollinger* 17–18, 106–107, 129; *Hernandez v. State of Texas* 116–118; *Loving v. Virginia* 91, 99, 127; *McCleskey v. Kemp* 80–82, 83; 'parade of horribles' and 83–84; *Parents Involved in Community Schools v. Seattle School District No. 1* 22–23, 125, 146; *Personnel Administrator of Massachusetts v. Feeney* 79–80; *Regents of the University of California v. Bakke* 14–16, 20, 91–93, 123, 129, 146; *Ricci v. DeStefano* 112–113; *Rodriguez, Milliken v. Bradley* 126–127; *Schuette v. Coalition to Defend Affirmative Action (BAMN)* 118–120; slow pace of changes on the Court and 49–50; standard of review in 77–82; *Sweatt v. Painter* 20n2; that displayed understanding of race 116–118; *United Jewish Organization of Williamsburg v. Carey* 89–93; *Village of Arlington Heights v. Metropolitan Housing Corp.* 79–80; *Washington v. Davis* 75–77; whiteness rising with assistance from 112–114; *see also* colorblindness, judicial; Constitution, U.S.
Sweatt, Herman 108
*Sweatt v. Painter* 20n2

Tate, William 42–43
Tatum, Beverly 26
Taylor, Stuart 26–27, 134
Thind, Bhagat Singh 3, 108
Thirteenth Amendment 35–36
Thomas, Clarence 16, 23–25, 26–27, 98, 109; citations of *Brown* by 69–70; on law treating us as equals 100; on reverse-racism discourse 133–134; on strict scrutiny 97
Trump, Donald 49, 50, 105, 113, 120, 143, 145

UCLA Civil Rights Project report 125
*United Jewish Organization of Williamsburg v. Carey* 89–93
University of North Carolina at Chapel Hill 123, 134–135
University of Texas at Austin 1–2, 19–20, 144; *see also Fisher v. University of Texas*
urban/suburban divide 127–128
*U.S. v. Barnett* 67

*Village of Arlington Heights v. Metropolitan Housing Corp.* 79–80
Virginia Prince Edward County Schools 67–68
Voting Rights Act of 1965 11, 108, 113

Wallace, George 73
Wallerstein, Immanuel 38
Warren, Earl 36, 55–56, 147; on equal protection 61; *Hernandez v. State of Texas* and 117–118; outcomes of *Brown* and 58–61
*Washington v. Davis* 75–77
*We Can't Teach What We Don't Know* 43
*White by Law: The Legal Construction of Race* 3
white flight 125–127
whiteness 4–5; abolition of 41–42; Critical Race Theory, education, and 36–42; reconstruction of 42; reverse racism as act of 124; rise of, with assistance from the Court 112–114; studies of 40–42; and white privilege via post-race discourse 109–112
white privilege via post-race discourse 109–112
Williams, Patricia 38
Winant, Howard 21, 37, 45, 51, 94, 110, 138
Woodworth, George 81

Yosso, Tara 26, 27